anglais

THE LAST ROMANTIC

"The Only Way"
From the poster by JOHN HASSALL, R.I.

THE LAST ROMANTIC

The Authorised Biography of
SIR JOHN MARTIN-HARVEY

by

MAURICE WILLSON DISHER

with a foreword by
D. L. MURRAY

With 46 Illustrations

HUTCHINSON & CO (Publishers) LTD
London   New York   Melbourne   Sydney   Cape Town

To

LADY MARTIN-HARVEY

Printed in Great Britain
by The Anchor Press, Ltd.,
Tiptree, Essex

George Meredith, speaking of Romance, says: "The young who avoid that religion, escape the title of Fool at the cost of a Celestial Crown." Good!

ELLEN TERRY.

Rien ne reste de nous; notre œuvre est un problème.
L'homme, fantôme errant, passe sans laisser même
Son ombre sur le mur.

VICTOR HUGO.

AUTHOR'S NOTE

THE greatness of Martin Harvey is the greatness of the tradition that ended with him. Separate him from it and he dwindles in importance. Regard him as part of it and he belongs to an imaginative force which influenced the history of our race.

What that tradition was before he became its champion, how it was formed and who upheld it, may seem to require a disproportionate number of pages, but these things are Sir John's spiritual genealogy and as such are of more account than the most distinguished family tree.

M. W. D.

CONTENTS

BOOK V

BOOK VI

LIST OF ILLUSTRATIONS

PLATES

IN THE TEXT

MARTIN HARVEY

A Memory by D. L. Murray

THE LAST ROMANTIC

MARTIN HARVEY has often been called "the last of the romantics" on the English stage. It is to be feared that many of those who use the phrase have but a poor idea of its meaning. They understand by "romanticism" what the latest generation has come to call "escapism". They think of it as the flight from reality into a world of self-pleasing illusion, as the improbable tale, the triumph of sentimentalism, the appeal of costume belonging to the past. Romantic actors may have fallen into these snares, but it is unfair to judge an art by its corruptions. Romanticism is an "escape from life" only in the sense that it draws on sources hidden from everyday experience. The romantic actor evokes the forces of the mysterious subconscious; he is their master, but also their subject. Romantic acting is possession.

Karl Mantzius in his "History of Theatrical Art" has given a terribly vivid portrait of the great German contemporary of Edmund Kean, Ludwig Devrient, and his sufferings. In playing Lear, Devrient would sometimes be so convulsed by the spirit inhabiting him as to be unable to complete his performance. One who saw it has told how he was carried out from the stage door "still dressed, in part, in the old king's costume. It was a strange scene. The disordered clothing, the pale face, the bright daylight . . . it was as if they were carrying a dead man from the battle-field". King Lear had not yet abandoned the body he had been recalled to inhabit.

The first time I met Martin Harvey was at the conclusion of a performance of *The Breed Of The Treshams* at the Theatre Royal in Brighton. He still carried his arm in a sling and bore on his face the other marks of the tortures to which he had been subjected in the last scenes of the drama. He rose to receive his visitors with his usual exquisite courtesy, then sank back into his chair, painfully feeling his arm—I realized that the heroic rapscallion, Lieut. Reresby, was still in possession. As we talked, Martin Harvey slowly became himself; but presently, the conversation turning to his Shakespearean parts, he began to expound his view of the character of Richard III. Lady Martin-Harvey softly touched my elbow. "Look!" she murmured. "Here comes the old villain!" It was true. The cruel eyes of crook-backed Gloucester were shiftily gazing at us out of Martin Harvey's armchair; yet he was not deliberately acting for us, only pursuing his thought.

This, my first impression of Martin Harvey, was almost one of my latest. It was in the early days of the War, in the dining-room of the Garrick Club, dismantled of its treasured portraits. "What do you think of Hitler?"

demanded Martin Harvey of me suddenly. I made some insignificant reply. "To me," he said dreamily, "he seems a *haunted* man." I nearly jumped out of my chair. For, as he spoke, I saw the *Führer* glaring at me, could almost swear I made out the dank lock drooping over his forehead. Harvey was not "putting on an act" over the luncheon-table; he was no *cabotin*; he had been visited by his daemon. "Your hat, Sir John!" said his dresser one night, as he wandered bareheaded out of his room to go on in the scene of Dr. Manette's garden. I thought the man should have said, "Your hat, Sydney!" for it was Carton already who was lurching absently towards the stage.

He was well aware of this quality of his genius, and, being more of a reflective thinker than most actors, had his theory to explain it. He believed that the actor in the fire of his inspiration burnt his way through to the stored memory of the race, drew fuel from the world-soul and expressed emotions and intuitions he had never known in his private experience. "I am certain," he affirmed to me, "that in *Œdipus* I uttered cries and groans that came to me out of the Greek past, sounds I had never rehearsed or planned." Whence, too, came that fearful voice from beyond the tomb that dignified the fustian of *The Corsican Brothers*?

The phrase "abysmal depths of personality" had an almost painful meaning for Harvey. He was always aware of the other selves that lie beneath the conscious, moral self of any man. The ferocious exultations that came to him sometimes when acting villainous characters alarmed him. The malignity of Richard, the cold criminality of Dubosc, the murderer in *The Lyons Mail*, were, he felt, himself and not himself. Irving is reported to have said that the actor is but a mirror over which reflections of good and evil pass, and disappear without leaving trace. For Harvey, I am sure, acting meant something deeper, and the necessity of embodying wickedness left him troubled.

More than any, diabolical rôles exposed the dualism of his acting temperament, for his sweet and sunny nature abhorred cruelty and cunning. One of his reasons for disliking Colley Cibber's stage version of *Richard III* was the brutality of the celebrated line : "Off with his head! So much for Buckingham!" When the daemon was not too strong for him, he tended to rob the characters he embodied of their more sinister traits.

> Thought and affliction, passion, hell itself,
> He turns to favour and to prettiness.

—so the critics sometimes complained, and one of them was quite furious at the gentleness of his Hamlet. Even more than Forbes-Robertson, of whom, it was said, did he deserve A. B. Walkley's praise for "giving Elsinore a thorough 'airing'". Even Richard he invested with a feline grace, and his Mathias in *The Bells* was a good man who had been goaded into a single crime to relieve the poverty of his family, not the tortuous self-deceiver that

Irving presented as the haunted innkeeper. He fervently repudiated my suggestion that he had found a great deal in Sydney Carton that Dickens had never put there. Yet that profound tenderness, those gleams of a fallen angel that held his audiences in hushed suspense, had been at the most only indicated in "A Tale of Two Cities". As for the whimsical, self-mocking humour, there is but a trace of it in Mr. Stryver's jackal in the novel. It was not interpretation; it was creation—but that is the privilege of the romantic tragedian.

For him, too, the spirit "bloweth where it listeth", and Martin Harvey would readily allow that his performances were unequal. Though they never fell below the level of finished technique which Mr. Lion mentions in the pages that follow, they varied in intensity according to the power that was vouchsafed at the moment. "Sometimes," he admitted, "I feel Carton's sadness with an almost overwhelming force." "Sometimes . . ." His characters were never—what some theorists consider the perfection of acting —carefully sculptured masks incapable of improvement; they were living flesh, his own.

To understand this essential character of his genius is to dispose of certain criticisms that pursued him all through his life. He had been nurtured in the tradition of romantic acting, as exemplified in his master and idol, Henry Irving, and this was a tradition in which the actor counted as much as the play. Harvey believed wholeheartedly in the "star". There is a good deal of injustice in saying that the interests of the drama were neglected by an actor whose repertory included Shakespeare, Shaw, Sophocles, Maëterlinck, Échegaray, Stephen Phillips, and Hugo von Hofmannsthal, but it is perfectly true that Harvey would put on plays of melodramatic or inferior literary quality if they gave him a powerful part. This was deliberate, and he was not ashamed of it. With the simple piety that was the root or his nature beneath all the subtleties and complexities with which his genius swayed him once he stepped before his audience, he declared, "My duty is to exercise as fully as I can the gift God has given me." He was an actor; he sought vehicles for acting; he could never regard the actor as a mere mouthpiece for the dramatist's thought.

Nor was he vain. Never was there a man more unaffected and ready to acknowledge his failures or to join in a joke against himself. He chuckled as he described how on a Canadian tour, at the start of which he was incapacitated by a serious illness, Lady Martin-Harvey and the company went on without him and did almost as well as if he had been with them. I was once praising his performance of Dubosc to him. "Did you see Irving play it?" he interrupted. "No? Ah! If you had you wouldn't talk about *me*!" And when the talk had fallen on some hostile criticisms of his acting, "I have had so many kind things said about me," he smilingly remarked, "things far too kind, that it's no doubt good for me to have a few hard knocks too."

Insensibly one is drawn from consideration of the actor to memories of the man. Unlike many actors, painters and musicians who exhaust the better part of themselves in their art, and as private individuals are colourless or even paltry personalities, he disclosed fresh treasures to those who had the privilege of knowing him in private life. Mr. Disher begins his study of Martin Harvey's stage-life with the "portrait of an idealist". The phrase would serve to describe any faithful study of the man as a whole. His rectitude, his unworldliness, his total devotion to his art, his courage and joyous zest in life had the effect of a tonic on those who met him. He tells in his autobiography how once, in spite of the apprehensions of his dresser, he received in his room a half-crazy wretch he had formerly known who had taken to drink and was sunk in despair. "I lectured him roundly about the unmanliness of it," he recounts briefly. "He bore my indignation lachrymosely . . . and sidled out. I never saw him again." The man must have been very far gone, though, if he did not pull up. There was an aroma about Harvey as of a day of keen wind and sunshine, that made it difficult after encountering him to persist in feebleness and sloth.

Those simple souls who identify actors and actresses of stage or screen with the noble and lovely traits they manifest in their performances in one case at least were not letting themselves be bemused by "glamour". Nobody in real life can be quite like the heroes of romantic dramas; they were not made for this sphere, and would not fit into our rooms without bumping the ceiling with their heads. But those admirers can be assured that the quint-essence of what they adored in the Harvey of the theatre, the courage of the reckless Reresby, the tenderness of Carton, the sympathy of the martyred Burgomaster of Stilemonde, could be found in the Harvey of real life, not to be obscured by a streak of hard-headedness and realism, derived, no doubt, from his shipbuilding ancestors in Essex, and shaped by his struggles with fortune and a resistant world. "Practical idealist" is the real label to fit his life. His orderliness was astounding. "The first time I saw *The Only Way*," I told him one day, "was as a young boy, at the Camden Town Theatre. I forget the exact year." He opened a drawer and took out a fat black volume. "I will tell you," he said, "the exact year, and the week, and the takings. I can do the same for every week of my career."

To anyone privileged to spend a day or a half-day with him at his stately country house on the borders of Richmond Park the many-sidedness of his culture was in a score of ways revealing. It was apparent in the collection of fine furniture, pictures, statuettes and other objects of art, the amassing of which had been his recreation for years. It was apparent from his conversation, the talk of a man of wide interests, of a discriminating reader with a delicate appreciation of style, of a philosopher for whom the seriousness and the riddles of human destiny were ever present in the background of his strivings.

This was an aspect of the man that could not fail to strike anyone acquainted with the general tone of the theatrical profession during the years of his apprenticeship. The actor then lived in a world of his own, preoccupied with the problems of his own craft, and it was rarely from books that he drew any of his inspiration. There has been loss as well as gain in the evolution that has assimilated the actor of to-day in education, interests, and habits, to the world in which he lives. But in Martin Harvey's case this breadth of culture was an asset of high value. Not only his historical impersonations, but his work as a producer, especially in Shakespeare and in such poetic drama as Hofmannsthal's *Via Crucis*, had a sensitiveness and distinction which disclosed the mind of the student.

There was another question that insistently demanded an answer for those who found Martin Harvey the most fascinating of studies. Oddly enough, it was often asked of Irving too. Were these two giants of the theatre really actors by vocation, or were they artists and thinkers who had only happened upon the stage by the accidents of their careers, and who might have been as great—perhaps even greater—in other fields of life? People often sensed in Irving a high ecclesiastic or profound statesman who had missed his vocation. In Harvey's case, the question was whether he might not have succeeded as well in some other of the arts as he did in acting. The query is by no means an idle one. He confesses in his autobiography that it was not he but his parents who were really responsible for his seeking a career on the stage. (It sounds incredible of well-to-do Victorian parents, but it is true.) And in one of the latest conversations I enjoyed with him, walking round an exhibition of pictures, he suddenly exclaimed with a groan: "*This* is what I ought to have done. Why didn't my parents understand? They knew I had always wanted to be a painter. Why didn't they help me to that?"

I knew that one reason why he envied the painter's lot was that with his canvas and brushes on his back the painter can travel at will and produce his greatest work upon a stool, without the burden of administering a huge theatre or the toil of training incompetent or indifferent actors to express his conceptions. That was a complaint not to be taken too seriously; but there seemed to me to lie in Harvey a deeper passion for painting than such trials of an actor-manager's life could explain. I am not qualified to give an artist's judgment on the specimens of his work with the pencil that are given in his autobiography, but I am struck by their life and point. They seem to betoken a gift.

A thing of which I can speak with more confidence is the undoubted literary powers that he developed late in life during periods of enforced leisure from acting. The autobiography is diffuse and badly constructed, but it contains chapters that any writer would be glad to sign. Read the pages on his childhood passed amid the shipyards of Wivenhoe, "to the music of the caulker's mallet and whining steam-saw". Read the account of the Lyceum under Irving—the grim and mighty chief, the quaint old mummers of a bygone day surrounding him, the magic cavern of the vast theatre, with its shadows and beams of light, its strange secrets and hidden chambers, like the Gothic hall of the famous Beefsteak Club—and a whole world of romantic Victorianism comes to life before you. Read the character-study of that quaint Irish cleric, "A. Fitzmaurice King", alias Canon Frederick Langbridge, part author of *The Only Way* and of Harvey's Eugene Aram drama, *After All,* and you will find yourself chuckling over a delicious piece of comedy, performed by Martin Harvey with the pen, not with his person.

"What a choice of words! By God, the man's a writer!" exclaimed a veteran member of the Royal Society of Literature with evident surprise when Harvey had finished reading his paper on the actor's art. Nevertheless, while saluting the embryo of a painter and an author in this amazingly rich personality, I find it hard to believe that Martin Harvey's gifts could have come to full fruition except through the medium that Providence and his parents found for him. His voice, his eyes, his face, his grace of movement—how could he have attained his full stature in any art that did not employ these? Something big would have been lacking from a Martin Harvey who had never been seen dominating by physical address as well as spiritual force a mob of frenzied *sans-culottes* in *The Only Way,* or a crowd of panicking Greek citizens at the steps of Œdipus' palace, or a tall and muscular Château-Renaud in the duel scene of *The Corsican Brothers.*

But if his destiny assumed a form that allowed him only to dabble in painting, and to take up the pen only as a brilliant amateur, there *was* another art beside acting which he assiduously practised and in which he reached the highest excellence—the art of living. I never knew any man who from all his days and from every circumstance of every day drew such an artist's satisfaction. Whether living *en grand seigneur* at the mansion I have spoken of; or "squiring it" (his own phrase) in a country estate he possessed for some years, and described in a delightfully written article; or transforming a hotel sitting-room on tour into some likeness of a home by bringing his own furniture with him; or finishing his last years more simply in a "cottage" —but Martin Harvey's idea of a cottage was a glorified one—he contrived to fill every corner, to occupy every moment, with beauty and order. His economy of living was wonderful; there was no place in it for a speck of ugliness, a second wasted in futility.

Pre-eminently was this artistry exercised in hospitality. Never was such a perfect host! The first warm greeting, that made the guest feel he was conferring as well as receiving pleasure by his visit, the enchanting conversation—touching turn by turn with lightness and grace on art, drama, and the whimsicalities of life, the exquisite table, a poem for the palate, and the final solicitude for the visitor's comfortable departure by car to catch his train, were all threads in a carefully woven design to give happiness. If I had been tempted to smile on a first visit at the almost tragic accent with which a failure in the fuelling of the kitchen stove was discussed, I soon realized that it was part of the insatiable artistic desire for a household without blemish.

How easy it would have been to jump to the conclusion that this was a man dependent on external things for his happiness, to ask whether he would be spiritually crippled if circumstances deprived him of this princely mode of existence. The answer to that question was to be given too. The storm that burst in 1939 made this life impossible for all but those ready to stoop to unworthy means to retain it, and conditions in the war-time theatre were unfavourable for the tours on the grand scale that had brought Martin Harvey at once artistic satisfaction and material prosperity. Financial worries clouded the prospect. Then was seen the genuine spirituality of the man. For he let go all that it was no longer convenient or practicable to retain with a perfect dignity and good humour. I ventured to condole with him on his having found it expedient to sell a good part of the artistic treasures he had spent so much labour in collecting. "I don't look at it that way," he replied. "The time had to come sooner or later when I should be parted from them; it has come a little sooner, that is all. And I remember simply that I have had the pleasure of looking at them daily for many years."

Perhaps what he found hardest to bear was the enforced inactivity from acting. Plans were formed and had to be abandoned through the difficulties of the time. He did not grumble, but I cannot think he was altogether happy if he could not be exercising his art. But the other deprivations did not trouble him overmuch. Short, like the rest of the world, of service and petrol, he became his own gardener with enthusiasm and learnt his way about tubes and bus routes. He was as much a prince in a crowded railway carriage as in a splendid car. There was nothing wrong about his scale of values.

Nor could his high spirit ever be beaten down. Always I had felt in the stride of the taut, confident figure the courage with which he went to meet every juncture of life. I did not have the opportunity of visiting him during the illness that ended his days on earth. But evidence of his unconquerable attitude reached me. It was a request that I would pass on to a great newspaper a statement he had drawn up to the effect that he was now out of danger, and hoped soon to be able to thank all friends who had inquired after him. A few days later he was gone—but how characteristic had been that last superb mistake! . . . He had gone; and while critics saluted the passing of the doyen of English actors, to many it seemed that the footlights on the stage of their life had been turned down. Until they remembered with what scorn he would have contemplated their despondency, and realized that the best of his spirit could still be theirs.

Those who have read thus far in these scattered memories and impressions will have been conscious of a great gap in them, and nobody has been more aware of this than the writer. But it has been very difficult to judge at precisely what point to introduce the figure of Angelita Helena Margarita

B

de Silva Ferro—I like to give her full romantic name as it is set forth by
Martin Harvey in the book of his life, because I am sure that for him the
first romance of the fiery-spirited little patrician with her mixed Spanish and
Stuart blood never faded. To the world she was known on the stage as
"Miss N. de Silva", and in private life as Lady Martin-Harvey. Was I in this
brief essay to single out for notice the part she played in helping him fight
early discouragements—"My splendid spur!" he loved to call her—or her
practical ability so invaluable to him in all business matters, or her artistic
sense that gave such delicate aid in pictorial productions like *Via Crucis* or
the beautiful modern drawing-room in *If Only Father* . . . or the organizing
power that perfected every detail of the beautiful homes in which his life
was passed?

Or was it as his leading actress that I should have appraised her support
and gifts, spoken of her daintily mocking French Princess in *Henry V*, or
her verve when the too rare chance came to play less than perfectly meek
and virtuous heroines? (If I had attempted this task I should have particularly
begged critics to remember also the strength she lent to his productions
by the concentrated energy of her *thought* in silent scenes like those of
Carton's farewell to his friends.) But it is at once apparent that I should have
had to bring her in on every page and develop this essay to twice its length!
I had rather quote Martin Harvey's own judgment on this long stage partnership, in which he replied to the objection that husband and wife in such a
combination cannot always be equally well fitted to the parts they have to
sustain.

To a wife like his, he writes, an actor "will owe a devotion to his interests
which it would be rare indeed to secure from a 'leading lady'; such a wife
will read her husband's every thought and impulse in the performance of
his part and will give him that instant understanding and support which
will bring to a scene its fullest mental expression; for this understanding
is the consequence of a community of interests bound together by mutual
and daily love and devotion". If I append to this, as Lady Martin-Harvey
kindly gives me permission to do, the inscription he wrote in the specially
bound copy of *The Only Way* which he presented to her, I shall complete a
tribute to which nothing can be added both to the actress and the woman.
It runs: "*To her who inspired it, who gave it its name, who helped me to weather the
storms which beset it, and was at my side for all its thousands of performances, and
who has left an undying memory in the hearts of all those who saw her as 'Mimi' and in
that of her 'Carton'.*"

THE LAST ROMANTIC

FRONTISPIECE

PORTRAIT OF AN IDEALIST

In our striped blazers or Norfolk jackets we basked beside a low sea wall, some of us sitting on it with feet up and hands around knees. Voices a little hushed praised actors. One boasted of having just seen Lewis Waller's Henry the Fifth which another scorned as not acting at all because Fred Terry, as the Scarlet Pimpernel, hid his heroic qualities under a foppish manner. Now that was acting.

The point told. No one could answer it. If you were something while pretending to be something else, then plainly you were acting.

The critic turned with a challenging stare no one could face. There was a pause until a quiet youth from Birmingham stopped scratching the gravel and tilted his chin so that his eyes, set on the horizon, shone.

"I like Martin Harvey," was all he said—all he needed to say, because it was beyond argument. A squatter on the wall murmured dreamily, "I saw him in *The Only Way*. French Revolution," and a basker, full-length on the grass, accumulated enthusiasm as he described "the best scene of all", where a prisoner, taking his turn at the guillotine, tapped his snuff-box as though very bored at being killed.

"It's Martin Harvey I like," said the schoolboy from Birmingham, still looking out to sea. There was no saying anything after that. It sounded like the Creed.

Later, in the winter, remembrance of this talk was stirred by a poster with the hero, mounted upon the scaffold, spending his last moments among the clouds. Playgoing, always an adventure, was now more. The clatter at the pigeon-hole as coins went in and metal tokens came out, the scramble past floor after floor of stone steps, the quick judgment at the top of a steep slope of benches whether to take middle places some way back or end seats near the front, the fever of mind at the prospect of half-an-hour's wait, the casual arrival of the orchestra with its exasperating air of being too early, were part of everybody's first plays. The difference began in our pride at being able to recognize "A Tale of Two Cities", and grew as Sydney Carton made himself felt.

"The fiery particle," breathed the young wit, as the hero swore he feared no man with a peculiarity of voice which always suggested that he said less than he could say. There was no denying his good looks or the grace

19

of his figure (for though short he was not short in the leg), but the long nose and the cock of brow over dauntless eye saved him from any charge of prettiness.

The very young, impressed by stature and brawn, may yet feel kinship through the lack of it. This was a new type of manhood, and in more ways than one. In the intervals we fell to discussing it. Subdued scraps of that bare language which gives schoolboys greater mental intimacy than any attained by men noted the idea of being waster and hero at the same time. Once again, here was evidence of acting.

Thinking had to be done on the long ride homewards by brand new motor-omnibus. Near the end, it turned into a side-street and the conductor announced a breakdown which would not take long to put right. In his absence the driver banged the engine vigorously. In the driver's absence the conductor, sucking the fringe of his drooping moustache beneath a street lamp, banged the engine gingerly.

As neighbouring churches sounded the twelve strokes of closing-time the bus went back to its route. On deck, with tree-tops rustling past, we still thought of Sydney Carton:

"Nothing like that in Shakespeare."

"Man, you're right."

This play you grew up with. It was always there, unchanging in the great change between school and career.

Young playgoers, fickle, let themselves be dazzled by Tree's zest for loading his face with false growths and features until the miner's admonishment to his erring daughter came to mind, "Tak' moock off face, lass, 'fore I belt thee." What resolved them, what made them plump for Martin Harvey both now and ever, was *Œdipus* at Covent Garden, with crowds storming through the auditorium.

These were the days of eagerness to judge the theatre by what belonged outside the theatre, of liking or disliking actors according to whether they played parts which ignored or forwarded Social Reform. Mere enthusiasts for the stage as the stage declared for Martin Harvey.

They still did so while standing four years later at the back of the dress circle at His Majesty's. One was a subaltern of that serious mind which could not treat war as part of life, which did not wish to be merry whenever opportunity offered, which kept to the spiritual significance of a crusade. They are rare, these minds, even among crusaders, but the subaltern took his seriousness as a matter of course. At his side the civilian *malgré lui* could not but see his friend's resemblance to this particular Hamlet overwhelmed by long shadows of gravestones on the skyline before the approaching night. It was a prince of the spirit vanishing into darkness, symbolical of the days of disillusionment.

Neither plays nor public testified greatly to any uplifting of the spirit for several years. In peace, far more than in war, eat, drink and be merry

was our all. Who cares about that now? History has recorded it as a period
of vitriolic cynicism, boasting several comedies as witty as some of post-
Restoration years and as free of restraint in real life as in make-believe.
In the midst of this bacchanalia, Martin Harvey staged a twentieth-
century morality adapted from one of the greatest stage poets of our
time.

Even if fashion forbade that this should make stage history, it still leaves
its mark there for its courage. Also, it gives the player's measure. Though
not intended to be a rebuke to debauchery, for he had cherished it as a darling
project for years, *Via Crucis* stood out as an isolated avowal of religious
faith.

Possibly the actor stayed unaware of the way of the world. Public
indifference to his play came, he thought, from post-war animosities—
although Hofmannsthal's native Vienna still evoked fond sentimentality.
In a city of alien sympathies, Martin Harvey made his house on the verge
of Richmond Park his ivory tower.

He never saw the generation surrounding him for what it was, never
troubled himself unduly over the minds of those elderly groups who masqueraded as infants in socks, shorts and singlets, and talked like infants with
exaggerated fervour about games of ball, in the four-ale bar "Arsenal",
in the saloon-lounge "Wimbledon". Where all stood topsy-turvy a taste
for acting became, naturally, juvenile.

To an actor-manager self-reared in the tradition of princely venture
no surprises exist in wayward changes of public taste. The Martin Harvey
Company of players could strike canvas at midnight; entrain, embark and
be at sea by morning. Better audiences always existed somewhere else. The
last of the actor-managers still looked out upon a universe and were admired.
Of this one in particular a practised provincial manager had said, "This
actor is the one 'star' who can visit each big town in the country twice every
year without showing the least falling-off in popularity."

The statement comes from the biography of Philip Rodway, whose
control of Birmingham theatres lasted too many years for a bouquet to be
suspected here. "Idol of the provinces"—it sounds like a sneer. How can
it be? London's idols prop themselves up merely to be toppled over in fame's
coconut-shy. But the actor who could "visit each big town in the country
twice every year" would not be forgotten even after the passing of that
strange life of Sundays spent on the railroad, where porters passed on the
true-word-spoken-in-jest of "fish and actors in the sidings".

Sophocles and Shakespeare owed their keep to profits on tour. Irving
had maintained his eminence to the last simply because he could, when
betrayed by his friends in town, trust to steadfast loyalty in the country.
But since the provinces kept faith without picking and choosing, their
idols moved in strange company. This is where the gibe came in. Bank
Holiday weeks were reserved by Rodway for a showman barely to be

restrained from standing on the steps and shouting, "Walk up!"—W. W. Kelly, who regularly arrived with *A Royal Divorce*.

Its natural appeal was heightened by the engagement, in order to appear as the Battle of Waterloo, of some local brass band; fellow-workers of the musicians in colliery or brewery would fill the theatre, and though they did not literally hang from the chandelier, they did lie on the umbrella over it with heads hanging over to watch the play, heads upside down. *A Royal Divorce* gave the popular imagination free play in its choice of Napoleons— English, Irish, Scots or Welsh, tall or short, fat or thin, lightweight or heavyweight. To the London playgoer the whole performance was a magic carpet back to the realm of Crummles. "Look here, W. W.," said Rodway, "this isn't quite the game, is it? I mean to say, four supers and two pans of red fire for the Battle of Waterloo——"

"Quite right, my boy, quite right," rumbled Kelly. "Jones, set off a couple more pans of red fire."

Hence the sneer implied by "Idol of the provinces". Hence also the Londoner's belief that his own taste in plays and players is rather better than his country cousin's. When it comes to acting the answer is simple. Where have our finest players found experience or training? But inquiry should not end there. The tale of Martin Harvey in town and on tour tells how little they know of England who only London know.

The graduate from the Royal Academy of Dramatic Art at his first provincial "date" might well feel he is in a strange land. Before he has passed more than a step from the stage door he might see evidence of the new way of life. There is, for example, a notice that gave warning of watchful eyes. The words have not been taken on trust from any book of traveller's tales but carefully transcribed from actuality. Here they are:

NOTICE

Artistes are requested to abstain from asking for permission for friends to visit them in their dressing-rooms.

The Justices of Birmingham, while recognizing that certain professional visits by Theatrical or Press agents may be necessary, do not look with favour on the admission of members of the Public to the Stage or Dressing-Rooms.

In no case should any person be admitted to the Stage area without a permit signed by the Stage or General Manager.

BY ORDER.

Victoria Courts,
    Birmingham.
    July, 1917.

Whether friends bring or carry away infection cannot be guessed at; nor is there a hint whether the evil feared, though not specified, will be caused when "artistes" merely come into contact with such different species as "members of the public" in the way that violence may result from the meeting of chemicals which are harmless when kept apart. Since courts, Victorian or otherwise, have no jurisdiction over such infection or chemical action ordinarily, the ominous shadow of crime hangs over theatricals in a manner incomprehensible to anyone from the outside world. But then, provincial theatres are not like cosmopolitan theatres. They are, to cite one all-important fact, often very much larger.

According to *The Stage Guide* of 1912, Birmingham's Theatre Royal and Belfast's Grand Opera House held 3,500; not a phenomenal figure, for even Leicester, with a population below a quarter of a million, had seats for 3,000 in its Opera House and nearly 2,000 in its Theatre Royal. As prices were "popular" there might be packed houses seven or eight times a week, which aggregates a vast concourse of people. In the West End the star acted to playgoers—in the provinces to populations.

The response was altogether different. Small assemblies in the West End of tired souls, with a suburban home so far distant that they were ready to be peeved if the entertainment did not warrant such long journeys, bestowed critical judgment upon what they saw. The masses, in quite different mood, came choked with emotion and demanded from the performance the chance to express emotion.

Swansea was so stirred at Irving's farewell that its public sang, unprompted, "God be with you till we meet again", and Glasgow was so stirred when Martin Harvey acted *The Only Way* there for the last time that unemotional Scots in their hundreds sang, "Will ye no' come back again?" But London occasions, even when they raise a cheer, do so from a voice here and there.

London audiences, being unemotional, normally prefer—not when a "floating population" takes charge—the happy ending. Provincial audiences for a century enjoyed a good cry over George Barnwell, the London 'prentice, who tasted the bitter fruit of passion's detested reign in a condemned cell with no reprieve, and over the penance in the snow of Jane Shore, the king's mistress, until Caroline Heath, who constantly played the part, died of low spirits.

Testimony in abundance proves the popularity of tears—Lady Isabel crying "Dead, and never called me mother" at Little Willie's last gasp; Lady Audley confessing her dreadful secrets of murderous bigamy in hysterics; Uncle Tom going the way of Little Eva, though here the last scene did show them at the Golden Gates; Little Jo continually moving on in the play named after him which prospered when all other versions of "Bleak House" had failed; Cigarette, heroine of Ouida's "Under Two Flags", dashing between her legionnaire and the firing-party to let the bullets lodge in her own breast, whatever ballistic experts might say. All these had toured steadily for years before perpetual Josephine infected Mrs. W. W. Kelly with melancholia, though not before *A Royal Divorce* had swept ahead of them all and made a deathless catch-phrase of a gallery boy's rude cry of "Not to-night, Josephine."

Such represents what playgoing had meant to some of the multitudes that acclaimed *The Only Way*, took to their hearts Martin Harvey and "Miss N. de Silva", thankfully received from them other popular entertainments, more particularly *The Breed Of The Treshams*, and still supported them when they turned to Sophocles and Shakespeare with poets of the modern world as well—a record such as no other players of the age could show.

From John Davidson to Stephen Phillips, from Maëterlinck to Hofmannsthal, from Zorilla to Binyon, their path was always the steep ascent of idealism. In a way other players gave them credit for it. At first it was rather grudging. Later it was acknowledged, generally with a smile. The proof that the theatre was at last genuinely impressed revealed itself curiously. At that time every fashionable player prided himself on his calm, his self-possession, his matter-of-fact air. There was a particular horror of any display of feelings off the stage, any hint of acting in private life.

Perhaps, though this is to risk mistaking cause for effect, it had something to do with a widely circulated story about anyone whose name happened to be handy: when told that at a funeral service he appeared to be "very cut up", he had said: "Ah! You should have seen me at the graveside."

Certainly memorial services for theatrical people now became as remarkable for the congregation's self-possession as for the absence of any lament in what was said to them from the pulpit. When Hawtrey died, Canon Hannay speculated in his address on the place of humour in the after-life. Coming from an author whose *General John Regan* had provided Hawtrey with one of his happiest parts, this was a break from conventional modes of mourning entirely in keeping with the twentieth-century outlook on life and death.

But of course all that had made the nineteenth century notable was not over; one splendid survival broke when Ellen Terry died. The next year the silver casket of her ashes was brought to St. Paul's, Covent Garden (which has the peculiar London magic denied to Cathedral or Abbey), and placed in a niche of the Lady Chapel. At the service, "Let us now praise famous men", was read by Martin Harvey, and his voice shook. There was the test. An actor who could be mastered by private feelings before a congregation of actors and be invulnerable against an obvious taunt had won the right to be judged by his own standard, not by theirs.

To a Christmas Annual's collection of anecdotes the young actor-manager contributed one which gives a glimpse of audiences elsewhere, remote from London and remote from any intimate knowledge of the stage. As a story there may not be much point to it, but as a study of the player and his public that hints at what each thought of the other it has its points in unintended ways:

"The scene was a certain town in the Midlands where the majority of the male population devote the scanty intervals of Industrialism to the cult of the Canine. But although on a Saturday or Sunday afternoon you might in the course of a short stroll meet some hundreds of dogs in the company of their owners, you would scarcely encounter a single animal which was not either a whippet or a lurcher.

"Once day Mrs. Harvey and I were walking in the town accompanied by the two rather venerable and very hirsute Skye terriers which invariably come with us on tour. We chanced to pass two very typical natives of the place, who were standing hands in pockets at the side of the pavement helping to support, Atlas-like, with their broad backs a hostelry which may or may not have been called 'The Globe'.

" 'Gawdstreurth, Bill,' said one of these gentry to his companion, whose eyes were fixed in a stare of absolute fascination on the portent embodied in our dogs, 'what breed do you call them?'

"For one second the oracle who had been addressed paused—quite nonplussed. His reputation as a canine wiseacre was trembling in the balance. Then he looked and caught sight of Mrs. Harvey and myself. With a masterly assumption of omniscience and composure, he replied, without a blush:

" 'What breed? Why, The Breed Of The Treshams, of course.' "

What *The Bells* was to Irving, *The Only Way* was to Martin Harvey, As the vision of one could be instantly recalled by anyone who murmured. "The bells! The bells!" so the wraith of the other instantly answered his cue of "It is a far, far better thing that I do"—often accepted as a line peculiar to the play. Possibly the vulgar might judge an actor by the standard of his most popular success, but critically it would be as inexcusable in one case as the other. At his highest the achievements of Sir John Martin-Harvey were his own, for there was none to set beside him as Œdipus or Everyman.

When he challenges comparison in Shakespeare he cannot stand out so clearly, and yet he does stand out because his Hamlet is not to be put in a group or class. In Dickens' dramas again his impersonations do not mingle with the Fagins and Micawbers, the Cuttleses and the Crummleses of various actor-managers. On his fourth plane, which is costume comedy, cloak-and-sword or Victorian stove-pipe hat, he fits into an Edwardian category of dearly-loved fustian which remains evergreen while much intellectual contemporary grandeur fades. On his fifth plane, which must not be reckoned lowest because it comes last, he inherits legendary figures like Don Juan, Edgar Ravenswood and Eugene Aram, or semi-legendary like the "doubles" of *The Lyons Mail* and *The Corsican Brothers*.

Here are two plays that stamp him as the last romantic beyond dispute. These were his roots in the tradition he consciously upheld. To explain what those plays were, whence they came and what they signified will take an unconscionable number of pages—without which there would be no full accounting for Martin Harvey. There was enough in his looks to make anyone understand why his father, yacht-builder of Wivenhoe, had positively encouraged him to go on the stage, which never can be an ordinary paternal idea of a calling. Here was a presence which demanded limelight. But what subdued this, what saved him from the charge of being a matinée idol when that charge was hurled at each of his rivals, was a very rare quality—strangeness. It constantly prompted a puzzled, "Where did he come from?" Some far more curious answer was expected than Essex.

Now if strangeness with beauty spells romance it might be pointed out that strangeness is the quality and beauty the tincture. As a label for Martin Harvey it is apt. That is what he stood for in the eyes of his audiences, that is the ideal he set himself. Is that what critics saw in him? But now, if only for once, critics here become unimportant, unidentifiable persons swallowed up in the masses. It is the masses that we have to think of, not the mere hundreds of thousands who go to the West End theatres, not even London's millions, but the whole population of the British Isles plus some considerable numbers in North America.

In order to understand what Martin Harvey meant to his own generation there must be no loose talk about theatres as though six of one were as good as half a dozen of the other. Any ordinary amusement seeker knows that the Little which caters for parties of two hundred and fifty cannot be compared with Drury Lane, where some two thousand and five hundred people sit at a time. These are extremes: most theatres in London hold rather more than a thousand each, a fact of importance to anyone interested in the subject of plays because the professional playwright consciously or unconsciously bears this in mind, and whenever Martin Harvey accepted such work, the consequence was not merely failure but oblivion—memory can bring back only fragments even when programmes and photographs are brought out to jog it.

He was not ordinary. If he stepped into the ordinary he became void. He was the very spirit of romance, so much so that if he stepped into the classic he made it one with romance. There was a wide sweep about the fling of his soul from Dickens to Ancient Greece and back again. If all his contemporaries could not look on in wonder that is because, like the hero of his own poster, he stood among the clouds.

That much his autobiography makes plain. It is well supported on the bookshelf by three or four memorials of his work which include an early biography. Why, then, yet another account of his life? The answer is that this, unlike most actors' "Lives", is strictly a book of the theatre, viewing the player as he existed among players, singling him out through opera-glasses now and then but measuring him regularly by the stature of all others. In this way his unique quality may become more manifest than if he were shown, in the conventional manner, as though he ran his race by himself.

BOOK I

CHAPTER I

ROMANCE AND THE REVOLUTION

ENGLAND never lacks good actors and never remembers them long. Betterton, father of our modern stage, lies buried somewhere beneath the Abbey Cloisters—somewhere, because at his tercentenary no gravestone was there for a wreath. Garrick, acclaimed the world's leading player, left a villa at Hampton to be in our own day "converted", like a heathen brought to see the error of its idle ways, into flats. Kemble, soaring to heights of the moral sublime, has been execrated for it by a posterity accustomed to virtue daily like porridge.

Grimaldi, beloved clown, had his grave bravely bedecked for his centenary, flowers from critics and laurels from a princess of the blood royal which were set aside when a live clown came to the churchyard with offerings from a circus; but when a wreath was brought to Richmond at Kean's centenary its bearers hunted for his last resting-place somewhere beneath the church in vain; said Sir Seymour Hicks, "A great man with all his vaults."

Why worry over dead men's bones? Those fine gentlemen and old rascals still gesture and grimace for the benefit of anyone who likes to let fancy roll backwards. In particular, there is a tippler—it was marvellous, said Byron, that a man should live so long drunk—named George Frederick Cooke. Almost to the end of his life he wandered about the provinces, acting brilliantly by fits and starts and drinking in grim earnest.

At Liverpool they hissed him for being alcoholically tongue-tied. He immediately found his voice: "What! Do you hiss me? Hiss George Frederick Cooke? You contemptible money-getters! You shall never have the honour of hissing me. Farewell, *I banish you*." And then, *basso profundo*, "There is not a brick in your dirty town but what is cemented by the blood of a negro."

At York they hissed him with a difference. He played Iago. Such a monster of enormity that he had learnt to pique himself even upon his own atrocious character, was how Scott summed up his terrible visage, his short, abrupt, savage utterance. Villainy was pure luxury in him; he hugged himself in its triumph, said Leigh Hunt.

Another compliment came from a Laertes who had seen this Hamlet sharpening his sword in the Green Room while muttering, "I and Mr. Laertes will to night in reality settle our little dispute." When it came to the

29

fencing match the scared rabbit dragged Hamlet to the ground and knelt on him. On or off the stage Cooke could behave, when he chose, like the devil. It was for this at York that they hissed him—the first time on record that stage villainy had received the compliment.

In 1800, when he was forty-four years of age, he blazed at Covent Garden into a star of the first magnitude admired above all, particularly in *Richard III*, which he made his own. In *Othello* his Iago triumphed beside Kemble and Mrs. Siddons: the date, 1804, deserves to be remembered, for then virtue's greatest stage upholders accepted the challenge of evil incarnate. There is no ignoring the moral issue, but at the same time that contest must be recognized as the birth of a legend. The Kembles, with their High Roman manner, their destiny in the empyrean, their aura of the supernatural, were classic.

Then came Cooke, of the earth earthy, wafted by the warmer air of romance. "Disorder" seemed part and parcel of it. There never was a more drunken age. Cooke, tottering forward as the curtain rose on *Richard III*, could not remember even as much as "Now is the winter . . ." Laying his hand impressively on his chest to insinuate that illness was the cause, he hiccupped out the unlucky words, "My old complaint." The pit agreed that it was. He went to America, arrived in triumph, got drunk before the curtain rose instead of when it fell, and found there a grave over which another drunken genius equally famous for playing, and not playing Richard III, raised a monument.

Is so much sordid "back history" necessary to the understanding of an idealist's art? Oddly, it is. Out of such a jumble—morals, romance, alcohol— emerges not only a particular repertoire of parts and plays. What can be seen in it also is the power of the actor to say far more than what is set down for him. Richards the Third by the dozen had not said what Cooke said. Setting "My old complaint" aside as an irrelevance and keeping to the nights when he did remember his words, he expressed a nineteenth-century spirit while acting an Elizabethan play.

Then another strolling player came from the provinces with an insatiable thirst for fame and liquor. Edmund Kean seemed to belong not so much to actuality as to the fevered imagination of his times. Like the heroes of many chapbooks and spectacles he was a mysterious long-lost child, without a father, uncertain who was his mother; no record of his birth could be traced, and he had no name.

"Master Carey" he was called in the booth of Muster Richardson, the Penny Showman, at Bartholomew Fair. There he was supposed to be the child of Ann Carey. If so, he belongs to a line of fatherless sons which would be the prize exhibit in the tables of hereditary genius, if its facts could be established. His grandfather would then be George Savile Carey, actor, author, composer, posthumous child of Henry Carey, whose wit as a playwright has been overshadowed by the belief that he gave us the familiar strains of "God Save The King" and "Sally in Our Alley", though he was the composer of neither.

He was supposed to be the son of George Savile, the Lord Halifax known to history as The Trimmer. Though many doubts arise from this chronicle, one thing is certain. No paternal influence guided its talents to fulfilment. Edmund Kean began life as a foundling in a doorway. In childhood he wore a dog-caller because he strayed. In manhood he starved. On his wanderings his first child died. When he came to Drury Lane the Theatre Royal had lost favour. He restored its fortunes and was idolized.

Rather than stupefy himself in good company he brawled in low company. After a scandal over his attachment to an alderman's wife his amours were too drab for scandal. Devoid of all respect for a world which had, like the patron of Dr. Johnson's indictment, stood by unconcerned while he was drowning and overwhelmed him when he was safe, he dragged the theatre down to the level of a brothel even as he illumined it with his fire. While wallowing in mental and physical squalor he constantly broke faith with the public, which knew well what his "illness" announced on the playbills might be, and in return the public has enshrined him for ever amid glamour as the most shining figure in that curious thing, the inherited theatrical memory.

Edmund Kean—the name is a flourish of stage trumpets. At his centenary in 1933 stage celebrities, standing before his statue in the Rotunda at Drury Lane, bracketed his fame with the British Empire, with the love of sport, more especially cricket, with the cult of character in the sense of respectability, with almost anything and everything he did not stand for, and this tribute to his memory closed with Sir Frank Benson's bold statement that his living heir was a certain actress who vigorously sustained the rôle in public life of the most brazen prude ever known.

As a jest it was exhilarating, and as nothing else should it ever be regarded. The simple truth remains that worthies who paid him homage now that he was safely dead would not in life have come within a yard of him. If we have any common unchallengeable faith left it is a belief in soap. That alone would separate our idol from us were he living. He would not so much as remove his make-up, though where he went to while still wearing Othello's burnished livery of the sun no one ever discovered.

Why, then, is he venerated and revered? The puzzle is solved by vague reference to romance. Here, in strictly indefinable shapes, is what nineteenth-century millions often thought they lived for, which explains the castellated waterworks, the public-house Italianate, the factory chimney lily-tipped, the Gothic railway-station and the former Memorial Theatre to Shakespeare, whose style found no other name than "Late Marzipan".

It also explains Kean. With him, as with Cooke before him, the romantic style of acting had an interest that was compelling. What is of more importance here is that he demonstrates how the actor's powers of expression

exist without dependence on the playwright. Tedious or not, this argument
must be maintained. Acting must be discussed in the life of an actor who did
not leave a legacy of good stories about golf.

In biographies which give the outstanding events in a theatrical career
as odd occurrences off the stage and mishaps upon it, the studied avoidance
of how a man acts suggests that it could be described only in a mass of
technicalities. Yet what the actor has to impart is not merely what is set
down for him. Even if he cannot stretch characters "quite beyond all the
authors meant or wished" to shock people too much for endurance, as Kean
shocked Dr. Johnson's Mrs. Piozzi, he still need not be just an author's
mouthpiece.

Some playwrights, of course, assert that he is, and object lustily when
he disobeys or rebels. Let the great dramatist train his own company to do
what he pleases, the whole history of the stage would still prove that the
great player has an idea to deliver over and above whatever the character
he impersonates may say. When an actor turns manager he presents those
plays which suit his own purpose, choosing what he will from the granary
of the past and employing what minor authors he favours to write what he
wills for the future.

Like all that is obvious, this is much less than the truth, how much
less becomes plain when the whole evidence comes to judgment. At the
zenith of acting its leading exponents did not choose their parts. The stars
had their courses fixed for them. Several of Shakespeare's tragic rôles had to
be essayed; not Hamlet, Lear, Macbeth, Othello, Iago and Romeo alone but
Richard III, Shylock, Coriolanus and Iachimo as well.

Which part suited which player best the audience decided with faculties
trained by constant comparison. Hence the inability to see any folly in the
casting of talented children for leading parts. Infant prodigies on the stage
then were what infant prodigies on the concert platform are now. Experts,
indifferent to all else, adjudged technical skill. Such detached critics delighted
not in the play but in acting for the sake of acting.

If a player did find a new part, then other players must act it. They had
to act, almost like prizefighters, *against* each other. Each, in consequence,
had a repertoire that included Sir Giles Overreach, the avaricious maniac in
Massinger's *A New Way To Pay Old Debts*; Jaffier, who nobly betrays his
fellow-conspirator, Pierre, and ends the lives of both of them on the scaffold
in Otway's *Venice Preserved*; Rolla, the virtuous Peruvian who rescues the
baby of his friends from the Spaniards, and also his country (if we can
disbelieve history) in Sheridan's *Pizarro*; young Norval, lofty-minded long-
lost son who causes his stepfather some uneasiness when beheld in the
embrace of his mother, amid enthusiasm voiced from a Scottish pit in the
memorable words, "Whaur's your Wullie Shakespeare noo?"—and Sir
Edward Mortimer, whose passion for honour causes him to do murder
and let others be hanged for it in Colman's *The Iron Chest*.

Martin Harvey as "Dick Dudgeon" in *The Devil's Disciple*

A scene from *The Only Way*

Miss de Silva as
"Mimi"

Martin Harvey as
"Sydney Carton"

The last on this list seemed likely for a time to survive the others. When the play was first performed in 1796, date with a significance to be noted, "Frogs in a marsh, flies in a bottle, wind in a crevice, a preacher in a field, the drone of a bagpipe, all, all yielded to the inimitable and soporific monotony of Mr. Kemble," so the author said. That play did not accord with the old tradition. Twenty years later, Kean gave it an enduring place in the new.

Certain temperaments would reveal themselves in one line of parts, just as different natures would shine in a line of different ones. While the High Roman manner emphasized what was noble and sublime, the romantics plumbed the depths of exultant evil and in that tussle the spirit of the nineteenth century took shape. From 1796 onwards the contrast of unadulterated virtue and inspissated villainy was (however clearly derived from Shakespeare) new. Throughout the eighteenth century such stress had been laid on the moral sway of Providence over all the world that the would-be murderers and ineffectual seducers of the stage had gone half-heartedly about their business, inclined almost from the start towards defeat, repentance or both.

The drama still aspired to the tragic dignity expressed by Mrs. Siddons and her brother as long as Kean stayed in the provinces, venting his baffled pride in invective against the unseeing eye. Birmingham withheld its applause. When he handed over the bride as Sir Giles Overreach he said to the lover, "Take her, sir, and the Birmingham audience into the bargain." At other times there was less humour and more venom in him, until at last the bloodthirstiness of his Shylock had thrilled Drury Lane and rendered dignity out of date.

What toppled the great John Philip off his pedestal was no breath of caprice. Almost a century of accumulating idealism had raised him there, that same idealism which welcomed the outbreak of revolution in Paris and then became bitterly disillusioned. How joyfully the news was received at first in London may be judged by the stage spectacles it inspired. Of these the most popular was the show at the Royal Circus (forerunner of the Surrey Theatre), which drew not only crowds from Lambeth but also the fashionable quidnuncs of Westminster.

The Triumph Of Liberty; or, The Fall Of The Bastille consisted of dramatized reports from "the various newspapers of the day, assisted by the aid of fiction", in the words of John Decastro, comedian, whose memoirs tell how:

"The whole of the dreadful sufferings, privations, and hardships of its wretched inmates, were most faithfully portrayed; and one feature of it was remarkably striking and effective, that of the release of the silver-headed, emaciated, decrepid old man from the *iron* cage, we believe the late Earl of Mazarene, who had been for such a long series of years immured in it in a low damp dungeon. This the audience were fired at, and the feelings of a liberal, enlightened, and public-spirited nation displayed its love for freedom with involuntary bursts of enthusiastic and electric applause."

This scrap of stage history has been very strongly inclined to repeat itself. It compels the question whether the persistence on the stage of the French Revolution throughout the entire length of the romantic revival had more in it than meets the eye. At least a theory may be hazarded that the genius of evil incarnate put upon the stage by George Frederick Cooke and Edmund Kean in the years of the Napoleonic Wars sprang from horror at the disclosure that the triumph of liberty had changed into a menace to liberty. Turmoil possessed every mind. Belief in civilization's onward march to the sublime had gone. Unsettled sympathies had to be expressed somehow. In fiction they heaved not so violently now the world was recovering from its shock, but still strongly enough.

That an enthusiastic playgoer should be the first novelist of the new romance was but natural. Theatre hacks seized the Waverley Novels as each came out and put each upon the stage well within the week. All that fever and excitement time's heavy dust has allayed, although not all Scott's work can be left out of reach on a high shelf. The liveliest have no part here. *The Heart Of Midlothian*, and *Ivanhoe*, though they have had more playwrights and players than the rest, are not in the grand succession of stage romance where Scott is best represented by an influence, seen in the figure of Lousi XI, derived from "Quentin Durward". The one Waverley Novel to fascinate the romantic actors regularly throughout a hundred years was *The Bride Of Lammermoor*. Directly it was published, half a dozen English hacks dramatized it (teaching the author how to spell the Scots tongue by changing the title to *The Bride Of Lammermuir*), and new versions were prepared for each new generation.

Next to Scott comes an earnest thinker of Liberal sympathies, politician, historian, Lord Rector of Glasgow University, Secretary of State for the Colonies and Privy Councillor, crowned with honours, created baron and buried in Westminster Abbey. No other author of celebrated works has suffered such neglect. Even in the midst of war's book famine his collected editions would be left over unsold at auction; and when an old misprint was noted which prophetically read:

Flakland
Pilgrims of the Rhine,

nobody in the group whose attention had been called to it had heard of "Falkland". Yet Lytton deserves better remembrance. Fashions for popular fiction down to and including the Penny Dreadful were set all unknowingly by him—plots based on the idealized highwayman, the disguised detective, the rapacious Roman, all make their first significant appearance in his pages, and with all Liberal philosophizing completely discarded they incontinently appeared on the popular stage.

SURREY THEATRE.

Under the Direction of Mr. OSBALDISTON.

EUGENE ARAM:—OVERWHELMING SUCCESS!!!

Every anticipation which the Proprietor had formed is now most fully and unequivocally realized; and EUGENE ARAM stands confessed the most successful Drama of the Season. The breathless anxiety with which each succeeding Scene was listened to—and the painfully intense interest it excited in every bosom, as the Drama drew towards its conclusion, can alone be equalled by that deafening applause which burst simultaneously from one of the most fashionable, crowded and delighted Audiences, the Proprietor has ever yet had the honor of witnessing since the pleasing task of catering for the Public has devolved upon him. He, therefore, seizes this opportunity, of acknowledging his most unfeigned thanks for the liberal support he has hitherto met with; and begs to assure his kind Patrons, that no exertion—no expense shall be spared, to render this Theatre worthy the high rank it now holds. The Drama of EUGENE ARAM will, in consequence of its GREAT SUCCESS, be performed EVERY EVENING till further notice, (Benefits excepted.)

NOT AN ORDER WILL BE ADMITTED, and the FREE LIST SUSPENDED.

UNDER THE		PATRONAGE OF
HIS ROYAL		HIGHNESS THE

DUKE OF  SUSSEX.

This Evening, TUESDAY, February 14th, 1832,
Will be presented (SIXTH TIME) an entirely new Domestic Drama, of interest, (in 3 Acts) with new Music, Scenery, Dresses & Decorations, called

Eugene Aram:
Or, ST. ROBERT'S CAVE.

Dramatized expressly for this Theatre, by Mr. MONCRIEFF, from Mr. BULWER's celebrated Novel,
The Music composed by Mr. JOLLY.—The Scenery, by Mr. MARSHALL.—The Dresses, by Mr. SHAKSPEARE and Miss FREELOVE.

> "Of lonely folk cut of, unseen, Of horrid stabs, in graves forlorn,
> And hid in sudden graves; And murders done in caves." T. Hood's Eugene Aram's Dream.

Eugene Aram, Mr. ELTON,
Rowland Lester, Mr. WILLIAMS, Richard Houseman, Mr. C. HILL, Corporal Bunting, Mr. VALE, Peter Dealtry, Mr. ROGERS,
Walter Lester, Mr. COBHAM,
Squire Courtland, Mr. DIBDIN PITT, Liptrap, Mr. HONNER, Heyward, Mr. MAITLAND, Summers, Mr. RANSFORD,
Tebbuts, Mr. LEE, Blacklock, Mr. ALMAR, Allbone, Mr. ASBURY, Thomas, Mr. Gardner, John, Mr. Grammer, Gaoler, Mr. Young.
Madeline Lester, Mrs. W. WEST,
Ellinor Lester, Miss VINCENT, Bess Airlie, Miss NICOL.
Dame Darkmans, Miss SILVER, Margery, Mrs. ROGERS, Sal Hammond, Miss JORDAN.

EXTERIOR OF THE SPOTTED DOG, AND GRASSDALE HAMLET---(SUNSET)
"A sequestered Hamlet, which I have often sought occasion to pass, and which I have never left without a certain reluctance and regret." *Vide Novel*

GARDENS OF LESTER HALL, BY MOONLIGHT.---(THE SISTERS' CONFERENCE)
"I do not know any thing in the world more lovely than such conferences between two beings, who have no secrets to relate but what arise all fresh from the springs of a guiltless heart." *Novel.*

DINGLE IN GRASSDALE FOREST.
"The evening had already deepened into night, along the sear and melancholy wood, the Autumnal winds crept with a lowly but gathering mean." *Novel.*

EXTERIOR OF LESTER HALL.
"A moderately sized and old-fashioned Mansion---the Manor House of the Parish---it stood at the very foot of the Hill, behind a rich, ancient and hanging Wood." *Novel.*

PARLOUR IN LESTER HALL.
"When Lester returned, Madeline, with a triumphant air, informed him that Aram had consented to be their guest for the night." *Novel.*

APARTMENT IN COURTLAND'S HOUSE.
"I, sir, never can have enough air: thorough draught or east wind, it is all the same to me, so that I do but breathe. Is that like Hypochondria? Psha!" *Novel.*

DEVIL'S CRAG AND PARRICIDE'S GIBBET---(MIDNIGHT)
"The Devil's Crag, as it was popularly called, was a spot consecrated by many a wild tradition, which would not, perhaps, be wholly out of character with the dark thread of this tale." *Novel.*

EXTERIOR OF ARAM'S HOUSE.
"The House had belonged to a Family of some note, whose heirs had outstripped their fortunes: the solitude of the place had been the main attraction to Aram." *Novel*

GYPSEY GLEN NEAR KNARESBRO'.
"A scene of this sort is perhaps one of the most striking that the green lanes of Old England afford." *Novel.*

EXTERIOR OF THE RAVEN, AND ST. ROBERT'S CAVE.
"To this desolate spot, called, from the name of its once celebrated Eremite, St. Robert's Cave, the crowd now swept." *Novel.*

PARSONAGE OF GRASSDALE AND VILLAGE CHURCH---(THE MARRIAGE MORNING)
"The heaven of their fate seemed calm and glowing: and Aram did not dream that the one small cloud of fear which was set within it, and which he alone beheld afar, and unprophetic of the storm, was charged with the thunderbolt of a doom he had protracted, not escaped." *Novel.*

EXTERIOR OF SESSIONS HOUSE, YORK.
"The third of August, 1759, rose bright, calm and clear: it was the morning of the Trial." *Novel.*

The Condemned Cell, (Two sudden blows with a ragged stick, One hundred gash with a hasty knife--- And one with a heavy stone; And then the deed was done." T. Hood.) **Denouement.**

From a Surrey Theatre play-bill, February, 1832

One among them found an enduring place to be defined in this chronicle. In Lytton's family a century earlier there had been a tutor named Eugene Aram, self-taught scholar of notable attainments and secret murderer. Understanding of the criminal's heart was ever the aim of Lytton's Liberal mind, and this inspired the novel of "Eugene Aram" in 1832. Thomas Hood had published his poem, "The Dream of Eugene Aram", a year earlier;

but it was the novel which caused the hero with his cry of "More blood! More blood! Still blood, blood, blood!" to haunt the stage before the first edition had sold out. In between such resounding literary triumphs as "The Last Days Of Pompeii" and "Harold", Lytton wrote a novel of the French Revolution called "Zanoni". A supernatural being is the chief character; at the climax he goes to the guillotine in another's place.

Here are the earliest nineteenth-century figures in the actor-manager's repertoire of romance. Why were they chosen? For the answer note what they have in common. Edgar Ravenswood, Louis XI and Eugene Aram are not heroes according to convention. As a triptych they exhibit no standard of honour or courage, but in some other manner they express romance in terms of portraiture. What appealed to the actor in each was the study of a character—somebody who felt this way or that, not somebody who did this or that. Since these diverse three are alike in nothing except that they are alike doomed themselves and murderously inclined towards others—a trait they share with Sir Edward Mortimer, whose company they would keep—they might be reduced to a type, *l'homme fatal*.

CHAPTER II

DYING FOR ROMANCE AT THE BARRICADES

PRECISELY what was meant by romance never troubled London playgoers much. Its presence became known, no matter what authors or actors intended, directly "French Revolution" set the scene. Martyrs awaiting their turn at the guillotine took all the magenta limelight so that little could be spared in this colour for any other heroes, except perhaps some Cavaliers. Your true romantic who died for romance in the Paris of Louis-Philippe, Chopin, Heine, and Mürger barely showed himself upon the stage.

While canvas Bastilles still fell nightly to the sound of tears, he still died in real revolutions. He wore a stove-pipe hat to keep a blood-soaked bandage in place as he leant upon an upturned flagstone and levelled his curio-shop musket at a bombardier with linstock, whose cannon the next instant would make one litter of dreaming brains and barricade.

If asked for what cause he fought his answer would have been, "Buona-partist", a faith, illogical in civilians who opposed the armed forces of tyranny, that glowed in the vague, far-off splendours. The student, the poet and the artist imagined a vain thing, laying down their lives for the sake of what, when it should be established, would cease to be. No other cause was ever such a lost cause as their romance. It blossomed in defeat and perished in victory.

Our modern world knows it in the opera-house as *La Bohème*. Possibly the lament of "Your tiny hand is frozen" stirs some stray visions of stove-pipe hats, particularly one over the gaunt face of Paganini the violinist, with the Devil ever at his elbow. There may be thoughts of George Sand and De Musset, conducting their love affair like an advertising campaign, of Chopin, of "*Les Misérables*", and then—with a shock to find it in the same world—of the perpetual clash of swords which calls itself Dumas.

Nothing matches, but it is all romance. Art and politics were one. In the early spring of 1830 you fought for the revolution of the drama night after night in the pit of the Théâtre Français. In the early summer you fought at the barricades. All of which took permanent effect upon a tradition of the English theatre.

As in London so in Paris, it began at the dawn of the century with an actor. Talma, friend of the Emperor, had a spirit that rebelled against the classic past; he ought to have changed places with Kemble, whose style was as well suited to the quiet dignity of French tragedy as Talma's turbulent passions were to Shakespeare. In Paris, Hamlet needed no other ghost than one imagined from a wild cry, a staggering and uncertain step, distended eyes, open mouth, widespread fingers and hands vaguely waving in the air.

One other part was shared by the two great players: Mortimer in *The Iron Chest* bore the name of Falkland both in the original novel and when played by Talma. He laid a further claim to a place in this theatrical ancestral tree by contributing to the standard debate whether acting should be as cold-blooded as murder or as spontaneous as manslaughter. Should the part be perfected in rehearsal, studied in every detail until complete and put before the audience as a finished work of art? Or should inspiration be the player's guide, moving him this way and that while keeping the company at arm's length, nobody knowing, least of all the player himself, which way genius—gin or djinn, according to his enemies—will take him next?

Kean, moved by inward spirits, brandy as well as his own fire, raged at will to such an extent that he would, after confessing, "hang me if I can recollect six consecutive lines of this infernal stuff", rely on the muscular workings of his face. Kemble calculated each controlled gesture to a hair's breadth. Garrick, who had taken a middle course, pronounced, "The greatest strokes of genius have been unknown to the actor himself, till circumstances, and the warmth of the scene, have sprung the mine, as much to his own surprise as that of his audience."

Talma added to this in his essay that was quoted both by Irving and Martin Harvey. In this, while not scorning the classic ideal of emotion remembered in tranquillity, he eloquently upholds the romantic principle of letting emotion carry you away. This is his notion of the actor:

"By repeated exercises he enters deeply into the emotions, and his speech acquires an accent proper to the personage he has to represent. This done, he goes to the theatre not only to give theatrical effect to his studies, but also to yield himself to the spontaneous flashes of sensibility and all the emotions which it involuntarily produces in him. What does he then do?

"In order that his inspirations may not be lost, his memory, in the silence of repose, recalls the accent of his voice, the expression of his features, his action—in a word, the spontaneous working in his mind, which he had suffered to have free course, and in fact everything which, in the moments of his exaltation, contributed to the effect he had produced.

"His intelligence then passes all these means in review, connecting them, and fixing them in his memory, to re-employ them at pleasure in succeeding representations. These impressions are often so evanescent, that, on retiring behind the scenes, he must repeat to himself what he had been playing, rather than what he had to play."

In other words, the flashes of lightning had to be controlled—which to a coming generation would sound like harnessing the powers of darkness. Whether Satan himself gripped the bow of Paganini may be doubted, but the Devil most certainly dogged the footsteps of Kean in those years when "Genius and Disorder" were supposed to be inseparable.

That the middle course had virtue enough to inspire a drama of its own was proved by a playwright, Casimir Delavigne. While a schoolboy he wrote an ode on the birth in 1811 of a son to the Man. Henceforward he was the National Poet. Vain dreams of glory for that son as Napoleon II inspired the ardent stove-pipe hats of Bohème as they toppled over the barricades to the sound of verses written by Delavigne—"La Parisienne".

Victory distended all lungs, but before the shouting died the romantics found themselves outwitted by a self-appointed citizen-king. The face, so like a pear that a cartoonist charged with *lese-majestie* easily proved that the resemblance was there before he indicated it, caused birds of the night to use *poire* for ever more as a term of derision, not for the bilker but for any poor dolt who paid what they asked.

In a city of disillusionment romance broke into petals again. Byron, Shelley and Scott inspired the more temperate blood. Delavigne, reading "Quentin Durward" and being impressed with the portrait of a craven hero, wrote *Louis XI*. Its rhymed alexandrines and its background of the monarchy in conflict with feudal lords accorded with the traditions of the Théâtre Français; its climax, where the king cringes before Nemours' threat of vengeance for the death of his father, upset time-honoured insistence on the august.

The demand made by romance for emotional turmoil was met, but there was still more in *Louis XI* to ensure it an abiding place on the nineteenth-century stage. Its appeal to actor-manager, to audience, to the spirit of the age, lay in its illogical glints of humour. That same year Delavigne's two illustrious rivals, both the offspring of generals in Napoleon's armies, brought out masterpieces that in theatrical annals would lag far behind it. Victor Hugo's *Le Roi S'Amuse* would be kept alive by Verdi in opera-houses, but notoriety was all Dumas's *Le Tour De Nesle* achieved. The queen who liked to fling the bodies of her lovers into the Seine each morning, with her long-lost sons among them, was first and most fatal of the *femmes fatales*.

Such parts were written for Mlle George, now admired less for her powers of acting than for being a genuine relic of the Empire. At fifteen, with a form remarkably mature, she upheld great classic rôles at the Théâtre Français. The First Consul sent for her and then and there added her to his conquests. Henceforth she gladly obeyed his commands; she would be ordered to disrobe, ordered to await his pleasure and then ordered to get dressed and go home if he had no time to spare.

When he crowned himself Emperor he included her in the royal divorce; but she, like Talma, made her steadfast loyalty to his cause known through the darkest days and to the end at St. Helena. All the stove-pipe hats of the Boulevard saluted her—but she had no glamour in English eyes. Thackeray was impressed solely by the morals of the parts she played. Dickens was direct:

"Once Napoleon's mistress, now of an immense size, from dropsy I suppose; and with little weak legs to stand upon. Her age, withal, somewhere about 80 or 90. I never in my life beheld such a sight. Every stage-conventionality she ever picked up (and she has them all), has got the dropsy too, and is swollen and bloated hideously."

For all that, for all the shocked remonstrance of the honest Englishman who (to quote Thackeray as a Paris correspondent) had a faith in his clergy-man and was a regular attendant at Sunday worship, Mlle George kept romance revived. Because her good name was what it was, and furthermore because she was far too generous in outline to play heroines, Hugo and Dumas spurred themselves to depict Lucrèce Borgia and Mary Tudor in grand dramas of murders, rapes, adulteries and other crimes.

"With what a number of moral emotions do they fill the breast; with what a hatred for vice and yet a true pity and respect for that grain of virtue that is to be found in us all," says Thackeray, and so supplies a clue.

Don Juan comes in nineteenth-century shape to point the same moral. He murders at the slightest provocation, and without the most trifling remorse; he overcomes ladies of rigid virtue, ladies of easy virtue, and ladies of no virtue. But when the nun comes to the rendezvous he tells her, "I am no longer Don Juan; I am brother Juan the Trappist. Sister Martha, recollect that you must die."

That suits her book, for she is an angel in disguise who in a scene of Heaven prays for the saving of his soul. Next to Don Juan's came Edmund Kean's turn to be romanticized, the one a hero of legend, the other a fellow creature whose death had just been announced. A biographical drama, bearing the title *Disorder And Genius*, had been written by a couple of hacks— the fascination of finding virtue amid debauchery affected authors generally— and Dumas merely added his master-strokes to the work while renaming it simply *Kean*, which was enough.

However funny it may have been to Thackeray as a French idea of London life its theme did come from England, and this much at least rang true. Kean, idol of rank and fashion, inspires hopeless passion in the heart of an ambassador's wife, who scorns the Prince of Wales:

"Then we have Kean at a place called the Trou de Charbon, 'The Coal Hole', where, to the edification of the public, he engaged in a fisty combat with a notorious boxer. The scene was received by the audience with loud exclamations of delight, and commented on, by the journals, as a faultless picture of English manners.

" 'The Coal Hole' being on the banks of the Thames, a nobleman —*Lord Melbourn!*—has chosen the tavern as a rendezvous for a gang of pirates who are to have their ship in waiting, in order to carry off a young lady with whom his Lordship is enamoured. It need not be said that Kean arrives at the nick of time, saves the innocent Meess Anna, and exposes the infamy of the Peer.

"A violent tirade against noblemen ensues, and Lord Melbourn slinks away, disappointed, to meditate revenge. Kean's triumphs continue through all the acts: the Ambassadress falls madly in love with him: the Prince becomes furious at his ill success, and the Ambassador dreadfully jealous. They pursue Kean to his dressing-room at the theatre; where, unluckily, the Ambassadress herself has taken refuge.

"Dreadful quarrels ensue; the tragedian grows suddenly mad upon the stage, and so cruelly insults the Prince of Wales that His Royal Highness determines to send him to *Botany Bay*. His sentence, however, is commuted to banishment to New York; whither, of course, Miss Anna accompanies him, rewarding him, previously, with her hand and twenty thousand a year!"

This pleased not only the Variétés in 1836 but also London when it came back to life as a film nearly a hundred years later. Heine, no mean critic either of theatre or life, approved the play as a picture of *la vieille Angleterre*, which he had visited, and as a portrait of the actor whom he had seen; and he gave great credit to Kean's impersonator, Frédérick-Lemaître. Though both had eyes that glared, the first romantic of the French bore little resemblance to the first romantic of the English stage. Yet between them, according to Heine, there was an astonishing affinity which was all the more remarkable considering how little their repertoires had in common.

Frédérick-Lemaître, though as "Edgard Ravenswood" he was so starkly devoured by wild melancholy that *La Fiancée De Lammermoor* triumphed in Paris, was not first and last a tragedian. From melodrama to romance was his range. When *Faust* was cut down for the Boulevard, Mephistopheles took flesh with a laughter like the sudden descent of Venetian blinds and a way of waltzing that made mesmerized rabbits of women in his arms.

Off the stage he lived according to the accepted notions of romance, filling the public eye wherever he went, behaving magnificently drunk or sober, and keeping the cafés interested in his love affairs. Everybody knew how he beat his favourite mistress, and how he told her trembling mother: "Why should you be frightened? D'you think you might get a beating? I'm not in love with you."

Disorder, strictly according to the formula, accompanied his genius. That satisfied the peculiar temper of the times without telling us how he acted. Did he pin his faith to study, did he, like Kean, trust to cognac and genius, or did he, like Talma, seek to recapture fine careless rapture? Evidence of his method exists in the surprise he sprang in *L'Auberge Des Adrêts*, an episode so often misrepresented by English writers that their accounts must be studiously ignored. The joke which they impracticably imagine to have been invented on the spur of the moment took shape in his mind as he brooded in disgust over his part; that joke was painstakingly rehearsed, though in secret, and could not have been devised without the most meticulous care. In one night it made Robert Macaire legendary.

Three authors had designed him as yet another dark-soul-lit-by-one-gleam-of-virtue. In the early summer of 1823 their melodrama went into rehearsal at the Ambigu-Comique on the Boulevard du Crime, French equivalent of London's Surreyside. Even for such dramatic tropics as these its crudity was too much.

The innkeeper of Les Adrêts, on the road from Grenoble to Chambéry, is making ready for the wedding of his adopted son, Charles. Two escaped felons, Macaire and Jacques Strop, arrive. A woman falls exhausted. Macaire recognizes her as his wife; she recognizes Charles as her son. Early the next morning she is trying to leave the inn when she drops her purse. It is a gift from the bride's father; the next moment his body is found, and she is accused. The two felons, trying to escape with the *dot*, are caught by gendarmes. Macaire swears that the murder was done by Strop, who attacks the traitor and wounds him. With his dying breath Macaire admits his guilt and restores the money, in order to make amends to his family.

Frédérick-Lemaître decided to anticipate the audience's mockery. The only one he took into his confidence was Firmin, cast for Strop. While the piece was in rehearsal they secretly went the rounds of old clo' shops. At the *répétition générale* they appeared in normal costume, but they caused some disquiet by refusing to enter furtively or employ the gesture of stealth customary in low-classed villains' byplay; instead they paraded like lover and noble father.

On the first night two of the strangest villains ever seen advanced to the footlights. Macaire wore a battered grey topper *en accordéon*, a woollen, wine-stained scarf to serve as a shirt, a patched, worn-out nondescript waistcoat, a green swallow-tailed coat from which hung a mass of rags as substitute for a dandy's silk handkerchief, soldier's threadbare pantaloons of red cloth patched in all colours, white socks, and for shoes a pair of feminine dancing-pumps held together by the laces.

In his left hand, partly gloved by a remnant of soiled white kid, he carried a formidable cudgel; his right toyed with the ribbons of a fantastic monocle. One eye was covered by a black patch. As for Strop, his meagre frame floated in a coat with flowing skirts puffed out by gaping pockets, and his emaciated legs were lost in down-at-heel boots; his neck was long and thin, his face livid; and on his prison-crop was perched a brimless shiny felt stove-pipe. He held a cudgel and had a derelict umbrella under his arm. Nor was their appearance the end of the joke. Macaire used a wooden snuff-box which squeaked every time he turned the lid round, as a commentary on his most sinister words and bloodthirsty deeds.

What the joke expressed as a whole was a critical spirit, firmly of opinion that extravagance could be carried too far. Thus as early as 1823 and for many succeeding years, for Robert Macaire lived his century out, a warning checked the wild fancies of romance.

How a sudden righteousness overcame it can be seen in the queer coincidence of 1839, when similar tales of virtue were told in two cities. In the February, Lord Lytton's *The Lady Of Lyons; or, Love And Pride* had presented Macready at Covent Garden as the humbly-born Claude Melnotte, who woos the wealthy heroine in the guise of a man of rank and station, at the instigation of her enemy. In the November Victor Hugo's *Ruy Blas* presented Frédérick-Lemaître at the Renaissance as the lackey who dresses like a man of quality and wins the love of a queen, also at the instigation of an enemy.

Late in the history of romance on the Boulevard an old hotel flanking the row of "blood tubs" was pulled down, and there the Théâtre Historique arose with the names of classic authors permanently on the façade and the name of Dumas permanently in the bill. Here *Le Chevalier De Maison Rouge* repeated on the stage the success it had had in print.

Geneviève, entering the prison of Marie-Antoinette, in order to facilitate her escape by an exchange of clothes, is arrested and sentenced to death. Maurice, her lover, enters the condemned cell to die with her. Originally they went to the guillotine together. But now Lorin, his friend, sets them free and himself mounts the scaffold.

Why this change? Circumstantial evidence supplies a reason. Dumas regularly borrowed effective scenes from the works of English writers. From Scott, for example, he took the episode in *Henry III*, where a door is barred by an arm of flesh-and-blood instead of a staple. Lytton published his novel, "Zanoni", in 1842, which gives time enough for it to have been digested in Paris.

Another piece by Dumas at the Historique was called *Hamlet*, and told a familiar story until the last minute when the Prince of Denmark, feeling responsible for the corpses around him, asks what his punishment shall be. "Thou," says the Ghost, "shalt live." That curse, of course, comes from the Wandering Jew, then at the height of his popularity.

Deserters from the Historique won a notable success near by with a common-or-garden melodrama, *Le Courrier De Lyon*, by Moreau, Siraudin and Delacour. It was founded on the facts of a miscarriage of justice. Towards the close of the eighteenth century the guard of the Lyons mail had been killed and robbed at a roadside inn. The murderer, an escaped galley slave, fastened the guilt upon a more or less respectable citizen, uncannily like him in appearance.

Some months later the Théâtre Historique enjoyed its last experience of popular favour with a melodrama in which, similarly, two leading parts were doubled. *Les Frères Corses*, Dumas dramatized by Grangé and de

Montépin, presented Fechter, a hero of great charm, as Fabien and Louis dei Franchi.

Louis leaves Corsica for Paris. Fabien his twin, stays at home. One night he senses danger; in a vision of the forest of Fontainebleau he sees his brother wounded to death in a duel. Time moves backwards and in the next scene, a masquerade at the opera, Louis is explaining how Mme de Lesparre has been left in his charge by her husband. She is now in the power of Château-Renaud, who has wagered that he will bring her to a supper-party at four in the morning.

By promising to return her letters if she will accompany him to the house of a respectable lady, he wins his wager. Louis challenges him. The duel is fought in the forest, where the dying Corsican sees in a vision that his brother is a witness of the event. Five days later in the same place at the same hour Château-Renaud is confronted by Fabien, ready with swords and seconds, to demand vengeance. The twins, one in life and the other in spirit, face each other over the body of their common adversary.

This, a semi-success of six weeks, could not save the theatre, and that same autumn of 1850 the unpaid company went on strike. *The Corsican Brothers* crossed the Channel to make English theatrical history, along with *The Courier Of Lyons, Louis XI, Eugene Aram, The Bride Of Lammermoor* and self-sacrificing heroes of the French Revolution in several variants of much the same story.

CHAPTER III

SETTING THE STANDARD

THAT Charles Kean should come into the chronicle is strange. Father and son were so unlike there seems no reason why the mantle of one should fall on the shoulders of the other. Inside Richmond Old Church a clue can be found where a memorial plaque bears witness of the love Queen Victoria's Master of Ceremonies had for the drunken, scapegrace vagabond; that love bound him to Edmund Kean's ideal, and though unfitted by temperament, physique and training to act in like fashion, he served romance by giving it magnificent trappings.

In Charles Kean the line of Carey attains respectability without forfeiting its claim to genius. This last of them, rather despised by a bias in inherited theatrical memory, has a place of honour in theatrical history. While mounting Shakespeare with unheard-of splendour, bringing both limelight and archaeology into play, he bestowed the same grand manner upon modern Parisian drama, and so graced it with glitter and fine bearing that it had social significance for a longer spell than its own day.

The Romantic Revival, driven from the Théâtre Historique, found a sure refuge with him throughout the eighteen-fifties at the Princess's, whose narrow stage, by means of scenes set obliquely, groaned beneath the weight of crowd, cavalcade, battle and bal masque. His repertoire, with Dumas by the side of Shakespeare, set the standard for actor-managers. His adaptations from the French were not always the first—Drury Lane's version of *Louis XI* preceded his—but they were always the most fashionable. It was he who made *The Corsican Brothers* acceptable (though even so there were misgivings).

George Henry Lewes, a critic who consistently damns Charles Kean's attempts at Shakespeare, argues that Kean's talent lies in melodramas, where, as high intellect is not *de rigueur*, he is not restricted by its fashion's exigencies:

"It is certainly worth a passing remark, to note how bad an actor he is in any part requiring the expression of intellect or emotion—in any part demanding some sympathy with things poetical, in any part calling for *representative* power; and how impressive, and, I may say, *unrivalled*, he is in gentlemanly melodrama."

This superior critic speaks of the "horrible termination", even though he admires the drawing-room manner which intensifies passion and gives it terrible reality. He is impressed by Kean's dogged, quiet, terrible walk in the duel:

45

"Fabien and Château-Renaud fight; during the pause, the latter leans upon his sword, and breaks it. Fabien, to equalize the combat, snaps his sword also; and both then take the broken halves, and fastening them in their grasp by cambric handkerchiefs, *they fight as with knives*. This does not *read* as horrible, perhaps; but to see it on the stage, represented with minute ferocity of detail, and with a truth on the part of the actors which enhances the terror, the effect is so intense, so horrible, so startling, that one gentleman indignantly exclaimed *unEnglish*!"

How anyone incapable of expressing emotion could act with a *truth* so horrible needs explaining. Since that drawing-room manner intensifies passion and gives it terrible reality then the critic is suffering from bias. The knot he tied himself into can best be explained if we suppose he was then wedded to the idea that emotion must be freely spontaneous like Edmund Kean's. The son had swung to the opposite extreme, calculated his effects down to "minute ferocity of detail", and acted with that self-composure which Lewes called gentlemanly.

This view is borne out by Herman Merivale. As a schoolboy, given the run of the theatre, he admired Charles Kean's intensity, so calm and so unutterably still:

"He simply turned and turned again upon his heel to face the duellist, who was round him, about him, savage and anxious and alert, everywhere —striking at Fabien fiercely, over and over again, to have the stroke turned easily aside, and always, by that iron wrist. Kean struck once, and once only, as the fate-clock of the forest rang the hour. And in a mass, and in a moment, Château-Renaud fell at his feet stone dead."

On the strength of Merivale's word, directly opposed to Ellen Terry's, the leading gentleman of the Princess's comes down to history as everlastingly in trouble with adenoids. Thus Merivale tells how he himself went to see *Louis XI* so often that the great man grew suspicious of Carlotta Leclercq's attractions, as the Dauphin, in the youth's eyes. "Herbad," he said, "you're rather precocious, you dow. I don't believe you come here to see be at all. It's Biss Leclercq's legs."

In the spring of 1854 *Mephistopheles* (by Michel Carré at the Gynmase four years earlier) became *Faust And Marguerite* by William Robertson. Objectors wondered how it passed the censorship of the Lord Chamberlain, and loudly questioned the orthodoxy of the conclusion when the soul of Marguerite, in white muslin, borne by angels in satin petticoats, was carried to heaven— "without wires", cried a critic, hysterical with admiration.

In keeping with its lowly Paris origin, *Le Courrier De Lyon* began its career in English at popular playhouses. It did not seem suitable to the drawing-room manner until Charles Reade's *The Courier Of Lyons; or, The Attack*

Upon The Mail was staged at the Princess's in 1854. In the last scene Dubosc leans out of a window to watch the procession to the scaffold. He is recognized by his victim, who is carried by the mob up the stairs to that room where the appearance of the double "was a mechanical mystery which many spectators witnessed for a score of times without satisfying themselves how such an instantaneous substitution could be contrived".

A sketch by Martin Harvey of Irving as Richelieu

Of these mechanical mysteries which Kean invented the most remarkable was the one referred to years later by Irving when he wrote: "The slote in *Faust* struck me on the head, instead of carrying me up into the flies above." In his "Life of Henry Irving", Austin Brereton describes the incident, but the word he uses is "slide". Possibly the only reference which is at all explanatory occurs in the printed version of *The Orange Girl*, by Henry Leslie and Nicholas Rowe, a Surrey melodrama of 1864. The scene is the Black Tarn, a sheet of "practicable" ice beneath a Druidical rocking-stone. Jenny, the heroine, is lured on to the ice and falls in. Mrs. Fryer, her friend, pushes the stone into the Tarn and leaps in after it. The stage directions explain that there are three traps, one for Jenny to descend, one for the Logan Stone to crash through, and another "through which Mrs. Fryer descends on a slote; the top of this slote represents a piece of projecting rock, on which she stands when dislodging the stone".

Players could be carried down through the stage as well as up into the flies on the slote, although this is not necessarily the full extent of its useful-ness. Merivale gives a clear account of its origin at the Princess's in the eighteen-fifties. Charles Kean, he says, made his Ariels and angels float in the apparent air by a mechanical contrivance all his own:

> "When six angels appeared to Queen Katherine in a vision in *Henry VIII*, I was the witness of a sad catastrophe. There were six of them sliding on invisible perches up and down a sunbeam. They were all pretty, and nicely graduated in years and height, so that the topmost angel was a little child. With keen youthful interest I watched them being tied on their perches in a kneeling attitude, and then draped with gauzy flowing mysteries till they all seemed sitting upon nothing. Then the soft music began to play, and the pulleys to work them up and down, and the gauzes to be withdrawn which were between them and Queen Katherine's dying couch; and then they began to sway their bodies and to wave their arms; and then the little child-angel at top, who had been eating too many oranges, began to feel the motion and was rather sick."

The most celebrated use of the slote was in *The Corsican Brothers*. Under lesser managements the ghost rose vertically through the usual kind of trap; but Charles Kean at the Princess's, Irving at the Lyceum and Martin Harvey at the Adelphi glided into view on the "celebrated sliding-trap" beneath which the slote ascended until it reached stage level—"a scenic effect," wrote G. H. Lewes, "more real and terrifying than anything I remember".

By mingling the Gallic drama with Shakespeare, Charles Kean shaped the future. In another way he linked himself with coming generations, for he gave children's parts—Mamillius in *The Winter's Tale* and Arthur in *King John*—to Ellen Terry after she had started her career by carrying a basket of doves in *The Merchant of Venice*, climbed up a pole in the celebrated street scene of *Richard II* and knelt as "top angel" in *Henry VIII*. "The heat of the gas at that dizzy height made me sick at dress rehearsal," she recalled. "Herbad" was wrong about the oranges.

Another figure who belongs to this book is described in Ellen Terry's "The Story of My Life". She acted at the Princess's by the side of John Ryder, who used to swear he had been engaged for his "d——d archaeo-logical figure". Together as Hubert and Arthur in *King John* they won such a round that Kean ordered them not to take their call before the curtain. Old

Martin Harvey in *The Corsican Brothers*: as "Louis"

as "Fabien dei Franchi"

Martin Harvey in *The Lyons Mail*

Royal Lyceum Theatre.

UNDER THE SOLE MANAGEMENT OF

MR. FECHTER.

THE

MASTER OF RAVENSWOOD
EVERY EVENING.

NO FEES TO BOX-KEEPERS.

THIS PROGRAMME IS SUPPLIED AND PERFUMED BY
EUGENE RIMMEL,
PERFUMER BY APPOINTMENT TO
H.M. THE EMPEROR OF THE FRENCH,
96, STRAND, 128. REGENT STREET, AND 24, CORNHILL.

Version of *The Bride Of Lammermoor*, which opened on December 23, 1865, and ran for 106 performances

Ryder, striding up and down the Green Room in a fury, told her, "When other people are rotting in their graves, ducky, you'll be up there"—with a terrific stare at dizzy heights of fame, and then they made their bow after all.

She gives another glimpse of him as he persists in making, night after night, a noisy exit which spoils Kean's effect, and explaining, "I'm a heavy man."

Tired of being dubbed a "sound, steady actor" in secondary rôles he left the Princess's for a while to lead the "heavy business" at the Bower Saloon, which stood low even in the Surreyside's social scale, with "Boxes 6d., Pit 4d., Gallery 2d." During his first week there, in the heat of August, he played Macbeth, Othello and the Stranger.

In the autumn he came back to the Princess's. When Kean went he stayed on for Fechter's Othello. Mr. Ryder's Iago, "Mephistophelean in appearance, quick in thought, picturesque in gesticulation", was deemed a creation of Mr. Fechter's, inasmuch as it could scarcely have emanated from a veteran of the London stage; yet Ryder was still the right side of fifty, still capable of linking himself with the stage of another century.

When Fechter turned to Shakespeare the old stage-doorkeeper told Merivale: "We all know Mr. Kean, Mr. Kean was great. But with 'im 'Amlet was a tragedy, with Mr. Fechter it's quite another thing. He has raised it to a mellerdram." In Othello he gazed at his black skin in a mirror before saying, "It is the cause"; and he dragged Iago to the bedside of Desdemona to make the villain kneel before her corpse. Then changing places with Ryder he played Iago. At the end of the council scene he stayed behind the rest, and having the stage all to himself, broke into a clear laugh of triumphant enjoyment.

After a clean sweep of tradition in Shakespeare he appeared in current romance at the Lyceum, playing Macaire in The Roadside Inn, Louis and Fabien in The Corsican Brothers, as well as Claude Melnotte in The Lady Of Lyons. Another of his parts was Edgar in The Master Of Ravenswood, by Palgrave Simpson, a piece that Dickens did "a good deal towards and about" because he desired to put Scott for once upon the stage in his own gallant manner. It ran for over a hundred performances.

Fechter undoubtedly restored the romantic style of acting. Iago's "clear laugh of triumphant enjoyment" alone suggests that, but stronger evidence still comes from his Ruy Blas. There is a "terribly jarring conflict" in the mind of the queen's lover, when his master returns and compels him to do petty menial offices. The "concentration of passionate rage" with which the valet accosted his oppressor, the obvious feeling that he was throwing from his soul a burden that had long crushed it to dust, the electrical effect when he snatched the sword from his master's side, the rapture he felt when dying that he was loved despite his livery, fired such a glow in the public's breast that for years he had no rival.

He left for America, where fiery temper, ill health, a broken leg, failing popularity, retirement to a farm, could not tame his wild spirit. When he died in 1879 the torch had long left his hands and burned more brightly than ever.

CHAPTER IV

RIVAL CLAIMS TO THE BASTILLE

SOME playgoers swore by Charles Kean, some by Madame Celeste, who cannot be ignored here if only because she has more to do with the stage history of the French Revolution than any other player.

The turning point in her career was unlike any dilemma in the whole range of drama, though common enough in life. After marrying and making her home in America she shouldered a heavy burden. As many others have done, she bore it willingly like a stage heroine—for a time. While publicly fêted, while rehearsing and acting, she had to bring up her child and nurse a sick husband; and this was the time of an ever-increasing popularity, mounting to a frenzy that expressed itself in the contemporary compliment paid by gallants in taking the horses from her carriage and dragging it themselves from hotel to theatre. Her season at Philadelphia in 1840 at the Walnut Street Theatre is described by its manager, Francis Courtney Wemyss, in "Theatrical Biography" (1848). He says of her:

"What an indefatigable lady she is—nothing tires—nothing daunts her. She nurses a sick husband all night, and appears as fresh as a lark at rehearsal again in the morning. We are for ever permitting her to say good-bye, and always glad to see her return to say good-bye again."

She took her farewell benefit as Vanderdecken and two other characters and went to New York, where her husband Eliott "played off the admitted attraction of Celeste with good effect against her all-powerful rival"—Fanny Ellsler. When the ballerina came to the Chestnut, Philadelphia, Wemyss arranged another season with Eliott, but in the middle of preparations for Celeste's reception at the Walnut Street he received a note "appealing to my forbearance and asking commiseration" from a sick and deserted husband:

"Deep must have been the provocation that could have induced a woman so devoted as Celeste appeared to be to him, to cast him off for ever, and on a bed of sickness—yes, of death, for he did not long survive the blow. Abandon husband and child and fortune, to seek protection in a land of strangers! Many rumours injurious to her reputation were circulated, but not one received credence from those who knew the parties intimately. She returned to the United States, on his death, to claim her child, and left America, so long her home, to think her dearly beloved daughter—whom to clasp once more to her heart, she had braved the perils of the ocean—had been taught to harbour thoughts derogatory to her mother's honour."

In London her future became entwined with that of Benjamin Webster, as rich a character as the richest Dickens drew, and yet as fine a figure of stage romance as any. He married at the age of nineteen a widow who started him in life with a ready-made family. To provide for them he trudged from theatre to theatre, from hall to hall, from barn to barn. He applied for "walking gentleman" at Croydon—"Full". For little business and utility—"Full." For harlequin and dancing—"Don't do pantomime or ballet; besides, don't like male dancers." For the orchestra—"Why, just now you were a walking gentleman."

So he was, sir, but he had had a musical education and necessity sometimes compelled him to make use of it. "Well, what's your instrument?"

Violin, tenor, violoncello, double bass and drums—"Well, by Nero! He played the fiddle, you know. Here, Harry (calling his son), bring the double—no, I mean violin, out of the orchestra."

Harry, as Webster told the story, came with the instrument.

"I was requested to give a taste of my quality. I began Tartini's 'Devil's Solo' and had not gone far when the old gentleman said that would do and engaged me as his leader at a guinea a week. Had a storm of gold fallen on me it could not have delighted Semele more than me. I felt myself plucked out of the slough of despond. I had others to support, board myself, and to get out of debt. I resolved to walk to Croydon, ten miles every day, to rehearsal, and back to Shoreditch on twopence a day—one pennyworth of oatmeal and one pennyworth of milk—and I did it for six weeks, Sundays excepted, when I indulged in the luxury of shin of beef and ox cheek. The gentlemen in the gallery pelted the orchestra with mutton pies. At first indignation was uppermost, but on reflection we made a virtue of necessity, and collecting the fragments of the not very light pastry, ate them under the stage, and whatever they were made of, considered them ambrosia."

After six weeks his chance came. He dashed on the stage to dance a sailor's hornpipe. He got through the double-shuffle, the toe and heel, though feeling faint, but at last broke down through starvation, and as the curtain fell on his hopes, burst into tears. But the manager engaged him for walking-gentleman and harlequin at the Tottenham Street Theatre.

In twelve years he established himself as a player in the West End and as a playwright on the Surreyside. At the age of thirty-six he turned actor-manager at the Haymarket where Madame Celeste, on her return to England in 1841, played a leading part or two. What happened next is not recorded,

THE DESTRUCTION OF THE BASTILE.

A DRAMA, IN TWO ACTS.

BY B. AND F. WEBSTER.

First Performed at the Adelphi Theatre, Whit Monday, 1844.

Dramatis Personæ.

[*See page* 6.

VICTOR ROLLANDE	... ... (Captain of the Swiss Guard) ...	Mr. Lyon.
ARNAUD GAUTIER	... ... (Officer of the National Guard) ...	Mr. Freeborn.
MAXIMILIEN ROBESPIERRE	(Assuming the Name of Paul Girard—The Man of the House with the Red Cross.)	Mr. Webster.
JEAN MARAT	(Jacobite Leaders and Members of the Convention)	Mr. Maynard
FREDERICK DANTON		Mr. Craven.
GUILLAUME LE ROUGE	... ... (Or Red Bill, a Blacksmith) ...	Mr. O. Smith.
HERMAN DUPLAY	... ... (Carpenter and Revolutionist) ...	Mr. C. J. Smith.
LEBLANC		Mr. P. Bedford.
PETARD	... ... } (Revolutionists)	Mr. Saunders.

No. 1,014. Dicks' Standard Plays.

One of the earlier attempts to stage the French Revolution
"Equality is my motto; but as I never kissed a lady, I'll see what it's like"

but when Webster boiled the French Revolution down to two acts he gave
her a small and far from satisfactory part.

In this *Destruction Of The Bastille* he took the name of Maximilien Robespierre, who denounces, to the sound of 'La Marseillaise' and the waving of
the Red Flag, "that abominable and inhuman engine of unrelenting despot-
ism, the Bastille." Celeste played Ninon (Countess of Montravers), who loves
Victor though "despised by this minion; and for a silly weak girl, too"—
meaning Ernestine. When Victor tries to arrest Robespierre he is at one
moment vanquished by Marat and Danton and at the next consigned by a
lettre de cachet to the Bastille. Nearly eleven months pass. Danton brings some
prisoners, "evidently spies", to the Bastille. Ernestine, one of them, makes
her way to the dungeon where Ninon gloats over her victim:

VIC.   I prefer honour to infamy; truth to perfidy.
NIN.   Night advances. Be mine or perish.
VIC.   Death, madame, brings no terror to the innocent.
NIN.   Enough! Now tremble at my vengeance! Know that Ernestine can never
        be yours. She is happy! She is another's!
                (ERNESTINE *rushes forward.*)
ERN.   No, woman; she is here to confound you in your guilt.
VIC.   'Tis she! Ha, ha, ha! Go, woman! Though you have striven to divide two
        faithful hearts, learn that pure affection never dies.

Danton appears. Ernestine places a noose over his head. Robespierre rescues
him and offers to save Victor:

ERN.   Oh, speak! Heaven will bless you for the act. Your name shall mingle in our
        prayers.
ROB.   Time presses. Let me whisper in your ear. (*He does so.*)
ERN.   Monster, I marvel the fires of Heaven do not strike you dead!

He wishes to hand her over to Guillaume Le Rouge (or Red Bill, a blacksmith). She prefers death:

Music—"Dead March" and muffled drum. Ernestine touches Robespierre, points
to Heaven, and goes out proudly with the Mob.

But she has left behind her a locket which he recognizes as he cries to Red
Bill:

ROB.   Fly, man; let her not perish! In pity's sake, spare me that! Let her not
        mount the scaffold, for she is——
GUIL.   What?
ROB.   My child!

This is too much for Red Bill. "Bah," he says, "I spit upon you!" Robespierre replies, "I am not the man I was, but feel that I am a father and will die to save my child." Though stabbed he dashes through the Mob:

An explosion takes place, the walls and prison falling discover Ernestine on the point of being executed. Robespierre staggers through ruins in time to save her. He bears her in his arms to C., and falls dead. Victor and the rest form a picture. Encounter between the Mob and Soldiery, and the Curtain descends on the DESTRUCTION OF THE BASTILLE.

What this establishes is a decided belief in the French Revolution as a setting for self-sacrifice nobly undergone in order that true lovers should not be parted. The public liked the play well enough for the authors to transfer it in 1844 to the Adelphi, where Celeste played no more bad parts. Nine years later *Le Chevalier De Maison Rouge* became for her and for Webster, *Geneviève; or, The Reign Of Terror.*

Here begins a fierce controversy which brings an unfounded charge of brain-picking against Watts Phillips, a stage-struck journalist. He once hoped to be an actor and stood prepared with swords, tights, boots and wardrobe, not unlike the amateur in "Great Expectations", for his first chance. It arrived as a note from Edinburgh to say he was to open in the part of Banquo to the Lady Macbeth of the American tragic actress, Charlotte Cushman. "Imagine me," he lamented, "with my five feet nothing as Banquo, beside that mature and majestic female."

Instead he cultivated a resemblance by bust to Shakespeare and sent MSS. to Webster. His first, *The Dead Heart*, was accepted but held back, because of its resemblance to *Geneviève*. Landry, a revolutionary, is sent to the Bastille for life because Catherine, his fiancée, is desired in matrimony by a nobleman and out of matrimony by the Abbé Latour. Years later, at the storming of the Bastille, Landry is dragged from his dungeon, numbed in mind, body and soul, recovers his wits and memory, and becomes a leader of the people. Behind closed doors he forces the Abbé to fight to the death. Catherine's husband is dead—her son must die—but at her entreaty Landry saves the boy by taking his place beneath the guillotine.

After three years of waiting, Watts Phillips saw urgent need for action in the resemblance of his own story to "A Tale of Two Cities", which he read week by week in "All the Year Round". Glorious Old Ben was as difficult of approach as a citadel, but at last the desperate author took him by storm and *The Dead Heart* opened at the New Adelphi (larger and more lavish than the old) in the November of 1859. Celeste was not in the cast; she had set up in management at the Lyceum. There, smarting from the sense of wrong, real or imaginary, she thought to take the wind out of Webster's sails in the January of 1860 by appearing in her third Revolution drama—

Tom Taylor's *A Tale Of Two Cities*, in which she played the boy in the prologue and then Madame Defarge.

What a masterpiece of romance Dickens had created could not be disguised by the clumsiest of dramatizations. Even at the Old Vic the sheer magic of its story-telling impressed an awed gallery that let fall upon the pit any stone bottles it had brought to throw at the stage. *The Tale Of Two Cities ; or, The Incarcerated Victim Of The Bastille* which opened there on July 7, 1860, was "adapted from Charles Dickens's story" by Fox Cooper, and had a very large cast of forceful players unknown to fame. With a technique born of no imperfect understanding of the Surreyside public the author exerted his powers to their utmost at the beginning.

The prologue was not skimped: in one scene Doctor Manette is forcibly abducted in "a retired part of the Quay, by the Seine"; in another he attends "the dying victim of St. Evremonde's Amour", who has several stirring last dying speeches because she is played by the manageress, E. F. Savile's widow. She dies. Manette's cries are stifled while the Marquis flings these words to the back wall of the gallery where they are understood full well: "Away with him to the Bastille!" In the Wine House Mrs. Savile reappears as Madame Defarge, and righteous anger in the audience fires a volley of oaths as the Marquis reappears:

(*A crash heard, followed by a shriek.*)

DEFARGE.　See—what's that?

JACQUES 1 (*looking out*). A child under the wheels of a carriage.

(*Enter* GASPARD *hurriedly*, C.)

GASPARD.　Dead, dead! My child is slaughtered!

Enter the MARQUIS DE ST. EVREMONDE, C. *Madame Defarge is observed immediately to place a rose in her head-dress selected from some she has on the counter. Jacques 4, by gestures, points him out as the party whose carriage had run over the Road-Mender.*

GASPARD (*frantically*).　See! look here! (*pointing off*, C.) Trampled to death by the feet of your horses—my child—one of us! Shame! shame!

MARQUIS (*taking out his purse*). It is extraordinary to me that you people cannot take care of yourselves and your children—one or other of you is for ever in the way. How do I know what injury you have done to my horses? Here—(*throwing down money*)—take that.

Madame Defarge, who is seated knitting, looks up and their eyes meet. The Marquis bows—an "improvement" on Dickens, who wrote "His contemptuous eye passed over her and over all the other rats." She tells him she is making shrouds. "*Looking in the face of the Marquis—their eyes meet— the Marquis clenches his teeth in anger*," and through his effort the actress-manager wins a round of applause. That act ends magnificently in the wretched garret where Manette, working at his bench, is found by Lucy and

THE TALE OF TWO CITIES;

OR, THE INCARCERATED VICTIM OF THE BASTILLE.

AN HISTORICAL DRAMA, IN A PROLOGUE AND FOUR ACTS.

ADAPTED FROM CHARLES DICKENS'S STORY, BY FOX COOPER.

First Performed at the Victoria Theatre, July 7th, 1860.

Dramatis Personæ.

[*See page 22.*

PROLOGUE.—A.D. 1763.

MARQUIS DE ST. EVREMONDE	{ (Aged 32, the Seducer—Haughty in Manner, and with a Face like a fine Mask)	Mr. Frederick Byefield.
CHEVALIER ST. EVREMONDE	{ (Aged 28—Brother to the Marquis, who looked on the Sufferer, whose Life was ebbing out)	Mr. Henderson.
DOCTOR MANETTE	{ (Aged 25—a Young Rising Physician of Beauvais, a good Husband and a Loving Son	Mr. W. Harmer.
SOLOMON BARSAD	{ (Aged 30—Gamekeeper to the Marquis, Aider and Abettor in his villanies)	Mr. J. Bradshaw.
GABRIELLE	{ (His Assistant, Tool, Lacquey, a Man who would do anything for Money)	Mr. N. Harrison.
LUCILLE	(The Betrayed—The Dying Victim of St. Evremonde's Amour)	Mrs. E. F. Saville.

No. 780. Dicks' Standard Plays.

Dramatized Dickens at the Old Vic

"No, you wicked foreign woman; I am your match"

recalled to life. Act II belongs to Sydney Carton and ends when he makes confession to Lucy, "In my degradation, I have not been so degraded but that the sight of you with your father, and of this home, made such a home by you, has stirred old shadows that I thought had died out of me."

Now Jerry Cruncher comes on in a "carpenter's scene", which signified nothing to the inhabitants of the New Cut except that frenzied preparations are going on behind. The big scene starts quietly with the Marquis at wine. He is disturbed by shadows and whispers. Madame Defarge appears:

MARQUIS.   Lucille! vision of horror. What sends you here to shake a heart that human peril never yet hath cowed?

MAD. D. (*coming forward*). 'Tis not Lucille's spirit, but her loving sister, that hovers around you, to embitter with her curses your last scene of guilt and misery—to remind you of yonder room stained with my brother's blood.

After that, for the conflagration without which no Surreyside drama can triumph, the entire back of scene falls, discovering the Marquis on couch with Gaspard's knife in his breast. The smoke clears away; the street beyond is crowded with people who exclaim loudly, "Extermination!" Madame Defarge, sitting on a stone, knitting, cries: "Burn! Burn! Burn! St. Evremonde! Sister, thou art avenged."

There may be only one more act, but it has six scenes, including public rejoicings in the Place of the Bastille and the Tribunal. The author, determined to put the whole of the novel on the stage, fails only when Darnay has been carried off and Carton, alone in the cell, goes to aperture, looks out and describes the carting away of prisoners in the tumbrils: "Look on it, ye despots—mighty as you are, you cannot conquer love!" The way has to be cleared for Mrs. Savile. Madame Defarge, shot in the struggle with Miss Pross, holds the stage with her death agonies until two minutes before the final curtain. After her inward eye has seen "the guillotine with a thousand faces gazing upwards at the condemned as from a sea of dark and troubled water", after the noise of the guillotine descending is heard amid suppressed cries, Carton comes in:

DARNAY.   The victim, then, was——

CARTON.   The traitor, Barsad.

The idea being that if the manageress could not have the final curtain nobody else should.

The next event in this chronicle is, most aptly, the birth at Wivenhoe of John Martin Harvey on June 22, 1863. His parentage and home are described in his autobiography. The usual idea that when any actor is born the entire theatrical industry marks time until he grows up can be ignored for once.

Instead, the opposite view may be held that when the make-believe phantasmagoria of a stage career comes up for debate, birthplaces, scenes of childhood and progress at schools dwindle in importance. Spiritual heredity ranks before material. A man's physical forbears fade into the past if he throws over their trade. When Martin Harvey turned his back on the Wivenhoe shipyard, where his father built yachts, he began to claim his descent from an ancestry of actors with particular reference to Irving, whose career had now just reached the point where he could play Hamlet on odd occasions in out-of-the-way places.

CHAPTER V

THE VICTORIAN SHAKESPEARE

PLAYS now began to sort themselves out. By haphazard choice some acquired a prestige denied to others; origin had nothing to do with it, for the Boulevard's *Courrier* of Lyons docked his scenes next to Covent Garden's Lady of Lyons. The bundle of acting editions looks strange when you pick out the favoured ones, yet these together form what might be termed "The Works of the Victorian Shakespeare". Imagine that impressive volume in some learned edition *de luxe*. Commentators in prefaces explain how, as in Queen Elizabeth's time, the world had to be ransacked for stories. There are borrowings from Goëthe but more particularly from Scott and Lytton, from Hugo and Dumas, from Goldsmith (as a novelist), from Dickens and from the calendars of crime. At heart that is very nearly all, although Byron comes in too at first and Tennyson at last. In bulk they may serve as Neo-Gothic Shakespeare, for they are invariably acted in the same repertoire as genuine Shakespeare. Yet their nineteenth-century spirit is not purely imitative. There is something else, something distinctive about their leading characters.

What did actor-manager romantics see in the portraits, Louis XI as well as Ruy Blas, Vanderdecken as well as Sydney Carton, hung in their oddly mixed gallery? Although the quality that these characters have in common cannot be reduced to a formula, it stamps, no matter how vaguely or unsurely, them all. The secret sorrow of some, the sense of guilt or the feeling of despair in others, lays upon each the burden of destiny. The lackey's shame at his imposture, the murderer's tortured conscience, the drunkard's contemplation of his own worthlessness, the innocent man's consternation when falsely convicted, the brother's mission of revenge, are the reactions of heroes who feel themselves oppressed.

The most significant figure is the Master of Ravenswood, since actor after actor preferred this star-crossed lover of the Lothians to Shakespeare's. Actor-managers riper in years than Romeo would naturally, it might be argued, prefer Scott's. The reasoning is too facile. View the collection as a whole. Note which portraits catch the light, which are hidden. Whether for tears or for laughter the greater the burden of fate the better.

Some other heroes invented by authors here laid under contribution remain steadfastly outside this tradition. None of the four "Three Musketeers" has a soul like a pack-horse: none bears a burden to make him melancholy. They are the very opposite of Byron's Manfred, who is bowed under the weight of sins uncommitted, of damnation not upon his head, of a load of evil that is not there. For sweet clarity's sake the kind of novel or drama which follows the fashion set by Waverley, Rob Roy and Ivanhoe should be classified as adventure—"costume" is the stage term—to indicate a difference which has always existed.

One of the most hardy examples in this carefree mood was *Le Bossu*, by Anicet Bourgeois and Paul Feval, staged at the Porte-Saint-Martin with Melingue, new idol of the Boulevard, as the hero, in September, 1862. As *The Duke's Motto* it began its English and American career of over forty years the next January, when Fechter appeared in it at the Lyceum. The title could not be translated because Sheridan Knowles's *The Hunchback* still held its place on every English-speaking stage, but the change was all for the good since the motto, "I am here," became a catchword to advertise the play.

In the prologue Fechter, a roving blade, climbs a rope hand-over-hand to a window, utters those words to pretend he is the duke and so abducts the duke's infant daughter. A sudden change of heart makes him fight for instead of against his sworn enemy, who is, despite his aid, killed by a covetous prince. The roving blade escapes with the babe, who grows up among a band of gypsies in the Pyrenées to love and be loved by her protector. The prince has for bodyguard a villainous hunchback, whom the hero impersonates in order to win back for the heroine the rich ducal possessions.

Light-hearted romance won a victory with this, but *Bel Demonio*, Fechter's next Lyceum play at the end of 1863, merged into melodrama. After carrying off his beloved just as she was about to take the veil, he escaped as a monk through his pursuers. Above all he tumbled wounded down a rock into a torrent in the "sensation-scene" manner of the day. "Bounce, conventional stage chivalry, agony of the boards, pop, enter-at-the-nick-of-time, tableau and flummery", it was called. So this is where we draw the line.

Yet another category of limelight romance came into being when a way was discovered of doing without sudden death. Swords and knives were all very well for the Gallic drama, but not for Charles Reade and Tom Taylor. They wrote for Ben Webster at the Haymarket an adaptation of Reade's novel on the subject of Peg Woffington, and called it *Masks And Faces*. In the cloak-minus-sword drama it is rivalled by another story (destined, this, for Martin Harvey's repertoire) of a heart of gold wrapped in a player's hide.

To cure a maiden of her love for him, Garrick exerts his histrionic powers to debase himself in her eyes; and this, so the gang of authors who evolved the story claimed, was supposed to be founded more or less on fact. So it was, even though that "fact" did belong to the life of somebody else. John Philip Kemble, according to the story told in his own day, had set a well-born lady sighing. In order to cure her he did not pretend to be drunken or ill-conditioned, but tried a remedy more desperate still. On the promise of a handsome sum if he would wed another, Kemble forthwith chose a widow, faithfully keeping his side of the bargain though the anxious parent never kept his.

All of this might be thoroughly in keeping with eighteenth-century comedy but it would not do for nineteenth-century romance. Another thing which impressed the Paris hack who wished to adapt the anecdote to his needs was that Kemble's name was not well enough known.

"Garrick Médecin", by J. Bouchardy, in "Le Monde Dramatique", Vol. II, 1835, tells how Lady Anna, daughter of milord Doney, Duc de Tavistock, refuses to read *les saintes lectures des clergymen* and turns to the dangerous works of Shakespeare instead, because she feels a fatal passion for Garrick. When offered a large bribe to disillusion her he refuses. She is sent to Richmond in the charge of one of those "old maidens", who invariably complain of having lost a fortune and smell strongly of Windsor soap.

Into their house bursts a drunken *cocher* who shouts, "Oh, pretty, pretty, miss, *vous êtes belle comme Venus*," and tells her that Garrick is as brutal as a sailor. "Sailors are the most gallant men in England," says the old maiden. He apologizes, and when her back is turned reveals to Lady Anna that he is Garrick—disguised because a visit from an actor would ruin her reputation.

Later the Duc de Tavistock arrives with a staid middle-aged man, doctor or lawyer, who will not agree that the king should be asked to suppress the theatres. When he leaves, the duke describes him as a friend he cannot acknowledge—an actor. On recovering from the shock of discovering that this visitor also is none other than Garrick, Lady Anna marries a baronet. Years pass. The baronet's wife, a duchess now that her father is dead, meets Garrick and asks why he sighs. For the first time he confesses his love. Their hands meet.

What it all amounts to is a whitewashing process. While Kean, much written about in "Le Monde Dramatique", stood for genius and disorder, Garrick now served to show how disorder could be assumed for virtue's sake. Victorian honour was satisfied. That the world agreed this table may show:

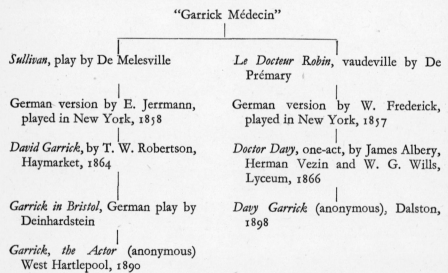

"Garrick Médecin"

Sullivan, play by De Melesville

German version by E. Jerrmann, played in New York, 1858

David Garrick, by T. W. Robertson, Haymarket, 1864

Garrick in Bristol, German play by Deinhardstein

Garrick, the Actor (anonymous) West Hartlepool, 1890

Le Docteur Robin, vaudeville by De Prémary

German version by W. Frederick, played in New York, 1857

Doctor Davy, one-act, by James Albery, Herman Vezin and W. G. Wills, Lyceum, 1866

Davy Garrick (anonymous), Dalston, 1898

With a reversal of sexes the story became *Tiridate ; ou, Comédie Et Tragédie*, by M. R. Fournier. *Comedy And Tragedy*, a translation by W. Robson (not to be confused with Gilbert's piece with the same title), was played at the Gymnase, Paris, in 1841, and with the new title of *The Tragedy Queen* at the Lyceum in 1847. Charles Reade changed it into *Art* (which he also wrote as a novel) at the St. James's in 1855. For New York in 1868 it became *An Actress By Daylight*, which was brought to the St. James's in 1871. Reade's version was cut down as *Nance Oldfield* to serve Ellen Terry as a one-act play, often with Martin Harvey's "support". Barrie's *Rosalind* also shows how a middle-aged player disillusions a young lover.

Though cloaks without swords merely mean domestic drama in costume, the plays which Tom Robertson wrote without costume shrivelled while *David Garrick* stayed alive. First Sothern, at a time when he was still inviting ridicule with his tomfoolery as Lord Dundreary, bestowed glamour upon himself as Garrick by personifying self-sacrifice in satin knee-breeches; then Charles Wyndham, after serving as a surgeon in the American Civil War, regarded it as his favourite part, and there were others in regular procession until Martin Harvey made it his own.

Yet another type of domestic-cum-historical dramas is indicated by Ellen Terry when she writes, "How many times Shakespeare draws fathers and daughters, and how little stock he seems to take of *mothers*!" though the nineteenth-century's grieving fathers came not from Brabantio but from Goldsmith's Vicar. Here was a variant of the man by fate oppressed; as such the Vicar of Wakefield was increasingly honoured as the century progressed, and Olivia had no rival until the twentieth century favoured another in a time of war—*The Burgomaster Of Stilemonde*.

Romance must be subdivided. The domestic is a class apart. There remain two distinct types. One is cloak-and-sword unfettered by "psychology"; the other wears its cloak with a difference. Keep tales of adventure separate from those romances which are not exploits of venturesome, healthy carcases, but experiences in spirit. There is a vital difference between *Henry V* and *Richard II*, even though both are Shakespeare and both English chronicles.

There is a difference between adventure's battle of friends *versus* foes and melodrama's contest of vice *versus* virtue; there is also a difference between these and the romance which is concerned with neither so much as with the struggle in some troubled soul. Ben Webster's very peculiar Robespierre, dodging in and out of the Bastille as though he owns it, makes some attempt at this, even as Macbeth does. Tampering with morality is what it was sometimes called, because it overthrew the popular desire for heroism and villainy to be as clearly distinguished as black and white. But while it offended the ethical, it gratified misgivings in the heart.

How this affected the actor was expounded by Sir John Martin-Harvey to members of the Royal Society of Literature in a lecture towards the end of his life. Quoting again from Talma he found truth in the argument that the actor, in delineating "odious characters and vile passions", paints them by analogy:

"In fact, amongst the irregular passions which disgrace humanity, there are some which possess points of contact with those that ennoble it. Thus the sentiment of a noble emulation enables us to define what envy may feel; the just resentment of wrongs shows us in miniature the excesses of hatred and vengeance. Reserve and prudence enable us to point dissimulation. The desires, the torments, and the jealousies of love enable us to conceive all its frenzies and initiate us into the secrets of its crimes. These combinations, these comparisons, are the result of a rapid and imperceptible labour of sensibility, united with intelligence, which secretly operates on the actor, as on the poet, and which reveals to him what is foreign in his own nature—the viler passions of guilty and corrupt minds."

Here is the seed from which twentieth-century romance grew. It certainly was not made according to any literary plan. It was not necessarily a struggle between good and evil, between courage and fear, between hope and despair, between resolve and fulfilment: it was not merely a perpetuated melancholy from Byron or from Hamlet. So many definitions which suggest themselves prove inadequate that it deserves to be treated with more respect than a mere literary or theatrical "influence". Playwright, player, playgoer were all in a conspiracy to imagine what the realist would decry as a vain thing; they agreed to find expressed in acting feelings not to be expressed in words—"To add the shades that are wanting or that language cannot express," said Talma. Such acting suffered the spontaneous workings of the mind to have "free course for moments of exaltation".

By the time Martin Harvey was old enough to gather vague ideas of what occupied adult minds the kind of fiction which constituted the Victorian Works of Shakespeare had permeated into every factory, every office, every shop, every home, every public-house, every school. Everybody knew who the lady of Lyons was, had gained a thoroughly mistaken idea of the private life of David Garrick, believed Olivia to be the chief character in "The Vicar of Wakefield", knew that the spiritual birthplace of the Mosaic law was Corsica, and thought of the French Revolution in terms of a life nobly laid down to save another's. If the reasons for all this have been made clear in the foregoing five chapters, Book I of this biography has not been written in vain.

Irving as "Mathias" in
The Bells

[*Photo: A. Corbett*

**Martin Harvey as
"Mathias"**

Dearer Than Life: three actors who helped at the start—
Wyndham (standing, left); Clayton (standing); Irving (extreme right)

BOOK II

CHAPTER I

FROM *THE BELLS* TO *LOUIS XI*

"My beloved master" is how Martin Harvey spoke of Irving. There is no doubting the discipleship. No actor ever sat more attentively at the feet of another. Yet this was in no frenzy of imitation, out of no desire to profit by borrowed glory, through no fault of servile idolatry. Why he stayed so long under one management might be ascribed to the need of a weekly pay-packet. But as other young actors in that company did not stay, the plain fact emerges that he was wanted there more than elsewhere.

He belonged there. Those were his natural surroundings, and they have to be explained in order to explain him. To understand the growth of his mind he must be seen against that background of romance by gaslight, a youth attaining manhood among a group of figures so glamorous that in retrospect they seem more than lifesize.

Justice so far has not been done to those personages, exalted in looks, noble in bearing and giving utterance to enchantment not so much noticed then as now, when the golden voices they made customary are rare. The inheritor of their tradition felt overawed at the tapestry created in his memory as these receded one by one. So imposing becomes this procession of them that he might wonder whether the human form could ever again in the theatre attain such majesty.

Enough time has gone by to warrant a spelling out of each name for the benefit of new generations who are barely conversant with any, which is not surprising because all the bright young pens of that day were writing addresses of welcome to the anti-romantical dawn. Irving, of course, is remembered, but even he needs a plain statement to show where he stood; and as the whole of that pageant is meaningless without him, his reign at the Lyceum will be recorded here. Whether familiar or not, the story must be considered anew, not this time as fact and anecdote but as evidence of a spirit which stirred men deeply, sometimes unaccountably.

The Lyceum had been taken by Hezekiah Linthicum Bateman, an American whose heritage of religious zeal had changed into stage-fever. Two of his daughters, starting as infant prodigies, had become actresses of note. Now it was the turn of Isabel, but the piece failed. When Bateman was thinking of shutting up shop, Irving persuaded him to stage a melodrama from the French called *The Bells*. It opened on November 25, 1871.

One act of idle gossip about the powers of a mesmerist at the fair, that mingles with recollections of the crime committed fifteen years ago, ends when Mathias hears sleigh-bells and sees a vision. The Jew, standing, reins in hand, "suddenly turns his face, which is ashy pale, and fixes his eyes sternly upon him; Mathias utters a prolonged cry of terror, and falls senseless—(hurried Music)". Another act ends with celebrations of his daughter's wedding:

(MATHIAS *is seated—in the midst of the waltz bells are heard off*—MATHIAS *starts up and rushes in the midst of the waltzers.*)

MATHIAS.   The Bells! The Bells!
CATHERINE. Are you mad?
          (MATHIAS *seizes her by the waist and waltzes wildly with her.*)
MATHIAS.   Ring on! Ring on! Houp! Houp!
          (*Music, forte—while the waltz is at its height the drop falls.*)

The shudder has yet to come. In his bedroom, when some revellers have bade him good night, Mathias dreams that he is on trial for murder: in the trance he is sent into by the mesmerist he demonstrates how he listened for the sleigh, how with a savage roar he struck down his victim, how he bore the body to the lime-kiln: "Go into the fire, Jew, go into the fire."

The vision ends. It is morning. The door is broken down by fearful neighbours. Mathias gasps: "The rope, the rope! Cut the rope!" As he stares vacantly about him his hands clutch at his throat, and then he dies.

In print, whatever difference existed between Erckmann-Chatrian's *Le Juif Polonais* and *The Bells* consisted mainly of new stage directions. The plot underwent very little change. Yet there were two distinct tales, opposite in meaning and effect. What had been the realistic study of a bovine mind, intent only upon material benefits to purse and stomach and self-satisfaction, now appeared as fresh romantic torment for the man accursed.

No more profitable study occurs in the development of nineteenth-century acting than the comparison between the Paris production and its London counterpart. English critics who saw Coquelin in the part complained that he went out of his way to represent himself as a common-or-garden innkeeper, who laughed to himself at having hoodwinked his neighbours and cheated the law. Thus would an unimaginative mind and insensitive nature, he seemed to argue, cause any twinge of conscience to be ignored.

Mathiss, the simple old fellow, comes home from the fair to tell his family about the clever mesmerist. Even when the murder of the Polish Jew is mentioned one quick change of expression is followed by a positive chuckle. When a Polish Jew, no wraith but just another traveller like the one he murdered, enters at the moment, he utters one sharp cry, not of terror but pain:

"We say to ourselves let M. Coquelin only be left alone on the stage, and he will become a totally different man. Not a bit of it. He goes on chuckling with his conscience, not wrestling with it. He hugs himself with delight that there are such fools in the world, but apparently he has no apprehension. The scene with the moneybags how tame—the discovery of the bit of gold left from the robbery, how it is slurred over! Mathiss puts the blood-money into his pocket without so much of a shudder. Who can forget the agonized look of Mr. Irving when he separated the blood-stained coin from the marriage portion?"

In the dream Coquelin was alternately angry and lachrymose, savage and weak. He had cast from his consideration all notion of a haunted man, showing instead what an everyday little Alsacian burgomaster would do if suddenly reminded of a crime which ordinarily would not disturb such mind as he possessed.

The Paris of Zola saw the point of this, but the English critic straight from the Lyceum, while admitting that the French play would not stand Irving's "elaborate embroidery", thought that Coquelin had neglected to observe its "psychology". Another, who did admire his effort to resist the mesmerist and his byplay when the spell was cast upon him, still doubted whether this study of the part was "essentially correct". A Redskin is not red to another Redskin, nor a Celestial yellow-skinned to another Celestial, and just so a romantic actor is normal to romantic critics.

Fifty years of imagining the Man Accursed had suddenly evoked the very spirit of him. Only in this way can the sense of what Irving meant in 1870 be conveyed. Earlier visions of conscience as a torture worse than every imaginable agony of death, which is what Ahasuerus and Vanderdecken amounted to, took on flesh in *The Bells*. Its leading gentleman had, of course, been respected for some half a dozen years as a capable actor; he had been known as such through the theatrical vogue of that "unwholesome subject" bigamy, when Lady Audley and Lady Isabel held the stage, but in these particular years conscience had been more esteemed in women than in men. Irving changed it round again.

Exactly why? You cannot blame it upon the play, because as *Le Juif Polonais*, in French or in translation, it had meant nothing of the kind. When the actor read it, he read *into* it a thing not to be described (unless by the magic of Poe when he put the maelstrom itself into print) but acted. Here is a fine peg to hang a zeitgeist on. Instead, taking a hint from the writings of Talma, Martin Harvey and other actors besides, we might inquire whether Irving found grief or torment within himself and magnified it.

Melancholy and the horrors,[1] according to Ellen Terry, stirred his

---

[1] In an age of sobriety it becomes necessary to explain that more than plain horror is intended. When drunkards clutched vainly at terrible shapes which floated before their eyes, unseen by others, somebody would explain to anybody green enough to stand aghast, "He's got the horrors."

soul. That is effect. There was cause for it. Burdened souls persisted in the theatre because they existed outside the theatre. Other entertainments set new fashions, seemed dazzling for a while, had their day. Compared with these the sorrows of the haunted man, expressed in poetry, fustian or downright doggerel, held a fascination which abided.

At one end of the century Manfred, by the strong curse which is upon him, tells the evil spirit

> I bear within
> A torture which could nothing gain from thine.

and at the century's other end an equally inexplicable wrongdoer became the hero of a public-house ballad, "I'm the Man What's Done Wrong to My Parents":

> And sadly I wanders about
> To earn some small mite
> For my shelter to-night,
> God help me, for now I'm cast out.

And what these two have in common is what Irving expressed as no other man expressed, no matter what his medium, upon the stage.

Before extolling him as the embodied spirit of his century we must see what there was in his own life to account for such impassioned outbursts of remorse, repentance, regret. That the iron should have entered into his soul has been explained at times by the ardour of his apprenticeship: the drudgery of "stock" at Edinburgh, where he played hundreds of parts in everything from farce to pantomime. But no man can complain of hardship who finds fame in his early thirties: by the ordinary standards of life Irving shot to the skies like a rocket. If some cause must be found for his craving to exercise his genius in horror, torment and despair, then not his career but his private life must be thought of.

Biographers too near to him omit facts essential to understanding. They forbear to mention, for example, that there was an actor with a prior right to his name. While turning over old playbills you may come across "Master Irving" at an unexpectedly early date. This was Joseph Henry Irving, who might have called himself the real Irving because he had a place on the London stage while Henry Brodribb, of the same age, was nothing but an amateur.

Joseph made his way to Drury Lane, where he was the hero in *Faw Fee Fo Fum; or, Harlequin Jack The Giant Killer* when Christmas pantomimes were still a matter of acting as well as antics. That was in 1867 when the Mr. Brodribb of private life appeared at the Queen's in Long Acre under a *nom de guerre*, not assumed in ignorance of its rightful owner because stage-struck youth takes very good note of youth so blessed as to be on the stage.

Literally to rob a fellow creature of his good name may seem funny, but such a clash to youngsters at the outset of their careers is not a joke; it constantly happens, and when one shines the other fades. As a fancy that invites the epithet of far-fetched the possibility suggests itself that Henry Irving felt acute regret when he uttered with soul-stirring sincerity Hood's "The Dream of Eugene Aram" at the time of his first London success:

> His hat was off, his vest apart,
>   To catch heaven's blessed breeze;
> For a burning thought was in his brow,
>   And his bosom ill at ease:
> So he lean'd his head on his hand, and read
>   The book between his knees.

Since the pangs of the conscience-smitten inspired his first overwhelming success, a surmise must be considered whether he felt any at the end of the real Irving's promising career in 1870 through death at the age of thirty-one. Many actors testify that the emotional experiences of real life can become the germ of great emotions on the stage.

The actor's private life may not always be solely a family affair. When biographers avoided the subject of Irving's marriage, the question mark they left proved more disturbing than the answer they withheld. The facts, not in any way scandalous, must be disclosed.

Strong parental disfavour, shown to the actor as suitor, was overcome by a bride fully prepared to endure poverty for his sake, before his successes at Drury Lane and the Gaiety in the autumn of 1869 showed that to be unlikely. They could not live without each other. They married only to discover they could not live with each other. To them in separation this began to appear incredible. Two years later they were reconciled. They were together for a very brief space before they had to accept its hopeless, inescapable truth.

The bitterness of the discovery was upon him at the time the mordant nature of his genius became apparent to him, when by chance he read the MS. of The Bells. There in the shuddering intake of breath, the hysterical gasp of terror, the distraught rigidity of limb, the petrified gaze at the mirage of despair, he gave vent to a secret misery of real despair.

That is the real Irving. That outward serenity of the academic dignitary in silk hat, *pince-nez* and frock-coat introduced make-believe into real life. How it succeeded, the maladroit terms of conventional praise disclosed. "Scholarly" was applied to Shakespearean productions which played havoc with the text, enlarged one part at the expense of the whole, and steadfastly pursued the *coup de théâtre* relentlessly and magnificently.

"Melodrama" was a word to anger him, though Ellen Terry used it when appreciating him with her zealous insight. His champions seemed angered by it too; instead of extolling *The Bells* in phrases that would amount to what we should call "theatre" they solemnly pronounced its "psychology" to be "correct". Romance was the norm of existence to people at the Lyceum.

As revival followed revival, critics noted Irving's far richer play of feature, bringing with it a variety of conflicting expression such as he had not used before, for he had "never hitherto so influenced his audience by a look or more thoroughly convinced them of the effect of a pause". When the daughter of Mathias cried, "Oh, Father, what a good man you are!" his look of supreme tenderness and speechless agony showed how the contentment of the present clashed with the "eternal memory of the irrevocable past". But the critic cannot leave it at that. "Actor" is not praise enough:

> "The difficulties of the last act, containing the realized dream, have been mastered by this indefatigable student. The excesses, the exaggerations, the undisciplined force have given way to a polished, a consistent, a truthful, and a very remarkable conception."

The praise cannot be truthful both times. What had once been "correct" now in retrospect becomes excess, exaggeration, undisciplined force. Studied effect never produced these torments, but critics wrote "student" and "scholarly" at all costs.

A battle of ideas follows. Coquelin expressed his in "Harper's" and Irving his in "The Nineteenth Century". It did not die down. Coquelin, who thought the reply unnecessarily indignant, declared he had been misrepresented. Inspirations might occur, during a performance, from what Irving had called the electric faculty, but serious scientific study came first. No amount of inspiration or electricity, said Coquelin, would produce anything like the effect of carefully considered intonation.

While lecturing thus, Coquelin would freely criticize Irving and mimic him to make the audience laugh. To clinch matters, he described his great rival, Mounet Sully, as "The French Irving". Beyond that, apparently, criticism could not go.

Correct or incorrect, *The Bells* triumphed. Bateman, so mindful of his family that he ranks as the foremost father-manager of the stage, wished to present his eldest and youngest daughters in his now prosperous theatre. While Irving took this play on tour they appeared in *Leah*, powerful drama of a persecuted Jewess, with John Ryder as the renegade villain.

After curtain-fall there were supper-parties to which came W. G. Wills, author of a new version of *Jane Shore*, so full of pathos that it toured continually until the leading lady died from melancholia. Throughout the eighteen-seventies and eighteen-eighties Wills brought poetry into the theatre in a regular supply. No doubt its quality fell below Shakespeare's, but he wrote about the same number of plays and in a not altogether dissimilar spirit.

There is a temptation to treat him as a joke since the one relic of his works is the ballad of "I'll sing thee songs of Araby" from *Lalla Rookh* dramatized. But no history of the stage would be comprehensive without him. No great genius was to hand, and so he went on as understudy; as such he performed marvels. That is the way his verse should be read. That is the way Irving read it.

"King of Bohemia" was Wills's rank and title. In a photograph that survives he looks it with curly bowler on wig, pipe stuck out of straggly white beard, caped overcoat to keep lumbago warm and bird-like eye fixed mildly aloft. In youth he came from Ireland to gaze upon the Tower of London. As a painter of children's portraits he had skill enough to win a royal command.

Actors who visited his studio found plays in MS. among palettes, easels, canvases and oil-paints. He had written one, *Ninon*, about the French Revolution at the time a friend took him to supper at the Lyceum. The manager read it, thought he had seen something like it before, and commissioned another play for his daughter instead. *Medea In Corinth* brought Isabel Bateman back to the footlights in the July of 1872.

Wills, appointed dramatist-in-ordinary to the Lyceum, wrote *Charles I* to the greater glory of both leading man and leading lady that September. It played havoc with history, but this should not blind any eye to the very notable service the author rendered the actor by revealing powers not suggested by *The Bells*.

When the time came for fresh horrors he responded to Irving's request for his favourite recitation to be turned into a play for the April of 1873. The poet liked to work at Brighton. To make ready for the journey he wrapped shirt, brush and comb and manuscript in the morning's newspaper, but could not go because his landlady's daughter had hidden his wig.

She had a habit of holding it to ransom for a guinea, and now he wanted guineas for his bill at the Old Ship. With nothing but a skull-cap to cover what made him blush like nakedness, he was a prisoner in his own house, having too strong a sense of honour merely to go and tell the child's mother. While still fretful over these scenes with the one young woman in his life, he wrote:

ARAM.   Put my hair from my eyes; I cannot see you, love.
RUTH.   There's nothing there—can you not see me? You are worn and weary but
          you are not ill.
ARAM (*trying to rise*). No, no, I am at peace. Come in—together we will see your
          father. Come in! The early cold strikes to my heart.
          (*He falls back.*)
RUTH (*watching him*). Your face seems altered! Why do you smile?
ARAM.   Oh, Ruth! I shall not die a death of shame.
RUTH.   No, you shall live.
ARAM (*shakes his head with a sad smile*). My hair—push it aside—I see you faintly.

Probably no more forcible example exists of romance as an alchemy able to change earthly dross into limelit art—actors are always citing examples of this on a far less impressive scale—but the self-same process can be examined by comparing the murder as done in Hood's ballad with the same murder as described in Wills's play:

> One that had never done me wrong—
> A feeble man and old;
> I led him to a lonely field,
> The moon shone clear and cold:
> Now here, said I, this man shall die,
> And I will have his gold.

> Two sudden blows with a ragged stick,
> And one with a heavy stone,
> One hurried gash with a hasty knife,
> And then the deed was done:
> There was nothing lying at my foot
> But lifeless flesh and bone!

> Nothing but lifeless flesh and bone,
> That could not do me ill;
> And yet I fear'd him all the more
> For lying there so still:
> There was a manhood in his look
> That murder could not kill!

As a realist—the greatest of his century, for his exposures of evil still shock—Hood took his criminology from the life: the efforts of Aram in his poem to find a hiding-place for the body copy details given in evidence at the most sensational murder trial of preceding years. As a romantic the bewhiskered and bald-headed stage-poet puffed at the short pipe in his moustache and drew entirely on his inward fancy, imagining himself a noble criminal. The portrait he drew and the portrait drawn by Hood compare like companion pictures of The Good Murderer and The Bad:

> I left her—straight into my breast there passes
> The soul of Cain—my will was not my own.
> In one fell thought I reckon a black score
> Against that—all that I might have won
> And all his villainy had robbed from me.
> Methinks, as I went out from her, the flame—
> The topaz crescent of the tiger's eye—
> Blazed into mine, as with a patient stealth
> He nears his prey before the thunderous bound.

I had refrained, but that the wretch held up
A woman's ornament—her name upon it
And read it with a mock. I sprang within—
Confronted him, and shouted "Coward! Thief!"
Close at his feet there lay a spade, this seized
I struck him down. I struck and struck again:
I only saw beneath my furious blows some writhing vermin—
Not a human life. Great God!
I can hear his cry, and see
The wild quenched gaze he fixed on me.

As a romantic Irving held the public imagination fast. While critics noted the "chronic disfigurement" of mannerisms that rendered him, so they said, unfit to walk or talk, audiences waved their hats or handkerchiefs and cheered. Years devoted to Kate and Isabel Bateman must be reckoned the prologue when *Richelieu*, *Hamlet*, *Macbeth*, *Othello* and *Richard III* won favour not so great as favour to come.

Had he kept loyal to masterpieces the fine frenzy with which his very name seemed charged like the shock of electricity would have vanished. Instead he turned aside from ways that belonged, more or less, to the idea behind "scholarly". His choice lighted by a surprising whim on *Le Courrier De Lyon*, known in England as *The Courier Of Lyons*, although people who saw not so much as the bare mention of a courier in the play cast doubts upon this pot-shot translation.

Irving asked Charles Reade to revise the script and took a hand in this as usual himself, but the result, *The Lyons Mail*, still remained stuff for the blood-tub. Now, unfettered by academic restraints, he could show how finely theatrical he could be as he switched from the despair of falsely-accused innocence to the sadistic delights of exultant guilt. He sprang the mine (in Garrick's phrase) when Dubosc, drunk with cognac and blood-lust, turned savage in the room he had hired in order to get a good view of his victim's dying agonies on the scaffold. He grinned and mocked at the raging people, crawled on his stomach to the open balcony, and beat a devil's tattoo with his heels; he smashed up the furniture, and flung bottles at the crowd in his impotent rage at being recognized. He knifed the arm thrust into the door which he tried to shut before the fight began between this wild beast at bay and the shrieking mob sworn to vengeance.

Only a few minutes before this Lesurques had moved his audience to tears over the heartbroken father's farewell in prison to his daughter. Save the beautiful farewell of Charles I, no stage pathos had been so true, so simple, and so unaffected as this, "Good-bye; God bless you."

Returning to Charles Kean's repertoire he pulled out *Louis XI*. "Irving is the more subtle. Kean was the more intense," was Herman Merivale's verdict. Though each made the part one of his greatest achievements their readings bore no resemblance. The trite remark that nineteenth-century romance suited nineteenth-century romantics must be made because critics to this day stand amazed at Irving's repertoire, as though Thomas Hardy had never written for their benefit the lines:

> Throbbing romance has waned and wanned
> No wizard wields the witching pen
> Of Bulwer, Scott, Dumas and Sand,
>   Gentlemen.

Praise ascended in chorus for the infinite variety, the jests and odd grimaces, the mind registered in the face, when Louis gave audience to the impetuous and insolent ambassador, or felt his youth revive at the sight of the cherry lips and buxon form of Martha, the peasant: for "the heterogeneous mixture of fervour and fawning, of craft and cunning, of terror and turpitude"; for the fearful agony of the half-frenzied King, after his terrible scene with Nemours, on seeing the phantom of his murdered victim; for the fight of the monarch over "the last inch of life with the king of terrors".

Already the Lyceum had begun to be a nursery of actor-managers. John Clayton left after playing Louis XIII in *Richelieu* and Cromwell in *Charles I* to make his fortune with a plot taken from "A Tale of Two Cities". One of the authors, Palgrave Simpson, had recently brought out *Marie Antoinette*, and therefore wanted to avoid the French Revolution. Accordingly, when collaborating with Herman Merivale in putting Sydney Carton on the stage, he changed him into a hero of the Rebellion of '45.

That method of dramatizing a novel, tried by Colman in *The Iron Chest*, makes a peculiar demand upon playgoers, for while they might lose themselves in fiction founded on fact there could be good reasons for quibbling over fiction founded on fiction and altered. Yet the Merivale-Simpson *All For Her* was approved in 1875 at the Mirror Theatre (formerly the Holborn, and then the Duke's before it made way for the First Avenue Hotel) because the authors scored a point Dickens missed when he made so little of the brave little seamstress.

Poor, reckless, good-for-nothing, drunken Hugh Trevor, whose fine nature showed through a mask of "cynicism and even of misanthropy", never lacked the love of a devoted little soul, Mary Rivers, who to be near him masqueraded in male attire. Hugh goes to the gallows under the pretence of being his double, Lord Edendale. Mary Rivers (disguised as a boy) perceives the impersonation:

MARY.   Ah! you are going to die for him! You shall not do it.
HUGH.   Peace.
MARY.   I cannot hold my peace. Here!
HUGH.   Silence I say. What right have you to question what I think right to do?
MARY.   What right! What right! The right of a woman who has loved you from a
                child. I am that Mary Rivers whose life and honour you saved—and
                I will not let you die! Help!

HUGH. Listen to me for a moment, Mary Rivers. You have loved me, you say.
MARY. All my life.
HUGH. I charge you by that love, Mary, to be silent now. We shall meet, I pray,
       where I am going. There is mercy in that great hereafter, which I am
       soon to understand.
MARY. Oh! Let me die with you!

"Soon to understand" is not an improvement on "than I have ever known", but the time for that to be transferred to the stage had yet to come.

That play was not seen by the Sydney Carton of the future, although it was at this time that he made his first acquaintance with the theatre. In order to see a performance by children of *H.M.S. Pinafore*, John Harvey, naval architect of Wivenhoe, Essex, took his four children to the Opera Comique while spending a holiday in London, and then and there had an inkling that his son John Martin, now aged fifteen, might do worse than take the stage as his career. This chance thought might help to explain why the boy became an actor, but not why he became a particular sort of actor. The records of his childhood give little hint of a trend towards spirituality. Facile reasoning might make a great deal of the long illness of his mother and the impression left on him by her death. Much might be made of the mysticism of Swedenborgianism, which was a family heritage. But nearly all such talk of early influences is vain until we can explain why religious surroundings will produce piety in one young breast, violent revolt in another similarly placed, and a mingling in yet a third of devout feelings combined with a profane resolve to subdue the saintly heart by acts of sin. The Autobiography of Sir John Martin-Harvey leaves us guessing.

CHAPTER II

EDUCATING AN ACTOR

FOR the leading lady of the Lyceum under his own management, Irving engaged Ellen Terry. She left the touring company of Charles Kelly (her second husband) and came to Town that summer of 1878 to bestow her rarity upon that overrated young woman, Ophelia. As she entered the theatre, one of a new generation of romantics passed the columns of its solemn portico. He was on his way to school in a narrow gorge called the Strand, through foul slums. All around lay authentic theatreland, the real, the blushful theatreland, glamour in a setting of mediaeval stench.

When Garrick managed Drury Lane he had bought a garden linked by alleys with the Strand and Catherine Street solely because he feared a rival playhouse on that site. He permitted a picture gallery to arise as a Lyceum, but even before Wellington Street (brought into being as the approach to Waterloo Bridge) gave the building new and imposing frontage nothing could keep performers out of that or any other hall on soil which produced plays as naturally as Covent Garden produced vegetables.

With its old Strand frontage turned into a wineshop besides which a tunnel was made for crowds to wait before they squeezed through a bottle-neck into the pit, the Lyceum now put up its columns to outvie Drury Lane in dignity. Behind these were spacious saloons and lobbies. Evening dress was "more commonly in vogue in the stalls and dress circles here" than at most theatres.

Across Wellington Street the Old Gaiety turned its back, where chorus girls hurried into their stage-door with a swish of long skirts, upon the sacred portico of the temple they had aptly dubbed "St. Lyceum". Eastwards the squalor of George Yard, Helmet Court, Eagle Court, Feathers Court, Angel Court and Maypole Alley—names echoing some forgotten legend where they ringed an iron-foundry—separated these theatres, royal or at least princely, from a group of less distinguished neighbours.

Outside the Gaiety's little frontage in the Strand the Penny-bus conductors put down their top-hatted fares from green Favourites, chocolate Westminsters, white Bromptons, red Hammersmiths and blue Blackwalls. When playgoers crossed Catherine Street, public-houses offered to refresh them, as though paving-slabs must parch their throats like a desert, at every few steps all the way to St. Mary-le-Strand.

On the south side of this island church, right fork to the pocket woodland round St. Clement Danes, the narrowest stretch of Strand—*the* Strand as distinct from wide West Strand—stood the Royal Strand Theatre (Aldwych Station, now that the whole place has gone sober). On the north side of St.

Mary's, left fork to the same sparrows' dusty forest, gables overhung the still narrower Holywell Street, with its booksellers' row for the delight of antiquarianism and for nasty minds shamelessly provoked by paper-backs which showed ladies sitting on gentlemen's knees and displaying ankles in a white froth as though in a pot of beer.

Where Drury Lane made a right-angle turn citywards stood the Olympic (the main entrance to Bush House was its stage). Newcastle Street had to be crossed here and on the other side Wych Street began; since its whereabouts start such catastrophic arguments in a story by Stacey Aumonier which deserves to be cherished, it might be described as Drury Lane's continuation to St. Clement Danes.

Gallery-doors for wall-rubbing tipplers to fall into indicated the side walls of the rickety twins which stood back to back with only a party-wall between them, so that a noisy performance in one could be heard above a quiet performance in the other. The Globe had its main entrance in Newcastle Street; the front of the Opera Comique stood afar off, opposite the Royal Strand, and its more opulent patrons, when they left the carriages by St. Mary-le-Strand, had to grope their way through dismal catacombs if they wanted to sit in boxes or stalls.

Yet Gilbert and Sullivan, whose partnership began with *Thespis* at the Gaiety that autumn when Irving first made himself felt at the house next door, drew the smart set to "Theatre Royal Tunnels" by bringing out *The Sorcerer, H.M.S. Pinafore, The Pirates Of Penzance* and *Patience* there. The Savoy Theatre, now being built for them, would be ready for the fourth of these to be transferred to it in the October of 1881. Rumours that the slum clearance fad from Paris would spread to this district had long been heard; in fact, the jerry-builder who ran up the rickety twins was commonly supposed to have got wind of it a little (from his own point of view) too soon. Somebody might be compensated but he would die first.

Such was the Strand. Just as ancestral ghosts fly from castles when plumbers come in, so its enchantment would leave behind nothing but a name when the sanitary inspectors should at last have demolition squads under their command. Though a queer country to be educated in, no *alma mater* could be apter for an actor. King's College, a deep cellar-like place beneath that unstormed bastille, Somerset House, was Martin Harvey's school, and this is how he described it when in the Chair at a King's annual dinner:

"The class-rooms were on each side of the foggy basement, stifling in summer and deadly cold in winter. For exercise we had the choice of a dreary expanse of asphalt, entirely enclosed by buildings, called—God help us!—the playground, or that flagged and foggy passage lighted by flickering gas-jets. Up and down that funereal tunnel the champions of the Sixth Form marched, half a dozen of them linked arm-in-arm, taking up as much room as they could—thereby causing the smaller boys to dodge round the end of the line when they had to pass them."

The names of the masters are in Sir John's autobiography. Omitting them here provides one last chance of insisting, for the benefit of obdurately conservative minds, that this is a stage biography.

.   .   .   .   .

At the other end of the public-houses in close array *Hamlet* went into rehearsal and Ellen Terry, arriving to be Irving's leading lady for the first time, looked around her at an auditorium "rather like the toy cardboard theatre which children used to be able to buy for sixpence". It was decorated in dull gold and dark crimson, and had "funny boxes with high fronts like old-fashioned church pews". Already it had a tradition that had to be served. She had prepared herself in deep earnest:

"Like all Ophelias before (and after) me, I went to the madhouse to study wits astray. I was disheartened at first. There was no beauty, no nature, no pity in most of the lunatics. Strange as it may sound, they were too *theatrical* to teach me anything . . . My experiences convinced me that the actor must imagine first and observe afterwards. It is no good observing life and bringing the result to the stage without selection, without a definite idea. The idea must come first, the realism afterwards."

Her impression of Irving matches, though unintentionally, what Mrs. Clive had recorded of Garrick whom she had seen with magic hammer in in hand, endeavouring "to beat your ideas into the heads of creatures who had none of their own". Garrick, with lamb-like patience, tried to make them comprehend him, and when that could not be done the lamb turned into a lion. By this great labour and pains the public were entertained. "They thought they all acted very fine; they did not see you pull the wires."

That was long ago, but not long enough to mean any break with tradition, for the Lyceum stage was still "set" for the royal box so that the monarch, even though never present, would not miss a point. With this in mind compare Kitty Clive's words with these of Ellen Terry's:

"He never got at anything *easily*, and often I felt angry that he would waste so much of his strength in trying to teach people to do things the right way. Very often it only ended in his producing actors who gave colourless, feeble, and unintelligent imitations of him. There were exceptions, of course."

Interior of the old Lyceum

When it came to the last ten days before the date named for the production of *Hamlet*, and her scenes with him were still unrehearsed, she grew "very anxious and miserable": though still a stranger in the theatre she plucked up enough courage to say: "I am very nervous about my first appearance with you. Couldn't we rehearse *our* scenes?"

He answered, "*We* shall be all right, but we are not going to run the risk of being bottled up by a gas-man or a fiddler." She was heartbroken:

"The only person who did not profit by Henry's ceaseless labours was poor Ophelia. When the first night came I did not play the part well, although the critics and the public were pleased. To myself I *failed*."

Should a complete list of opening performances "bottled up by a gas-man" ever be made, Irving's point of view will be evident. Seas ganged dry and the burning of Rome ended in soot regularly everywhere but at the Lyceum.

No word expressed in Irving's day exactly what he stood for. In our own day young actors would have called it "Theatre". Realism and naturalism were other worlds to him. All the virtues of the artistic conscience yielded to his sense of the stage. "With what passionate longing his hands hovered over Ophelia," Ellen Terry says in passing, as one of the merits of his style. In other words he "raised *Hamlet* to a mellerdram".

There was ridicule of him even then. Early in 1879, at a special matinée, the Royal Strand Theatre revived an old burlesque of *Hamlet* so that Odell, who had had one very brief engagement at the Lyceum, should burlesque Irving. "Now is the winter of our discontent," he began, until told by the prompter he was in the wrong play. At the height of his interview with Gertrude he broke off to catch a bluebottle, and his advice to the players amounted to "Speak as if you had plums in your mouth. I know an actor of great eminence would never have been heard of had he not spoken as though his mouth were full of plums."

Odell, exiled from the London stage, long outlived Irving, to become the idol of his club and to utter the classic retort to the young man who wanted his five-pound note back, "My boy, I haven't finished with it yet."

For the summer of 1879 the Lyceum came under the rule of Geneviève Ward. If ever she dwindles into a mere name the way we write history will be at fault, for no actress ever was made of sterner stuff. Death-defying Antigone, ready to be buried alive rather than deny her brother's body funeral rites, was her chosen part, for she was classic; because the times were not she walked into romance and walked away with it, so establishing a royal place in these chronicles for forty years.

She was born in New York the year Victoria ascended the throne in London and therefore represented America before the footlights in those clarion years when France, Italy and England all claimed the crown of wild

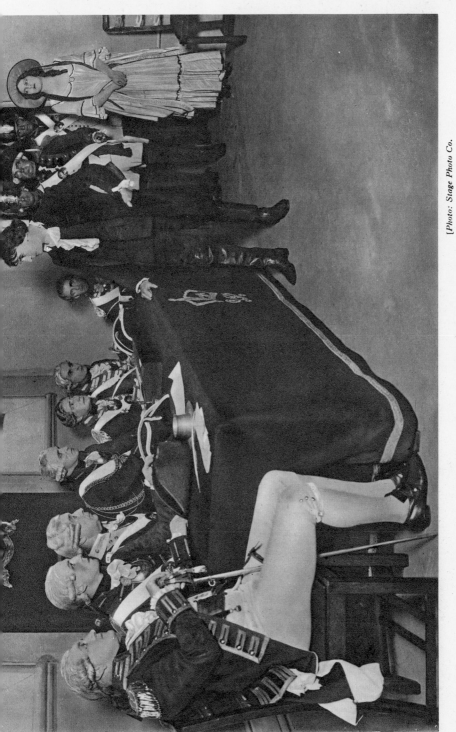

[Photo: Stage Photo Co.

The court-martial in The Devil's Disciple

The Tribunal in *The Only Way*

olives along with pounds, dollars and cents as well. While training for opera in Italy she married Count Constantine de Guerbal before appearing at the Scala, Milan, as Lucretia Borgia.

Her husband, a Russian, neglected to ratify the marriage according to the rites of the Greek Church until an appeal had been made to the Czar: bride and bridegroom parted at the church door. Strain injured a voice that ranged from contralto to soprano. She came to England as an actress, played Lady Macbeth and Lucretia Borgia at Manchester, and when London had nothing to offer her except the Adelphi there she went and bowled them over, even in the shoes of Celeste.

As Portia at the Crystal Palace or Rebecca in *Ivanhoe* at Drury Lane; as the heroine of Wills' *Sappho* in Dublin, or of Sophocles' *Antigone* and *Œdipus At Colonus* at the Crystal Palace, her triumphs left her dissatisfied:

> "After three years of acting I felt I should like to know more of the principles on which my art was based, and so I went to Paris and studied the French classic drama under M. Regnier. The parts themselves I knew I should never play, but what I wanted to know was not only how things should be done but why they were done."

In this classic spirit she played Lady Macbeth in French at the Porte-Saint-Martin. Her personality, she decided, suited ruthlessness, unflinching resolve, no matter how bloodthirsty:

> "Unsympathetic parts? I have played nothing else. I felt they suited my personality. My friends protested against my accentuation of the less redeeming features of a character, but my theory is if you have to play a villain—play it. I have no sympathy with such a character myself, and why should *I expect* an audience to feel otherwise?"

All she lacked was a classically minded audience. She found an actor of the High Roman manner in Johnston Forbes Robertson when she took the Lyceum. After two failures they acted together in the romantic drama which she performed two thousand times—with Medea, Sarah Churchill and Meg Merrilies in between—on a tour of the world.

Forget-Me-Not (the theatre's most misleading title) was founded by Herman Merivale and F. C. Grove on Article 148 of the Code Napoleon, which gave parents power to annul a son's secret marriage.

Stephanie de Mohrivart, called Forget-Me-Not, has been the vampire of a gambling-hell for the wealthy. Her son, the Vicomte de Brissac, marries without permission an English girl. When he dies his mother still has the power to make a dishonest woman of the widow, and with this she blackmails her way into the best society of Rome. She is thwarted by one of her old lovers, who convinces her that a victim of her gambling-hell is in pursuit

F

with a knife. Stephanie yields, but not before she has asked why men should "talk about blight and contamination" to the partners of their luxuries.

Some notice must be taken of plays nearer West Strand, for Wills had at last placed *Ninon*. "New and original" was the label of this Revolutionary romance, because in it neither the Bastille nor the guillotine's blade fell. Also it was written in blank verse. After being considered by Ben Webster and by Ellen Terry, as well as by the managers of Drury Lane and other theatres, it at length saw the footlights at the Adelphi in the February of 1880.

The heroine is a seamstress. Before the Revolution her sister died, betrayed by St. Cyr, and her brother lost his reason. Ninon, now a spy employed by Marat, wins the seducer's love, enters his house, finds the Dauphin there, hides him under her cloak, and learns that St. Cyr is innocent of the crimes committed by a villain under his name. In future, as the husband of a seamstress, he loses his aristocratic status—at least so the acting version argued, although in the original MS., as it left the hand of Wills, she died for love's sake.

In the years when Londoners saw life in the Strand it was still habitable, still full of homes. Almost opposite the Adelphi Theatre Salisbury Street ran down to the Thames, and there John Ryder was ending his days by bestowing, at not immoderate charges, the priceless heritage of Charles Kean and Fechter, with a little of the Bower Saloon thrown in, upon youths worthy to act as torch-bearers. When a meeting was held to champion an academy of dramatic art he attended to denounce it. The stage itself was the only school for acting. "I'm damned if anything else is any good, and I think your whole scheme, so far as I understand it, is blasted nonsense." With that he jammed his hat on his head, left the platform and went back to his pupils.

When Ellen Wallis (now playing Ninon) was among them she had praised an actress who shed real tears. "Look at me, my dear," said Ryder, and instantly a tear lurked in his eye before glistening on his rugged cheek.

How many benefited from his teaching may never be known. Somebody swore he could always tell them by the way they wagged their index fingers. That is wrong: other histrionic pedagogues for years to come still spread the admonitory epidemic. But what he undoubtedly possessed was authority, and a seed of this entered one young soul. Before finishing the course on that sitting-room carpet, with John Ryder bestriding the hearthrug between him and the fire, Martin Harvey had acquired a sense of the dignity of the stage. That he never lost.

Would the acting of that day impress us nowadays? The question must be considered, even if it is impossible to answer. Memory is volatile, no scenes are static in it. Old playgoers who long suspected this were startled all the same to find how acutely even the most vivid recollections of a film differ from the film itself: it follows that what survives of a performance in our remembrance is not what we actually saw.

Nowadays all investigation has to be conducted in the detective spirit. There has to be a strict regard for evidence. Photographs? They must be looked at askance because many sitters were camera-shy. Newspaper reports? These also must be circumspectly treated, for when you read how severely playgoers were overcome just realize how much easier it is to faint in a crowded, badly ventilated auditorium than in a modern one.

What then is trustworthy? The most eloquent clues come from stage-directions, and it is unfortunate that these are rare in acting editions of Shakespeare or emotional drama. Comedies whose horseplay is important carefully indicate all "bus.", and so prove the most profitable study.

These observations bear on "The Art of Acting", a pamphlet which might be docketed among absurdities were it not published (in the eighteen-seventies) by so professional a firm as French's of the Strand and East 14th Street, literary pillars of drama's transatlantic temples. Incidentally it led another life as "The Actor's Handbook", published by Dick's.

However preposterous the style, it may not unreasonably be regarded as the work of some such veteran as John Ryder with an urge to bestow the fruits of long experience upon the young. Chapter I consists of definitions which undoubtedly fit the characterization of contemporary plays. Here is part of one:

> "*Gentlemen*.—The requisites to *persuade this character completely* are many, and difficult to indeed attain; they are perfect ease of deportment, even under the most embarrassing circumstances! manners that conciliate and gain universal esteem; good breeding so disciplined as never to be thrown from its guard, or, except on the most extraordinary occasions, betrayed to the discovery of passion."

Next come tradesmen whose manner is subservient and, on extraordinary occasions, servile. It is not by this intended "to deprecate a class of men, but to describe habits, which are inevitably fostered by barter and sale, unless counteracted by superiority of mind". Heroines need a pervading force of sensibility which shall never vanquish though it shall often endanger heroism, as distinct from *Fine Ladies*, who should add to the almost un-attainable gracefulness of the gentleman, a continued playfulness, a visible coquetry which though perfectly at her command should appear spontaneous, and an ample mixture of delightful caprice, which she evidently indulges only to make herself more captivating.

All of this so faithfully represents the characterization in comedies at London's most fashionable theatre in the eighteen-sixties that the chapter on "Expression of Character" cannot be ignored when it supplies these definitions:

> "*Love*, when successful, lights up the countenance into smiles; the forehead is smooth and enlarged; the eyebrows are arched; the mouth a little open and smiling; the eyes languishing and half shut, or gazing on the beloved object. The accents are soft and winning, the tone of voice persuasive, flattering, pathetic, various, musical, rapturous, as in Joy. Kneeling is often necessary in all suppliant passion; but it is only necessary to bend one knee in case of love, desire, etc., which must never be the one that is next the audience."

(The actor has tripped over his pen here. What he means is that the knee that is knelt on must be the one next to the audience, who otherwise would see a twisted torso. Artists might pride themselves on their contraposto; actors never.)

> "*Jealousy*, which is a mixture of passions, directly contrary to one another, can only be justly represented by one who is capable of delineating all the passions by turns. Jealousy shows itself by restlessness, peevishness, thoughtfulness, anxiety, absence of mind, etc.
> "*Rage* or *Anger* expresses itself with rapidity, interruption, violence, harshness, and trepidation. The neck is stretched out, the head forward, often nodding and shaking in a menacing manner against the object of the passion; the mouth open and drawn on each side towards the ears, showing the teeth in a gnashing posture; the feet often stamping; the right arm frequently thrown out menacingly, with the clenched fist shaken, and a general and violent agitation of the whole body."

Visions of John Ryder playing Othello and other heavy business to the tuppenny gallery and thrippenny pit of the Bower precisely in this fashion are not to be curtly dismissed. It is possible that he taught his pupils to assume it, for even in the eighteen-nineties John Ryder the Younger was upholding a still more archaic tradition. In the reminiscences of Leon M. Lion there is a vivid picture of the way the great John's nephew always made his speeches in the place ordained when the centre of the floats was lit by a "rose" of candles; he always made way at the last words for the next speaker.

In some such style Martin Harvey mastered the art. At his first engagement the soubrette complained that he made love as though he were her father. As she played a French chambermaid, that is how a romantic should have made love to her. But there had been a tussle with fate before he had got as far as that. He described the start of his career in "The Era Almanack" for 1900 with some details lacking from his autobiography. When "badly bitten with Footlight Fever" he read this advertisement:

STAGE: ASPIRANTS WANTED.—Ladies and Gentleman, Talented and Untalented, wanted to join the THEATRICAL PROFESSION at once. Splendid Opportunities. Terms moderate. Engagements secured. Call or write: Montague Montressor, 19 Blynde Street, Hampstead.

When interviewed in his garret, Mr. Montressor said Martin Harvey was just the right kind of man to get on if coached in the art of make-up, which would cost two guineas.

By means of water-colours—no grease-paints then—the stage aspirant received instruction every day, first lesson, young man; second lesson, old man. By means of Clapham Junctioning forehead and cheeks, Mr. Montressor tried to impress his pupil by making him more hideous every time, then handed him a list of "props" that would be needed by anyone who wished to be like Edmund Kean, and told him to join the Profession forthwith.

There was a Mr. Bedford at Barrow-in-Furness who accepted his signature to a month's contract on payment of a premium. When Harvey arrived at the Theatre Royal, "about as dirty and ramshackle an edifice as I had ever dreamed of", nobody had heard of the play. By pawning his dress suit and his watch the Stage Aspirant raised his fare home:

"I saw on the platform a tall, greasy-looking man, wearing a high hat, an old astrakhan-trimmed frock-coat, and a very dirty shave. That was Mr. John Bedford I was convinced, though I had never seen him; come after me I knew, so I hid myself away and watched him pace up and down the platform. When the train for London steamed in I bolted into a third-class carriage and buried myself in the darkest corner. Twice Mr. Bedford passed the carriage and I trembled. I believed he might have the power to haul me out and make me fulfil my contract there and then, but at last the train moved and I was relieved."

Only a score of years had passed since Irving, precisely in the manner of Kean, had carried his "props" to the Lyceum, Sunderland, and Mr. Bedford expected the company he had engaged for *The Brigand Of The Abruzzi*, a drama belonging to the days of drunken genius, to behave in like manner. In the Theatres Royal of what had been the old "circuits", where stock companies went round and round, no change had been noticed or would be considered worthy of notice. Peaceful methods, and all that went with them, could still be dismissed as "under-playing".

Stage history can be viewed as a constant wavering of scales with illusion and effect in the balance. Half-way through the nineteenth-century the play strove to "knock 'em" or "hit 'em hard". That ideal would never entirely vanish as long as actors liked applause, although it had never been the sole criterion, for the worst ranter could convince himself that he did not make the judicious grieve.

The next phase in dramatic art's development can best be illustrated by an actual incident. Here is in one great player's very words the remembrance of another great player's very words. In an address at Harvard, Irving recalled his apprenticeship at Sunderland where, during the season of 1856-7, he supported the great celebrities who visited its Lyceum.

With *Guy Mannering* came Charlotte Cushman, an American actress of living granite; when she played Romeo her sister was the only Juliet who could stand up to it. For a raw young juvenile (juveniles were not always young) to be taught by such a star shows what veterans meant when they extolled the training undergone in "stock". Nearly thirty years later the lesson was still fresh in Irving's mind:

> "By-play must be unobtrusive; the student should remember that the most minute expression attracts attention; that nothing is lost, that by-play is as mischievous when it is injudicious as it is effective when rightly conceived, and that while trifles make perfection, perfection is no trifle.

> "This lesson was enjoined on me when I was a very young man by that remarkable actress, Charlotte Cushman. I remember that when she played Meg Merrilies I was cast for Henry Bertram, on the principle, seemingly, that an actor with no singing voice is admirably fitted for a singing part.

> "It was my duty to give Meg Merrilies a piece of money and I did it after the traditional fashion by handing her a large purse full of coin of the realm, in the shape of broken crockery, which was generally used in financial transactions on the stage, because when the virtuous maiden rejected with scorn the advances of the lordly libertine, and threw his pernicious bribe upon the ground, the clatter of the broken crockery suggested fabulous wealth.

> "But after the play, Miss Cushman, in the course of some kindly advice, said to me: 'Instead of giving me that purse, don't you think it would have been much more natural if you had taken a number of coins from your pocket and given me the smallest? That is the way one gives alms to a beggar, and it would have added greatly to the realism of the scene.' "

"Much more natural but far less effective," a veteran of the Bower would reply, but in vain. Such small changes were being made in every company in order to add "greatly to the realism of the scene". Even when realism had no particular end in view the changes would still be made—as, for example, by Irving, when the die-hard of romance—for there was no conscious knowledge of the schisms in acting that made the virtues of one style the vices of another. However sharply divided the warring creeds of those days are to the modern eye, both saw their theatre as one and indivisible, with every disagreement as a sign merely of some minor heresy over their equivalent of the Thirty-nine Articles. Martin Harvey never saw himself as a romantic in a class apart. On visiting the Lyceum as a schoolboy he observed that Irving, as Hamlet, wrote "with an excited up-and-down movement which must have formed letters quite twelve inches high"; and over half a century later he set down this "trivial reminiscence" without agreeing with the theory (which he observed in practice) that the very nature of romance called for movements more than life-size. His observing eye was typical of 1878, when by a very gradual change each auditorium was growing darker and each backcloth brighter. The cult of realism in acting depended on artificial light so diffused that an actor's gestures could be understood even when his back was turned.

Much of what was happening psychologically is indicated by that very significant term, "up-stage". Actors spoke of coming *up to the floats* as long as lighting remained dim, for then the one commanding position was the centre of the platform or float in front of the proscenium arch. In remote theatres lamps and even candles still remained in use, but where gas-jets had long supplanted them, the whole attitude of the leading gentleman towards his supporting cast turned round. When "up-stage" was by the floats he had had his back to them. Henceforward he would be up-stage when farthest from the floats; there he faced them—so that their backs would be to the house. "Come down to the floats" became the expression for the new generation—or rather those members of it engaged by up-to-date managements. Even at the time this book was being written, old actors spoke of the footlights as up-stage when recollecting their youth and then, in the next breath, as down-stage when referring to the twentieth century. In Martin Harvey's youth exponents of naturalism, progressing with the times, addressed one another as though in a room with four walls; romantics still played to the audience.

Irving's concern for illusion was merely an ameliorating influence. When it came to being "natural" according to the sense it acquired in the eighteen-sixties he could not hold a cup and saucer to his juniors. The everyday manner of social comedy, defined by its opponents as "Step on the chalk mark and count fifteen," had for some dozen years been the distinctive style of the management who belonged to "the Marlborough House set".

Under that new moon the tide had turned against melodrama. To a modern the old style became impossible. Ellen Terry knew exactly how the big scene in *The Lady Of Lyons* might be done but she "never could do it". It occurs in the fourth act, where Beauseant, after Pauline has been disillusioned, thinks it will be an easy matter to induce her to fly with him. In "The Story of My Life" this is how it is quoted:

"Go! (*White to the lips.*) Sir, leave this house! It is humble; but a husband's roof, however lowly, is, in the eyes of God and men, the temple of a wife's honour. (*Tumultuous applause.*) Know that I would rather starve—aye, starve—with him who has betrayed me than accept your lawful hand, even were you the prince whose name he bore. (*Hurrying on quickly to prevent applause before the finish.*) Go!"

The play was Irving's choice, not hers. That brilliant partnership universally accepted as destined, inevitable, was odd. Irving was "always attracted by fustian". Terry protested, even to tears.

While giving praise to him in the height, she is his severest critic. How did they stay together? Centuries divided them. Not merely his love of old ways, his affinity with melancholy and the horrors, his respect for unvenerable tradition, astonished her. Even in great scenes that they made their own for all time, even when they seemed like twin stars set in the heavens, they were secretly at odds.

Irving, by turning Shylock into yet another *homme fatal*, necessitated an entire revision of Ellen Terry's conception of Portia; in the trial scene she wished to be very quiet, but as his Shylock was quiet she "had to give it up"; his heroic, martyred patriarch was splendid, "but it wasn't good for Portia".

The divergence began with authorship—"Just the dullest play to read as ever was," she noted of *Werner*—and steadily widened. She stood aghast at his treatment of Shakespeare's text, worried over his methods of rehearsal and submitted against her own desires to his style of acting. If there is a time in the history of acting when the old order met the new, it happened when Henry Irving acted with Ellen Terry. Both were romantics. There was no clash of styles. There was no disharmony in the audience's sight even though he represented the past and she the future. It was an armistice in time.

If you think of Hamlet and Ophelia, of Claude and Pauline, of Shylock and Portia, somehow that spiritual relationship takes a vague form better than any that could be put into words. When he turned macabre she could not partner him. Though she would play as small a part as Jeannette in *The Lyons Mail* someone else had to be leading lady in *Louis XI* and *The Bells*.

That also happened when at one performance of *The Iron Chest* in 1879 he made Sir Edward Mortimer more concerned with torments of guilt than with honour rooted in dishonour. It happened yet again in 1880 when he revived in splendour *The Corsican Brothers*, till the whole town raved over the duel amid the bare trees of the silent forest, snow falling on the frozen waters, the sky red in the glow of the setting sun.

Great argument about acting must evermore end as it begins as personal opinion. Nothing can be demonstrated, nothing proved, and all the evidence is based on memory with its trick of shifting scenes unknowingly. When a majority, so vast and overwhelming that its desire to see an actor makes even his failures last one hundred nights, has agreed upon the greatness of an actor, then the minority serves the same cause, for without adverse criticism there is no ring to his praises.

Such actors as Ben Webster were admired all their days unremittingly, unanimously, which means that nobody claimed greatness for them—the proof being that nobody objected. To Irving's claim a score or so of strident voices objected. Each reasoned plausibly. No two reasoned alike. In the end they contradict each other and cancel out. All that they have achieved by their shouts is to point the moral that no such noise is heard when critics have nothing to shout about.

CHAPTER III

ACOLYTES OF THE LYCEUM

NATURAL aptitude, that inscrutable mystery, black despair to all who lack it, made acting very easy for some. William Terriss, sailor, planter, rancher, thought of it when shipwrecked and turned player the moment he trod the boards in all manner of plays, contemporary, eighteenth-century, Elizabethan. Others began, as George Alexander did, by making a pleasant hobby of amateur theatricals; others inherited, like Ellen Terry, both a place in the limelight and gifts to be worthy of it, while others drudged their way, by study, labour and devotion, to achieve through love and sacrifice, nothing.

Many pupils spouted Shakespeare to a score or more of old actors well qualified to teach them, in side-turnings off the Strand. What became of them all? "Stock", which had made an actor of Irving by thrusting over four hundred parts upon him in under three years, faded away in the eighteen-seventies. "Tours" took players everywhere and left them stranded anywhere, but this was how a start was to be made, and Harvey made it.

Several celebrities put themselves out to sponsor his baptism of grease-paint. One morning he passed a stage-door for the first time and beheld the T light that then lit rehearsals; he had an interview on the stage of the Opera Comique with W. S. Gilbert, who gave him a word of advice. One actor-manager passed him on to another until he actually "appeared" at the Court, a fairly new little house, remote from Theatreland, which had arisen through somebody else's demonstration that fashionable people would buy stalls anywhere as long as the fancy pleased them.

John Clayton starred here. With his consent the recruit had a brief chance to show himself when Charles Wyndham was in front. Through the good offices of at least half-a-dozen of London's busiest stage folk, the youth for three pounds ten shillings a week chased the chambermaid in a farce at Newcastle-on-Tyne, and did so with a dignity that did credit to John Ryder.

That tour ended. Nothing came of it. Friends knew Henry Irving. Letters passed to and fro. Now an engagement at the Lyceum, as a mirage, glowed in rainbow hues. In terms of hard cash the glory faded, for while Irving bestowed his princely generosity upon painters and composers, forcing upon them fees higher than they asked, his salary list hurt nobody's feelings in that way.

Varied and abundant information about the financing of his company happened to be preserved by some human magpie who for a quarter of a century collected scraps thrown into Bram Stoker's wastepaper basket. The untidy mess, in a large wooden apple-box, came under the hammer at a book sale at a distant date. Now it has been emptied over two tables, a desk and several chairs, to give verisimilitude to this otherwise bald and unconvincing narrative.

"Salary List Friday 16th Sept. paid Alexandra Theatre Liverpool," still showing, in the indelible pencil ticks against each name, how the ghost walked from dressing-room to dressing-room, ends "Recd. £481 18s. Total £482 19s.", delicately implying a guinea for the ghost. Others earn their pay less easily since five take twenty-five shillings for the week. Out of the forty-five members of the company, including dressers, five exceed ten pounds; of the rest but eight exceed five pounds (and only two had said when engaged, "Make it guineas"). Irving values himself at £60 and Terriss at £20, leaving Ellen Terry alone in the glory of three figures—£200.

When expenses amounted almost to £10,000 the receipts would more than double the figure, but many other bills, including costs of productions, rose to dizzy heights. Another scrap from the wastepaper basket comes out of the shuffle:

Mr. Irving's Company.
Supers acc. from 12 *to* 17 *September,* 1881.

Date 1881	No. of Men	Remarks	Rate	£	s.	d.
12 Sept	19	at	1s. 3d.	1	3	9
13	19	at	do.	1	3	9
14	18	at	do.	1	2	6
15	18	at	do.	1	2	6
16	12	at	do.		15	0
17	12	at	do.		15	0
		Extra allowance for Master Super			1	6
			Total	£6	4	0

Liverpool, 17th September, 1881.

In the summer of 1882 Martin Harvey asked leave to join the company. The moment seemed ill-chosen, because critics had turned. But theatrical triumphs often prove costly, failure sometimes profitable. *Romeo And Juliet* at the Lyceum that spring had occasioned as much grief among actors and newspapers as a public funeral. After a day of national mourning when Ellen Terry broke her heart and Irving felt his years, the public manifested its will to pack the auditorium nightly.

Of course several minor performances won praise. William Terris raised cheers for Queen Mab (as Mercutio usually does); in the rôle of Paris an actor from the Standard, Shoreditch, caused programmes to be scanned for the name of George Alexander; and yet another young man of melodrama,

Charles Glenny, from the Duke's, Holborn, arrived as Tybalt. More admired than all the handsome faces was the wrinkled brow of Mrs. Stirling, then most dearly loved of Nurses.

No fault was found with the production as such, for critics advised "students" that liberties taken with the text were scholarly, and "artists" that the donkeys in the market-place of Verona were real. The leading lady and the leading gentleman alone were blamed; and yet despite all expert opinion the public came to see Henry Irving and Ellen Terry until the end of July.

During the August holiday Alexander resigned his part, preferring to spend the autumn as Romeo with Miss Wallis, the star-maker, on tour. In his place the athletic Clytemnestra from a celebrated performance of *Agamemnon* in Greek at Oxford, now arrived in order to illustrate the practical advantages of beginning at the top. Vacancies also occurred in the crowd, whose sudden onrush in hand-to-hand encounter made the differences of opinion between Montagues and Capulets seem "main incidents of the story."

While Martin Harvey with a letter of introduction to Irving entered the vestibule where Bram Stoker read it disparagingly before passing him on to be engaged as a super, Frank Benson strode through the stage-door with the resolve: "Now was my opportunity. Romantic acting on the stage had lost much of its poetry, its sense of rhythm: Oxford culture would restore all this to the stage."

When *Romeo And Juliet* resumed its run on September 2 these two newcomers, one eager to impress, the other to be impressed, stood in the wings of the Lyceum while property-men in blue coats and scene-shifters in white scurried past before the curtain rose. As a humiliated professional, Martin Harvey was duly mauled and hustled in the crowd, then left to kick his heels until the last act. As a respected amateur Benson was mauled by Irving himself:

"With one hand he seized my foil, hit me over the knuckles with his own, prodded me in the stomach with his knee, again dashed his blade against mine, said, 'Die, my boy, die; down, down,' and elbowed and kneed me into the mouth of the tomb, and stood in front of the dying Paris, brandishing a torch, amidst shouts of applause for Romeo, and little, if any, regret for Paris."

Here Martin Harvey came on in the crowd of mourners, and that night of stars ended. When *Much Ado About Nothing* went into rehearsal the new Paris departed on tour like the Paris before him, to play Shakespeare's greatest rôles. The super grimly resolved to make do with the smallest ones, so as to have a share, no matter how insignificant, in the next production—the most memorable revival of *Much Ado About Nothing*.

Yet the stars of that firmament never came nearer to a clash of opinions than when they were being hailed as a Beatrice and a Benedick beyond compare. Ellen Terry shed tears because they descended to "buffoonery", and owing to his "rather finicking deliberate method" she could never put "the right pace" into her part. There were no differences of opinion over their next Shakespearean venture, and their most devoted admirers went away explaining to each other that *Twelfth Night* was a poor play even with Ellen Terry and Fred Terry as brother and sister. In between came the special performance of *Robert Macaire*, which she herself describes:

"It was funny to see Toole and Henry rehearsing together for *Macaire*. Henry was always *plotting* to be funny. When Toole as Jacques Strop hid the dinner in his pocket, Henry, after much labour, thought of hiding the plate in his waistcoat. There was much laughter later on when Macaire, playfully tapping Strop with his stick, cracked the plate and the pieces fell out! Toole hadn't to bother about such subtleties, and Henry's deep-laid plans for getting a laugh must have seemed funny to dear Toole, who had only to come on and say 'Whoop!' and the audience roared!

"Henry's death as Macaire was one of a long list of splendid deaths. Macaire knows the game is up, and makes a rush for the french windows at the back of the stage. The soldiers on the stage shoot him before he gets away. Henry did not drop, but turned round, swaggered impudently down to the table, leaned on it, then suddenly rolled over, dead."

Martin Harvey had little to do, but he felt himself to be an acolyte. There was another who felt like that. "Irving's Page" indicated her rank in the company. As a very small schoolgirl she had written so solemn a letter to Irving that the reply began, "Dear Sir". She went with a doll in her arms to see him and set so pleasant a picture before his eyes that she became a member of his company.

There had to be children to run about in his market-places, but her destiny promised higher things than that. Behind the scenes of the Lyceum the air tended to be academic. Young ladies and gentlemen formed a group distinguished as students from ordinary supers. The child's bright intelligence marked her out even among these, especially as so slight a form contrasted itself dramatically against the now celebrated length of leg.

Angelita Helena Margarita de Silva Ferro, who liked to be called "Nell" and to be billed "N. de Silva", had the prestige of a definite place in the romantic scheme of things when Martin Harvey felt like a "new boy". It was a privilege to speak to her, more than a privilege when he saw deep understanding in the large blue eyes—somewhere in colour between the periwinkle and wild violet. She had the rare *listening* intelligence.

Manlike, he loved to talk—as the women novelists of the period were extremely fond of saying about their heroes. He saw her on her way after rehearsals, and explored with her that London maze which existed before Charing Cross Road, Shaftesbury Avenue and Rosebery Avenue simplified the map, before Regent Circus had taken its new name from Piccadilly and before the War Office had had to remove to Whitehall because the palatial clubs objected to it as an eyesore in Pall Mall—where the building itself still stands.

At that time, incidentally, a go-ahead Post Office was persuading the public to have private telegraph-wires laid on. It helps to show you what sort of world it was—on the very brink of change.

From Irving's classic columns to Bow Street, where Order and Opera faced each other, was one step; another took the young players to that odd jumble between Oxford Street and High Holborn, where a king stood on a church and a group in stone who might from their prominence be expected to be the Four Georges, the Sons of Aymon or some legendary ill-assorted quadruplets, turned out to be, when tourists peered in sight-seeing eagerness, immodestly proclaiming the advantages of wearing wool next the skin.

Like a triangular lighthouse facing the sunset, the Vienna Café near at hand demonstrated how cosmopolitan London could be. It was Vienna, and there these two, so proudly Thespian, could drink coffee stoppered with cream and eat cakes of outlandish flavour while they talked the best of all possible "shop". Round by St. Giles's Circus where a brewery, a jam factory and a pickle factory contributed to a veritable Christmas pudding of rich smells, they turned into Tottenham Court Road and ignored a shout from a yellow Hampstead just before the conductor pulled at his bell to let his driver race past a station bus on its way from Victoria to St. Pancras with nothing but trunks "outside".

The Thespians thought nothing of that length of pavement even with Hampstead Road added; then they took short cuts through one of those unsuspected enchanted lands which endear London to the Londoner more than all its antiquities and sights. By way of the mock village of Prince Regent's fantasy they gained his park, now of particular theatrical interest since the real chair-boy had been engaged for a Regent's Park scene on the stage; and they looked into the waters of the canal from the bridge where a hero of melodrama at the Princess's dived nightly to the rescue of the second villain, by whom he had been disinherited and undone. Not that realistic melodrama meant anything to upholders of romantic melodrama, but as an Arden for courtship London had nothing better than this.

Players, the public supposes, lack stable and enduring love. To give that the lie this Rosalind and her Orlando built on unshakeable foundations. Any mention of true love prompts an immediate charge of sentimentality.

That be damned. Love this time was true if ever it were. In roundabout phrases, the difficulties two people encounter before they can think as one had been overcome, the loyalty that no future difficulties can weaken was created.

Put it in whatever words you like. The particular mental relationship, which characters in fiction manage with consummate ease, came on this occasion under the control of two real human beings. They tended to old fashions in their tastes, and perhaps that helped. Heart and soul they believed in the drama where their watchword would be "God is in the Theatre". No matter how objective their biographer might aim at being, all this would still have to be set down as statement of fact. After rehearsals and between performances at the Lyceum a design for living was perfected between two of the youngest members of the company. It formed the basis of the last romantic's not inconsiderable history.

Thick wads of wastepaper in the apple-box filled from Irving's basket now bear on this story, especially one particular batch collected on a round trip of the Atlantic by the unknown tenacious magpie. Bills from a Soho firm of basket manufacturers merely for the repair of those large hampers always used for stage costumes amount to over a hundred pounds, but that is a mere money matter. Evidence of heartache is here when the facts of Irving's first American tour, 1883-4, are compared with the second, 1884-5. Plan of Cabins, S.S. *City of Rome*, shows Terriss in 1, Harvey and two others in 71, "Miss Eleanor de Silva" and one other in 85, outward bound.

Saloon Passenger List of *City of Chester* homeward bound in the April of 1884 is dominated by Mr. Jeremiah Devlin, Mrs. Devlin and infant and quite a number of Masters and Misses Devlins, who perhaps talk of the voyage to this day. Less obtrusively the list contains the names of Mr. M. Harvey, Miss de Silva and others destined for the Lyceum, but not, of course, those of a leading gentleman and leading lady bound by the ancient etiquette of "stock" to dwell apart (these rites cannot be abolished in a moment). So ends the salt-wind's romance, for on American Tour forms dated September, 1884, "Mr. M. Harvey" appears but not "Miss de Silva"—parental control kept her at home. He sailed, Mr. Irving and Miss Terry aboard this time, in S.S. *Parisian*.

Advancement at last came his way. He had had a small part when *Richelieu* was revived in 1884, but it had been very small. In printed casts so little importance is attached to "Clermont (a Courtier)" that blanks are left opposite. While "looking on" in Act I, Scene i, he says to the bankrupt gamester:

> Ay, take the sword
> To Cardinal Richelieu; he gives gold for steel,
> When worn by brave men.

That was something, even though after three or four words more he had to hold his peace for three acts.

Actors made history unknowingly, and Martin Harvey never prided himself on slightly upsetting one stage convention that had lasted two centuries and would last another fifty years more. Actresses, as though to revenge themselves on the boys who created Shakespeare's heroines, claimed boys' parts. Since the days when Miss de Camp had looked so lovely in breeches that the august John Philip Kemble had attempted rape in her dressing-room, the immature male had always been represented upon the stage by the (sometimes fairly mature) female.

Pages, urchins and princes usually appeared at the Lyceum after this fashion, and when the company sailed in the autumn of 1884 even the Dauphin (an actor's part hitherto at the Lyceum) was meant once more to follow suit. Not until the young woman who had been engaged to impersonate him failed to exhibit any of the graces of Carlotta Leclercq did Irving notice natural princeliness in any of his younger actors.

At Quebec that autumn Martin Harvey had the chance to grace that part and others as well. Of Joliquet, the boy who hops up and down cellar steps in *The Lyons Mail*, he made a miniature work of art. As the Dauphin he was the Dauphin. Throughout the tour from Toronto to Buffalo, from New York to Chicago, from Washington to Philadelphia and back to New York, he looked upon himself as a principal, and returned to London full of this natural pride.

When the Lyceum reopened in the May of 1885—somewhat boisterously because of protests against reserved seats in the pit to which people too busy to reserve them always objected with good reason—he could deny Pope's couplet on the subject of hope because he felt himself already blessed. As Osric he played face to face with his "beloved master". Within one glorious fortnight he was to play two other parts. His career seemed to have reached that rung where the pens of biographers could be heard scratching in the future, "From that moment he never looked back."

When *Louis XI* came into the bill he was the Dauphin, second only to Irving in the masterly death scene. The king has made his last gasp. Marie, hoping for a reprieve to save her lover from the headsman, knows that the hour is about to strike. The Dauphin takes up the crown in order to pronounce the royal pardon, but even in the shadow of death Louis finds strength to clutch the crown. "The young Dauphin has never been better played than by Mr. Harvey," was one verdict.

When *The Merchant Of Venice* came next he was Lorenzo, that blessing Shakespeare conferred upon time's endless queue of young actors, a minor part whose scene cannot be cut, whose lines in such a night cannot be stolen. More than one stalwart of to-day credits the turning point of his struggles to some sudden reshuffling of parts in *The Merchant* that brought him

The duel in *Don Juan's Last Wager*

A scene from *Don Juan's Last Wager*

[Photo: Stereoscopic Co.

Lorenzo while somebody in front was looking for a juvenile lead. Osric hides that light under a bushel of "character" but in Lorenzo it shines. One might imagine that Shakespeare, when he put forth his white hand at the opening of that last act without a principal upon the stage, had his mind this once upon his own beginnings or upon an extraordinarily fortunate beginner.

But the gentle rain from heaven did not take the Lyceum's stage for its "place beneath", that May night of 1885. One critic, instead of setting down the usual "did justice to", wrote, "and though Lorenzo's lines might well have been better spoken, seeing that they are among the most beautiful and descriptive ever written, still to make up for the loss of them we had the prettiest and gentlest Jessica possible".

Many "love lines" were spoken that night without fervour, without poetry, without appreciation, the critic lamented. This Lorenzo rarely, in the course of fifty years to come, ever attempted to. No actor-manager ever played so few love-scenes: he chose many not sweetened by "love lines". To the new male generation this was a virtue. Youth that, rightly or wrongly, despised courtship in any form as unmanly would make Martin Harvey its idol for that among other reasons.

Rehearsals for *Olivia*, Wills's dramatized Goldsmith already played at the Court with Ellen Terry as the heroine, were in full swing and Martin Harvey walked on. For the winter, *Faust*, Wills's dramatized Goëthe, was in preparation and in that he would, apart from an exclamation, have to walk on again, though it was consoling to find Miss de Silva's name down as an angel.

Meanwhile across the road *The Vicar Of Wideawakefield* had gone into rehearsal with Birdie Irving, who had a prior right to the name as Joseph Irving's daughter, in the chorus. When the autumn season began, *Olivia* and the neighbouring burlesque ran concurrently, each with an Irving in it, until Mephistopheles had all things ready to dazzle the public eye with visions of hell.

Coquelin's comments were lively. He could quite understand that from the director's point of view it might have been thought desirable to play Mephistopheles in such a manner as to put Faust in the shade, but from the artist's point of view it was reprehensible. Notwithstanding that he was both director and artist, Irving "would not have played the devil as he did were his theory of dramatic art the right one". Not that any ill-feeling existed. At a Lyceum matinée for the Actors' Benevolent Fund four years later Coquelin recited "Le Mouche" as a curtain-raiser to *The Bells*, when Martin Harvey was Clerk of the Court who hands to Mathias his deposition and commands, "Read it."

Whatever the Lyceum company, from Ellen Terry (Margaret) to Martin Harvey (Soldier), might think of it as dramatic art, there were never any doubts about *Faust's* success. When revived in the December of

G

1886 it gave Mephisto the chance to play Santa Claus. The caterer's bill inventoried:

		£	s.	d.
26	Cock turkeys at 10s. 6d.	13	13	0
105	Geese—1229 lbs. 10 oz. at 8d. lb.	40	19	9
1	Barrel of Apples	0	18	0
1	Bag of Onions	0	5	0
2	doz. ,, Sage	0	2	0
1¼	gross ,, Baskets	0	19	0
		56	17	6
	Mr. Clark	1	10	0
	Received W. J. Clark	58	7	6

Whiskey at forty-one shillings the dozen bottles and plain gin at twenty shillings the dozen brought in another bill for £14 13s. 10d. and "money gratuities" sent the total up to £115.

London had an up-to-date look in the summer of 1887, for the Duke of Cambridge had just opened the grand red-brick thoroughfare called Charing Cross Road. But Irving's thought, more retrogressive than ever, turned to one of Byron's most faded works. *Werner* now excites curiosity as the first murder mystery of the English stage. Three suspects, all capable of the deed and ready to profit by it, remain under suspicion until the author lets the cat out of the bag at the end; and although there is no detective, a holy father is perplexed by the remorse of a man who in the next breath swears he is not guilty. This particular shape of things to come still had no interest at Irving's one-performance revival, for in the process of adapting Byron to the stage a scene was added in Act I to catch crime red-handed and so solve the mystery before it could mystify.

Martin Harvey played Ludwig, a part created solely for the supply of useful information; it is, in fact, the epitome of all such parts, with a speech which seems designed as a mockery of young players' hopes. What can be done with such lines?

> He rode round the other way,
> With some young nobles; but he left them soon;
> And, if I err not, not a minute since
> I heard his excellency, with his train,
> Gallop o'er the west drawbridge.

"And the boat sails Wednesday" is the addition which suggests itself—according to the story of the English actor in New York who thus embellished his one speech, after being told (as Irving had been told at Sunderland) that unless he put more life into his work he had better take the next boat home.

The splendour of the Lyceum has been acclaimed by critics and actors in many a style. However frequent their praises, nothing dims the testimony of the little acolyte. The homage felt by the small-part player, who served his seven years and then another seven with Biblical patience, finds no equal among the tributes which range from grudging compliments to fulsome flattery. In his autobiography Martin Harvey records the bitter total of disappointments without facing the bitter truth.

Irving hardly foresaw him as the wearer of his mantle: that "bad notice" of his as Lorenzo at the start of his career fettered him like a ball and chain. The acolyte was not without honour save in his own temple. From the first flush of youth to early manhood, when the human spirit chafes most fiercely against hindrances, the resolute will of the master kept the young man in his place, no matter how strong the bond of affection between them.

Regular employment at an increasing salary, not only in Town but on provincial and American tours, compensated for the lack of advancement. Any attempt to leave the company excited remonstrance. That Martin Harvey belonged there could admit of no doubt whatever. Nothing disturbed the peace except his frenzy to act. Pierre, a boy with a basket of bottles in *Robert Macaire*, was all that came his way in the spring of 1888.

Irving had a morbid dread of being watched from the wings, and though it was not actually forbidden the company were given to understand he did not like it. Martin Harvey ignored this once, boldly taking his stand in the prompt box, during his scene with Cromwell in *Charles The First*. What he witnessed was described in a lecture many years later in a way which revealed the worshipper as well as his idol. This explains why Martin Harvey held fast to the belief, "Making your clothes act is the most difficult feat of all," all his life:

"The last act is reached, and nothing remains to that sweet, misguided Stuart but to part from his Queen and children, and go forth to the scaffold. Cromwell's offers of compromise have been rejected by the King, and the usurper, apostrophizing his monarch as 'Thou shadow of a King', leaves the stage, consigning his master to his fate.

"Another scene, and the 'shadow of a King' enters and we see indeed the *shadow* of Charles. The sweet dignity, the patient resignation, the quiet but unquenchable belief in the holiness of his anointment, shine about him like a dim aureole, as about a being of another world. Faded, colourless, unreal, how is it that, as he closes the door behind him unattended, unannounced, how is it that this wraith of kingship breathes such new humility about him? How is it that he seems already to wear that 'incorruptible crown', in which not all his misfortunes and common human mistakes could dim his belief?

"I wonder if the author who wrote in his manuscript, 'Enter Charles' conceived such a spectacle of purged suffering as Sir Henry Irving presented at that moment? Or was it created by the deep sympathy of the actor for human error, evoked perhaps from the remembrance of some moment of personal emotion when, like Charles, he had hit the dust of disaster and touched the depths of worldly ruin?

"We cannot say, but from my experience, theatre management, with its alternations of triumph and disaster, might well have given Irving the inspiration for that moment, which the marvellous command of his Art he possessed would illustrate. *The change in his costume* from the lustrous velvet of former days to the colourless linsey he now wore, the old elegance of his bright Cavalier locks now thinned and greying, hanging in a strange tail over his meagre lace collar, conveying such a poignant note of neglect, and the air of humble but dignified acquiescence and departed attendance, as he opened and closed the door while turning his back to the audience—it was an imperishable moment, illuminating the power of creative imagination aided by a faultless technique.

"This is not an instance of occasional inspiration flashing from unsuspected heredity 'in the warmth of the scene', as Garrick expresses it, but the use Irving could make of a personal sorrow—a valuable and poignant fountain of inspiration."

As a record this is valuable. It photographs the scene so accurately that past and present can be compared. In our thoughts we know how we would like those moments to be acted, and it happens that we saw one of our own generation act them when the centenary of Irving's birth was celebrated at the Lyceum in a programme of excerpts from his plays. The new generation finds very little to admire in "new humility" and "humble but dignified acquiescence". If the martyr king were acted like that now it could be justified only as realistic truth, and would need close documentary at that.

"The greater the ruin the greater the pride" wins modern sympathy. When Owen Nares stepped into Irving's shoes that afternoon in 1938 he won approval by choosing naturalism—a father bidding his family farewell with as little fuss as possible. Being certain that every single person in the theatre was aware of the crown and the scaffold, Nares left history to act itself and made us feel instead the ordinary family ties which are what school-books seldom think worth mentioning.

Though that might be more to modern taste nobody could argue that Owen Nares was to his time what Irving was to his; the argument, in fact, works the other way round; for Irving to have been impressive in ways not approved by the twentieth-century's advance guard, his genius needed to burn all the fiercer. Which leads, where it is meant to lead, back to Martin Harvey. It indicates how remote he stood from "naturalism" derived not from inner nature but from everyday exteriors. "New humility" for him expressed the Sermon on the Mount. No misgivings of a questing new world shook the last romantic. There was nothing in him of fashion's fool. He remained where he had sent down roots in those long years of waiting.

If the master had suffered in his 'prentice days from too much work the disciple certainly suffered from too little. The problem solved itself in a way which to the end of his life he called "thrice blessed". Several small-part players banded themselves together and obtained Irving's permission to tour, when he took a summer holiday, as the Lyceum Vacation Company. Three leading gentlemen and three leading ladies chose whatever great rôles they desired most out of the whole realm of romance. In this way, Martin Harvey, in his early twenties, came to play Ruy Blas.

Some fifteen years had passed since Fechter had revived, at his last appearance in London, the English version of Hugo's drama. Though an opera and a Gaiety burlesque were being made of it, the name still conjured up visions of a hero who swept aside all rivalry like a tornado. Ruy Blas still recalled his blithe form: to play his part was to be haunted by his shadow. But what else were the Lyceum Vacation Companions set upon but the challenging of overaweing comparisons?

Wearing their hair long, walking a little ungainly, speaking somewhat awkwardly, they demanded to be judged by the standards set by Irving. Who was Fechter, anyway? Those who set themselves by Irving's side ran the greater risk of being dwarfed. Martin Harvey wisely took the character his "beloved master" had never essayed, though it might well be considered the most significant in all the works of the Nineteenth-Century Shakespeare. What Hamlet was to the Renaissance Ruy Blas was to Industrialism.

To that class-conscious world the lackey-overlord ought to have been mounted as a portent into the firmament. In order to make his meaning plain Hugo handed the part to an idol of the Boulevard who should have known best how to make Ruy Blas typify the People. But romance was bound to run away with a hero who died for the love of a lady. That he also bore democracy upon his back was merely the token that he belonged to the brotherhood of the burdened. He had no message for the age of social reform.

When the Lyceum Vacation Company brought him to the Theatre Royal, Bristol, quaint toy playhouse with doors still standing at either side of the proscenium in the Georgian manner, he had the shape not of a revolutionary democrat but of some wistful dreamer in a fragrant past. The slim, fragile figure, bullied by Don Salluste until driven for the queen's sake to take up arms, came into his own at this performance. He proved in a night what a lifetime of engagements might never have proved. He discovered his bent for self-sacrificing devotion. He showed, as Lorenzo, Salarino, Dauphin, Osric, De Clerment and all such never could show, how finely he could die. To gain the queen's pardon he pours the phial of poison into his throat. Her arms are around him as he prays for blessings to fall upon her with his last breath. There is a photograph extant to show how beautifully he did it.

When his partners had their innings, Martin Harvey supported them, and in *The Lady Of Lyons* submitted to the rebukes villainy deserved. Early Victorian romance still blossomed; *The Corsican Brothers* was another example of it in their brief repertoire. Benson dropped in to see what they made of it one night at Cheltenham; his wife was ill, and when he saw what spirit Miss de Silva imparted to the masquerade, Shakespeare's heroines were laid at her feet. When she played Ophelia at Shanklin Town Hall, Martin Harvey came to look on and was impressed by the Ghost—Stephen Phillips, whose father was Precentor of Peterborough Cathedral. Heıbert Ross, a member of the company who had started life in India, he also picked out because of the organ-roll of his voice. All seemed to glow with ardour, fired by the torch their Hamlet had lit when he had played Paris at the Lyceum.

The actor of Ruy Blas returned to Town merely to "Enter" and "Exit" as a character who breaks silence only to announce his permanent disappearance—Donalbain, one of Duncan's sons-at-heel in *Macbeth*. To have trained, disciplined men around him was necessary to Irving, for one restless figure would mar both his scenic splendours and the stillness preceding his own coiled-serpent effects. In return he saved his servitors from that bane of stage life, "No continuity", and gave them the chance to make a home. Life had this one great compensation.

In the January of 1889 there was a Lyceum marriage. "N. de Silva", as Mrs. Martin Harvey, set up house in Cockspur Street, overlooking that equestrian statue of George III which London urchins admire as "Nelson on 'is 'orse". Marriage gave them new dignity on their Vacation Tours, especially when they played Katherine and Petruchio in *The Taming Of The Shrew*. Another of the partners wanted *Robert Macaire*. Mr. Harvey was Jacques Strop and Miss de Silva the boy with the bottles.

The Gaiety presented *Ruy Blas; or, The Blasé Roué* at the end of September, 1889, with Birdie Irving as one of the dancers. There was a burlesque *pas de quatre* by four comedians, dressed below the waist as ballerine and above as well-known actors. When Irving saw his own bust copied by Fred Leslie above female fleshings he was shocked by such "indecency". Both the dancer and the manager of the Gaiety let the newspapers know that they had considered the protest and that they chose to ignore it. Irving wrote to the Lord Chamberlain's Office, calling attention to an offence under Regulation 21 in theatre licences which had forbidden representations of living persons ever since W. S. Gilbert caused Gladstone to be impersonated in *Happy Land* at the Court. Leslie had to change his ways. A newspaper published this report:

"Mr. Irving is no longer represented as a woman in the new Gaiety burlesque. On Saturday night Fred Leslie appeared in the burlesque *pas de quatre* without the flowing locks and the *pince-nez*, and the visage of elongated intellectuality above the ballet skirts. He came on with a perfectly bald head, as unlike Irving's as any head could possibly be, and with any possible resemblance he may bear to the tragedian carefully hidden behind a black mask.

"There was no suggestion in the make-up of Irving or anybody else. Leslie was a mystery in ballet skirts. And still the people laughed. They laughed louder than ever when Leslie walked on the stage with a slow swinging angular strut from the hips. When he stood on the stage with his head thrust forward and his arms dangling they roared again. Leslie did not speak. He imitated no one's voice. He represented no one's face. But in ballet skirts and a mask he strutted and stood with a suggestion of mannerism that seemed to convey a good deal to the audience.

"It is the funniest thing in the burlesque. Mr. Irving cannot object because he is not represented. The Lord Chamberlain cannot interfere. Leslie has scored."

But ridicule could not harm so great a prestige. Irving's fame was at its zenith now that his thoughts turned to the most popular subject of all. As long as the romantic tradition should last the French Revolution would remain part of it. In the midst of *Macbeth*, Irving thought of *The Dead Heart*. Ellen Terry overcame her dislike of fustian because the "juvenile" offered itself as a promising first appearance for her son, Gordon Craig. Otherwise Arthur de St. Valery might have seemed destined for an experienced member of the company who possessed the requisite wistfulness in his youthful good looks.

The vacationists returned to find the new production already cast. There was a small part for Martin Harvey. He accepted without demur, innocent of the so-called stage jealousy (shown by farmers towards each other's crops and by dentists towards each other's fillings) and ready to make of the recruit a lifelong friend. "The best actor that the company ever produced," Craig said of him.

"I'm full of French Revolution," Irving wrote to Ellen Terry in a letter she includes in her autobiography. The storming of the Bastille by a starving crowd would be "very terrible", and then he would be the liberated prisoner whose dumb show would astonish yet another generation as though unaware that such "business" could never fail, and be cited as a peculiar manifestation of Irving's powers by critics who used phrases very similar to those applied to Ben Webster and to the super at the Surrey a hundred years before.

"I see in Landry," said Irving, "a great deal of Manette—the same vacant gaze into years gone by when he crouched in his dungeon nursing his wrongs." The letter ended with samples of the few lines he had added to her part which are the very fustian she detested:

"Ah, Robert, pity me. By the recollection of our youth, I implore you to save
my boy!" (*Now* for 'em!)
"If my voice recalls a tone that can fall quietly upon your ear, have pity on me!
If the past is not a blank, if you once loved, have pity on me!" (Bravo!)

Unlike Shakespeare this might be, and that was its virtue. In order to
keep romance theatrical the worthy had to alternate with the garish. Civilization's nightmare, compulsory education, had to be borne in mind. The love
of learning, the love of books, the love of poetry, might well perish now that
the fine frenzy of lovers became a rod to beat infants with.

"Compulsory Shakespeare" (sets of questions senile enough to make
imagination retch) drove youth to the theatre as to a tin chapel. Compulsory
drama took the place of puritanical hatred of the stage. Acting too would be
seen with compulsory eyes. But as Irving instinctively loved the garish play
as well as "dramatic literature", romance in his style would never be "compulsory". *The Corsican Brothers* could not be reduced to loathsome examina-
tion-papers for schools. Neither could *The Dead Heart* with its "ifs" and its
"pities" introduced by the great Shakespearean scholar to bring down, so
he said, the house. This they did on the opening night, September 28, 1889.

What the audience felt was described by Burne-Jones in his congratulations to the leading lady. He was very glad "Mr. Irving was ready to have his
head cut off for you, so it had what I call a good ending". In the souvenir
of the play there is a picture of Landry on the scaffold where the guillotine
stands against the sky, and the letterpress quotes "his spirit leaps within
him, as lightened by an unknown burden, and mounts upwards where sorrow
is unknown".

As far as the popular imagination was concerned, French Revolution
meant self-sacrifice at the guillotine. That was clearly indicated when Sardou
tried to make it mean something else in his *Thermidor*, first played at the
Comédie Française in 1891 and brought to the Opera Comique in 1892.

The plot tried hard to be original, though the heroine was all too plainly
the Geneviève of Dumas over again. Her lover and his friend try to secure
her release. When they set her down as an Ursuline they see the Ursulines
file past condemned. When they draw up a form to say she is with child she
refuses to sign. Then they look through the list of prisoners to send someone
to death in her place.

Even in Paris the audience knew at once that this was where the hero
should come in, but Sardou had not thought of that. There was no substitute—an oversight which wrecked his play because all the sympathy was for
that completely non-existent cipher. According to a monograph by Blanche
Roosevelt, Sardou himself confessed:

"The success of the evening was the rôle played by an individual
not on the bills, one who never comes on the stage, whom no one has

ever seen, and when you come down to it, one in fact who has never even existed but as a possible victim—*toute la sympathie du public etait pour lui*. In writing my drama, I must confess I scarcely expected this creature to play a star part, but such he did."

To what extent this satisfied Coquelin's artistic conscience may be unknown, though *The Times* declared that realism had never been brought to greater perfection. Though his constant intervention filled the piece, as an Executor of the Decrees whose secret resolve is to keep as many heads on shoulders as possible, all the lives he saved could not equal the customary one of sacrifice.

BOOK III

CHAPTER I

THE MADDING EIGHTEEN-NINETIES

ACOLYTES in the Lyceum formed their character as though in a temple. Under Irving they observed rules of dignity, grace, beauty, serenity in a rigid code of behaviour. Outside its walls, outside the life that it ordered, on duty or off, a battle of ideas raised the dust. Whether Martin Harvey and Miss de Silva wanted to stay out of it or take part in it their destiny as romantics brought them, whenever they did take a hand in the fray, back to their tradition. As "St. Lyceum" increased in awe so it severed itself more and more from other theatres, even from those with players and playwrights once members of its own company.

Everywhere the ancient search for some new thing had been aggrandized into a belief in the New as another name for the millenium. The Old Order made the Lyceum its citadel. As though to solemnize its passing, Irving set on his stage the great sunsets of history, reviving *Charles I* in between *Henry VIII*, *Lear*, *Becket* and *King Arthur*; and with these his own sun sank in splendour, sublime in an age that invited ridicule.

"Shock or be shocked" governed London life: Swinburne's ballads upset Carlyle, Whistler's paintings upset Ruskin, and the Prince of Wales's Turf attendance on Fridays instead of Wednesdays upset Queen Victoria, until it became the inescapable law of human nature. Everybody either extolled or reviled Marie Lloyd's wink, Grant Allen's novel, "The Woman Who Did", the plays of Ibsen, the Albert Hall, Wagner's operas—almost everything. The lifting of a skirt's hem out of the mud sent bystanders into fits of delight or horror. At the mere mention outside church of hell or God, strong men, bearded like the pard, might swoon.

Intellectuals suffered from the same complaint. Ibsen's foremost champion, seizing an opportunity to be shocked at an age-old notion in *All For Her*, argued, "in point of taste, a woman masquerading in male attire is always questionable". While the old puritans raged together as never before at many such things, the new puritans made offences out of everything else— tea, coffee, tobacco, meat, military service, the shaving of the chin, any sports that happened to make use of a ball, trouser creases, high starched collars and unnudity at the photographers.

Downright vice seemed to give immunity from this raging fever; a pretence of being "wicked" gained the same effect with far less trouble. The vogue of anecdotes and verses which touched somewhat coyly on the subject of sex—some prominent people put their names to them in Christmas annuals—gave the eighteen-nineties that schoolboy air which found its label in "naughty".

On the stage the bedridden drama discussed who slept with whom and (forensically) at what date. When the right kind of clothes were worn in the right kind of setting, fashionable audiences flocked to hear this debated, and resounding fame could be won overnight. In the autumn of 1890 Martin Harvey, without a part in the Lyceum's new Bride-of-Lammermoor play, *Ravenswood*, by Herman Merivale, saw how Pinero, once a small-part player at the Lyceum, set this fashion, and watched the ascent of others who had left the temple, notably Alexander and Forbes Robertson. At the Globe close by, Benson's young men displayed their progress in Shakespeare. Ross, after playing Laertes (which at the Lyceum seemed the unattainable), signed a contract for the Strand. Even without envy in his soul, Martin Harvey had to contemplate his own undeserved backslidings.

When *Much Ado About Nothing* came back in 1891, "Mr. Harvey" appeared midway between Mr. Irving and Miss Ellen Terry on the programmes, opposite yet another of those small fry upon whom Shakespeare wreaks his vengeance for having once been himself a small-part actor. Conrade is simply a "follower". To Don John he makes his one speech: "Yea, but you must not make the full show of this, till you may do it without controlment. You have of late stood out against your brother, and he hath ta'en you newly into his grace; where it is impossible you should take true root, but by the fair weather that you make yourself: it is needful that you frame the season for your own harvest."

There is more such word-spinning when he listens under the pent-house to Borachio's guilty secrets until apprehended by Dogberry and Verges, to be called a false knave and answer, "Marry, sir, we say we are none," to call Dogberry a coxcomb and be called "thou naughty varlet", to be bound and then brought on again while others talk. The actor of such parts becomes the Chestertonian invisible man.

The Lyons Mail reappeared with some effective changes in the business— notably the elaborate rifling of the contents of the malle post by the light of lanterns on the roadway in front of the lonely inn. Now Martin Harvey could not be ignored, however small his part. "Great spirit is imparted to Joliquet," ran one notice. Another ran:

> "Two of the best and most earnestly played characters were the Jeannette of Miss Frances Ivor and the Joliquet of Mr. Harvey. Miss Ivor's Jeannette was a thoroughly sound and pathetic rendering of a character, slight it may be, but of great importance to the play, whilst the boy Joliquet was played like a boy by Mr. Harvey. It was in this character that Miss Kate Terry came first into notice as a child actress at the Princess's in the Charles Kean days."

He also had a part in the curtain-raiser *The King And The Miller; or, Cramond Brig*.

In the next revival of *The Corsican Brothers* he played Antonio. It was a longer part, mainly consisting of

JUDGE (*reading*). "Before us, Antonio Sanola, Judge of the Peace at Sullacaro, Province of Sartene, between Gretano Orlando and Marco Colonna— it has been solemnly agreed as follows: dating from this day, 22nd of March, 1841, the vendetta that broke out between them on the 11th of February, 1830, shall cease. In faith of which they have signed these presents in the presence of the principal inhabitants of the village, with their witnesses, M. Fabien dei Franchi, arbitrator, the relations of the two contracting parties, and ourselves, Judge of the Peace."

After two more lines, namely, "Now then, sign," and, "Make your cross there," he folds up document and all *exeunt*. There was a small part for Miss de Silva.

At this time the old dramatist-in-ordinary to the Lyceum was dying. His last energies had been expended upon the revision of a Napoleon play from America, but he had to surrender the task, and though included in his list of works it had others to sponsor it when beginning record-breaking travels at the Olympic in 1891 as *A Royal Divorce*. Wills died that year on December 13. Irving and Ellen Terry attended his funeral service in the Chapel Royal Savoy.

The young actor made slow progress: after the legal manner of the judge, the bedside manner of the doctor .In *The Bells* Martin Harvey had to ask Irving if he felt better: "No more pains in the head?" and, "No more strange noises in the ears?" Then he had to tell him to take more care of himself and not to drink so much white wine. "His nerves are still very much shaken," and "Don't forget what I have said," were his final words as he moved towards the door.

While he served the Old Order his wife helped to usher in the New. Young Mr. Shaw, the Socialist, had written a play. His argument was that all the talk about the New drama, though a society called the Independent Theatre existed to foster it, might soon end as "a figment of the revolutionary imagination". Having "rashly taken up the case" he preferred, rather than let it collapse, to manufacture the evidence.

In this way *Widowers' Houses* came to be acted at the Royalty on December 9, 1892, with Miss de Silva as the maid whose semi-strangulation by the heroine shocked even those broadminded critics who prided themselves on being prepared to see slum-landlordism dramatized. At the Lyceum her best chance was in Tennyson's *The Foresters*, a special performance given that year without Irving in the cast; it blended Shakespeare and Christmas pantomime in its tale of Maid Marian and Robin Hood among midsummer-night fairies. Miss de Silva as Titania had a scene to suit her lightest mood:

TITANIA.	Nip him not, but let him snore.
	We must flit for evermore
FAIRY.	Tit, my queen, must it be so?
	Wherefore, wherefore, should we go?
TITANIA.	I, Titania, bid you flit,
	And you dare to call me Tit.
FAIRY.	Tit, for love and brevity,
	Not for love of levity.
TITANIA.	Pertest of our flickering mob,
	Wouldst thou call my Oberon Ob?
FAIRY.	Nay, an please your Elfin Grace,
	Never Ob before his face.
TITANIA.	Fairy realm is breaking down
	When the fairy slights the crown.

Nothing as prominent came her husband's way. The small-part player cudgels his brain over a Shakespeare unknown to the lazy reader and the eager audience. Scraps that the eye skips and the ear never heeds are handed to him as indiarubber bones are tossed to puppies. There was rarely any idea, in the days when a part that did not fit you was supposed to be your chance to show how good you were, of bestowing them suitably—"Good parts make bad actors," was the answer to any complaints. Small-part players were as important as scene-shifters, neither more nor less, and as long as they entered on the right cue nobody saw them. In the Lyceum's glittering pageantry of *Henry VIII* in 1892, Martin Harvey had to announce:

"Ladies, a general welcome from his grace
Salutes ye all: this night he dedicates
To fair content and you: none here, he hopes,
In all this noble bevy, has brought with her
One care abroad: he would have all as merry
As first, good company, good wine, good welcome,
Can make good people,"

all of which amounts to "good evening", though that is rather more than most of such speeches convey.

For over two hundred nights the actor, in all the pride and assurance of his thirtieth year, had to open the banquet scene with this mockery of ambition before Sir Harry Guildford, when told, "Place you that side," subsided gibbering and grimacing among the eighteenpenny supernumeraries. Why has no frustrated, indomitable mummer written, "Small Parts I have Played", in order to revenge himself upon poetry's greatest genius for all these utility aristocrats, these unremembered earls, lords of oblivion, all meticulously docketed in old chronicles as having been pillars of the State in their day, although now like names which catch the eye by chance in some out-of-date Post Office Directory?

When poetry is written thousands of words at a time there have to be lines that tell the mind it can slumber. Nobody pays the slightest attention to them. Veterans of stock, dreaming of the great parts they wish to play while engaged for general utility, would put the words of Macbeth into the mouth of First Gentleman or Second Murderer without anyone being the wiser. "In Shakespeare nobody worries about meaning" became their conviction.

In the February of 1893, Irving played *Becket*. What Victorian England could accomplish when threatened with extinction by the New Age was manifested by the Lyceum with a performance as majestic as a State occasion. The playwright was the Poet Laureate. Quite a number of years had passed since Alfred, Lord Tennyson, wrote this play, and he had died full of years in the autumn of 1892, but his successor lacked the stature to fill his place.

Changes in the scenes had been made by Irving (for the author himself had described his work as "not intended in its present form to meet the exigencies of our modern theatre"), but though "cuts" were drastic there was no improving upon the great climax provided by historic fact. Becket might have been intended for Irving's maturity, and Rosamond matched Ellen Terry, however limited the part's scope.

Eleanor of Aquitaine, Queen of England (divorced from Louis of France), had in her the stuff of drama, especially for Geneviève Ward, whose ecstasy in cursing made itself heard in, "I shall live to trample on thy grave." There was the king for Terriss and a knight templar for Gordon Craig. Martin Harvey found himself cast for Lord Leicester, who brings the king's commands and goes away confounded—a part that so conjures itself up in terms of brawn that it would make any but a tall man embarrassed by his lack of inches.

When *The Merchant Of Venice* came back into the bill in the June of 1893 Gordon Craig played Lorenzo. Salarino was for Martin Harvey. Salanio, Salarino and Salerio sound more like a troupe of acrobats than characters in a play, but though they bear little evidence of an author's love they have work of importance to do. In performance the play requires of them some powerful listening, in particular to, "Hath not a Jew eyes?"

For the most to be made of this, fine speaking was not enough. Its effects had to be well, though not too well, recorded on attentive faces. That Martin Harvey, having once played Salarino, found himself so cast for each revival might mean that he was uncommonly to be trusted. Shylock, as a character, might be put out by Lorenzo, but Shylock, as Mr. Irving's part, hardly noticed the young man.

At length Irving relented. In casting Dagonet, the Jester at King Arthur's

Court, he remembered how the small-part player had played the Court fool of Elsinore in years gone by. That had been for the new acolyte a figure with one grimace to make, though not one word to say. The same player, now seasoned, could have a scene or two with Ellen Terry by donning motley once more. This was in *King Arthur*, written for the Lyceum in 1895 by Joseph W. Comyns Carr.

"Insinuant" describes this poet of the trim beard—genial companion witty after-dinner speaker, ingratiatingly well mannered, always at the elbow of the man-of-the-moment—who stepped into the shoes of W. G. Wills both as Shakespearean-vicegerent and king of Bohemia. From the Temple he passed to Fleet Street as a critic with Art under his hat. When Hardy suddenly became popular, Carr helped him to turn "Far From The Madding Crowd" into a drama with a strong smack of the murder in the Red Barn about it. When Hugh Conway rose high in favour, Carr collaborated with him; and no sooner had a young Australian journalist, Haddon Chambers won resounding success single-handed with his drama of a bushranger *Captain Swift*, than he listened spellbound to Carr's version of "a bicycle made for two".

Aided by his wife, a brilliant designer of costume, Carr installed himself at the Lyceum, after preparing the way with a pamphlet concerning Irving's *Macbeth*. Literature now kept Art company under his hat and he turned reader of plays. When Wills died what remained of his aspiring spirit was a poetic drama, *King Arthur*, in the Lyceum offices. The MS., paid for handsomely had lain there seven years when Irving, hankering once more after a theme very near his heart, asked Carr whether he could make something of it.

Since riding tandem displeased him this time, Carr wrote *King Arthur* anew by himself (for the general good, since his blank verse never lapsed into bits of awkward prose). It served the purposes of scenic magnificence—and it gave heart of grace to a young actor, thwarted until he was heart-sick, with the best part he had had so far, even though it did recall Shallow's idle boast "I remember at Mile-end Green, when I lay at Clement's Inn, I was then Sir Dagonet in Arthur's show."

In a Camelot after the style of St. Sophia there was an imposing array of Byzantine Britons who upheld both traditional schools of acting. Irving was Arthur and Ellen Terry his Guinevere. Forbes Robertson was the Lancelot and Geneviève Ward the Morgan Le Fay. Thus a balance was achieved between romantic and classic which then and there proved that one offsets the other to the benefit of both. No comment was passed on the contrast, and yet how different they were could not be denied. Nothing better has been said since on the subject than this:

"Romantic acting, like other romantic art, is adventure, almost gambling; it comes off and it seems to have found new worlds or lit on the door of magic, or it fails and flops into grotesqueness. Classical

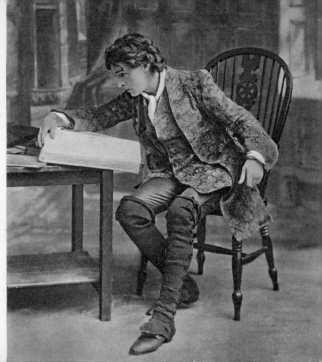

[Photo: Stereoscopic Co.

Martin Harvey as
"Eugene Aram" in
After All

Martin Harvey as
"Richard III"

A scene from *Great Possessions*

[Photo: A. Ellis & Walery]

acting like Mr. Forbes Robertson's runs lesser risks; it may not take your breath away, or send a momentary wave of coldness across your face, or elicit whatever your special bodily signal may be of your mind's amazed and sudden surrender to some stroke of passionate genius.

"But there is one glory of the sun and another glory of the moon. This acting, at least, never makes you yawn; and it never amuses you meanly; indeed, you might almost wholly describe it by negatives, in terms of the trances of imaginative exploration that it does not easily give you, and also of the inflation, feverishness, turbidity that it never approaches.

"Or you might say that this art is less like that of one artist of rare gift than of a commission of artists highly accomplished; it is what they would all unite in approving, so far as it goes; it has no freakish faults; it is standardized. Or you might just take Pater's wording, and say that the principle you find ruling it is that of order in beauty as distinct from that of strangeness in beauty."

The critic who wrote that, C. E. Montague, belonged to the Manchester School, believed in the natural and showed no partiality towards romantic plays. That "new worlds" could be found by such means is from him a noteworthy admission. He was not writing of *King Arthur* and his theory of order in beauty is not applied, as well it might be, to Geneviève Ward. The note of her voice rings out even more in a newspaper interview published at the time:

"I have to make my effects decisively and instantly. There is no preparation for my scenes. Each time I appear I have unhesitatingly to strike the right note, or my opportunity would be gone."

Irving himself avoided all such "standing jumps" into emotion at white heat directly the player enters. Even though his preparations were hidden from the public eye he felt them himself, like the rising anger of a man outwardly controlled. An enthralled audience awards less merit to the player who has to be impassioned the moment he appears. Yet it is a test of skill. Macready had sparring partners willing to be almost throttled in the wings the moment before he had to enter, violently agitated. He asked after one of these who had given satisfaction. He was a stranger, there by accident, and he had been taken to hospital.

In the spring of 1895 when a new double bill went into rehearsal there was for Martin Harvey fresh disappointment. Old Corporal Gregory Brewster in the curtain-raiser, Conan Doyle's *A Story Of Waterloo*, called for support from three only. *A Chapter From The Life Of Don Quixote*, all that remained of an ambitious effort by poor, vanished Wills, needed eleven. There was a boy, Antonio, among them. Irving handed the part to Miss de

H

Silva. But he knew the effect he wanted and she helped to create his vision of Cervantes' Spain where mockery turned against romance—in order to create romance.

Though *Cymbeline* was not seen at the Lyceum until the September of 1896, Ellen Terry's prompt copy has "Cleveland, 1895" under her autograph. Pasted in it is the reproduction of a Greek portrait which resembles a caricature of Irving's Hamlet. Against the passage where Imogen falls into Iachimo's trap, she has written, "Believe him—(he the greater villain). No distrust—An *impulsive* lady."

The notes at the end of the copy are commented upon. "Idiot—why of course," is written against one trite observation, "Somebody must have told him" against an explanation cited from Dr. Johnson, and "good old Johnson!" appears ironically elsewhere. Cowden Clarke, on the other hand, wins great favour—"'Clarke' is a Dear." When the editor writes "Clarke may be right," she has crossed out "may be" and written "is".

Against Hazlitt's comment that Imogen has "no need of an outrageous antipathy to vice" in pardoning Iachimo, she sets down, "She'll never *forget* it though!" Concerning the lines

> Give him that parting kiss which I had set
> Betwixt two charming words,

the editor's note is, "Warb. informs us that they were 'Adieu, Posthumous!'" Underlining "informs" and placing "!!!" beneath it, Ellen Terry asks, "How does this brute know?" and suggests "God's—blessing: My—Love: Sweet—Heart."

.   .   .   .

There seemed to be a waning awe of Irving's name. *Cymbeline* was heckled with one of the many catch-phrases of the day. You cannot understand public imagination without some knowledge of these. What began in Hazlitt's day as a love of quoting Shakespeare came up-to-date with sayings from recent plays.

"What will Mrs. Grundy say?" was (without any reference to propriety) one. "Praise from Sir Hubert is praise indeed" and "I hope I don't intrude" were others which lasted, though not for so long. Proverbial wisdom sounded well throughout the long years when it was not laughed at. Proverbial humour to match it dropped from the lips of the comedians of the day, especially from those of the Adelphi dramas where "I believe you, my bh-oy" originated. The process went into reverse at *The Dead Heart*: directly Ben Webster said his heart was dead, a galleryite shouted, "How's yore pore feet?"

The music-halls now coined a new catch-phrase in every new song. When Iachimo turned down the nightdress of the slumbering Imogen the cry rose unbidden to some not necessarily ill-meaning lips, "Now we shan't be long." No immunity could be secured against such Shakespearean-commentary, because the popular idols of the halls had by now provided a concordance equal to every possible occasion of public life. But that shout, while it plainly does not show deliberate disrespect, indicates a fall in prestige—unconscious tribute paid by Demos to the power of capricious fortune.

When *Richard III*, with Miss Terry and Miss Ward still present, went into rehearsal, Harvey felt another rebuff. After fourteen years of steadfast discipleship he expected some kind of part in order to maintain the position he had won the year before. Clarence might have come his way, but instead he found himself cast as Clarence's escort, Sir Robert Brackenbury, another of those self-propelling "properties" whose existence no Bardolater suspects.

This one is worse than most because while Richard and his brother swap speeches, he enjoins them, whenever they pause for breath, to forbear this converse. Someone of stature could carry it off with dignity, but someone short enough for the royal dukes to talk through his hat was bound to feel small, on top of which the performance had barely begun when Harvey's part in it was over.

That night Irving slipped on the stairs when returning to his chambers in Grafton Street and severely injured his knee. It was an accident of the kind to be expected in the course of a lifetime, and only the soothsayers in Bond Street close by would see in it the first ebb of fortune. That was not evident when Martin Harvey gave up the security of his permanent place in the company and the Lyceum. He would return whenever there was a part for him; otherwise he would now go to any London theatre where there was a part for him.

Only those who have tried it can know what a nerve-racking experience this is—with its recurring lesson concerning what critical momentum means when it is constantly lost by freakish chance.

CHAPTER II

FROM IBSEN TO MAETERLINCK

LUCK, according to stage-door proverbial philosophy, depends on whether you turn to the right or to the left when leaving the house. What that means the early years of Martin Harvey clearly show. If he had found golden chance either before or after his years at the Lyceum he could not have meant what he does mean now.

Instead of "luck", say "fate". The facts warrant it. All the frustrations as a boy of twenty lead to that long, arduous training under Irving. All the withheld rewards of his adventures among masterpieces and other plays as the prey of fortune in the London of the Diamond Jubilee brought him back to fulfil what looked so uncommonly like his destiny.

The struggles of 1897, even though his name soon appeared "By kind permission of Sir Henry Irving", were hard. Long rehearsals twice resulted in a few special matinées when he attempted something ambitious. In such ventures the actor looks to the critics in the hope of reward. Martin Harvey gave himself heart and soul to the project of making the work of Jose Échegaray known at the Court Theatre; he appeared in *Mariana*—a bride, when her old love enters her room, calls her husband, who kills her and challenges him to a duel. Only an actor could fully understand what he felt after the performance on reading, towards the end of a full-page critique by G.B.S. in the *Saturday Review*, "Mr. Martin Harvey, Mr. George Bancroft, and Miss Mabel Hackney take care of the minor parts." At this point in an actor's career he becomes aware how many, how very many, never pass beyond it. Even those who do win critical honours may do so without winning any other.

That very notice of *Mariana* asked why players of known ability were seen only when certain parts made them absolutely indispensable. Why was it morally certain that if the leaders of the stage had not gone into management they would have been heard of as everybody's dearest friend, only so "dry", so "unlucky", so any-excuse-for-engaging-third-rate-nonentities-in-their-place, only a name to young playgoers? Why would Sir Henry Irving and Mr. Wyndham vanish instantly from the stage if they did not hold their places by the strong hand as managers? The possession of skill was fatal, Shaw contended. His moral was digested by one of those who had taken care of a minor part.

What Martin Harvey demonstrated, perhaps unknowingly, all his life was the advantage of cultivating one style of acting. Great players in the past never felt the temptation to do otherwise; fashion either made no demands upon them at all, or else changed too late for them to conform. Make-believe they accepted unashamedly as make-believe.

"All lies," said the wise man of Ancient Greece at Europe's first theatrical performance, and the centuries have laughed at the words in error, for as the first critic he laid the foundation-stone of the faculty. Drama should never be mistaken for truth; its faked evidence proves nothing. But when the Victorian stage began to represent railway-trains, prisons and delirium tremens the fad called realism passed for reality. Real chairs and tables furnished three-walled rooms, and really wet umbrellas glistened in canvas gardens.

From the acceptance of such cup-and-saucer "naturalism" as nature, or at least the only nature worth mirroring, the power of Irving saved the stage. Without the Lyceum, romance would have been discredited; without the Lyceum, Martin Harvey might have been jack of all styles and master of none. Whatever he would have learnt in London he could not have become paramount in Ibsen because enthusiasts staged that master's plays without first learning how to.

Many years had to pass before the problem of foreign plays would be faced; to know how to act a French play the actor sometimes visited Paris, but Christiania and Copenhagen seemed more remote than New York. We have Mr. Shaw's word for it that the first London performances (the only performances there in the nineteenth century) of *John Gabriel Borkman* blundered.

Four months after its Scandinavian *première* it was staged at the Strand one May afternoon in 1897, with a cast which indicated how willing players were to sacrifice time and energy for Ibsen. Most of them were of note, whether suitable or not for that half-real, half-mystic play where the fraudulent banker, suffering self-imposed captivity since serving his sentence, dreams of the illimitable kingdom he might develop by the wizardry of finance.

Geneviève Ward was the hard, unforgiving wife (not nearly hard enough for the chiselled marble of her style), and Martin Harvey the son with a mission in life to save the family honour, which he gaily refuses. You can sense the romance in his style while reading comments by G.B.S., which also indicate the prestige he had achieved:

"Mr. Martin Harvey, as Erhart, was clever enough to seize the main idea of the part—the impulse towards happiness—but not experienced enough to know that the actor's business is not to supply an idea with a sounding-board, but with a credible, simple and natural human being to utter it when its time comes and not before. He showed, as we all know he would show, considerable stage talent, and more than ordinary dramatic intelligence; but in the first act he was not the embarrassed young gentleman of Ibsen, but rather the 'soaring human boy' imagined by Mr. Chadband."

After *John Gabriel Borkman*, Ibsen excitedly wrote his "dramatic epilogue", *When We Dead Awaken*, about a sculptor whose life's work has been disfigured by a swarm, round the plinth, of men and women with faces rather like beasts. The point was as plain as a pikestaff and as sharp as the pike. Rather than feel it, one of Ibsen's champions declared the play to be the product of a great brain in its dotage, another translated it into English words arranged grammatically in unheard-of phrases, and another used it as propaganda for standing stripped before the camera: London could not claim to understand Ibsen after that.

The old master who liked to smoke his cutty, drink his wine and laugh over the tricks of wild young women meant little in the life of any English actor, least of all for one who belonged to what was, for better or worse, the enduring tradition of the English stage. Yet the romantic style, played consistently, might have suited Ibsen better than the realistic. Many of his plays, more particularly these later ones, make very little pretence of being "true to life"; they begin in an everyday manner, but such preliminaries in *John Gabriel Borkman* are deceptive. How could its climax of symbolism be presented as though of domestic interest?

Such problems might not be solved because they had not been recognized. That Martin Harvey was a romantic actor could not be doubted, but only the younger critics consciously differentiated styles. Interest in the theory of acting had been keen for years without reaching the diagnosis that what was bad in one style might be good in another. The English school upheld the Shakespearean principle defined in Hamlet's

> . . . . . this player here,
> But in a fiction, in a dream of passion,
> Could force his soul so to his own conceit,
> That from her working, all his visage wann'd;
> Tears in his eyes, distraction in's aspect,
> A broken voice, and his whole function suiting
> With forms to this conceit?   And all for nothing
> For Hecuba . . .

Conflicting methods originated in the classic dignity of the French stage, which put order and regularity first and passion last. Shakespeare had to be played from the heart, Corneille and Racine from the head. Out of that clear divergence arose a fog of argument thickened by many disputants down to Irving and Coquelin and beyond. The French case was put by Diderot in his "Paradoxe sur le Comédien", translated by Walter Herries Pollock and published with a preface by Irving in 1883. The gist of it is that all real feeling should be in the auditorium, none on the stage:

"The actor who plays from thought, from study of human nature, from constant imitation of some ideal type . . . from memory, will be one and the same at all performances, will be always at his best mark; he has considered, combined, learnt and arranged the whole thing in his head. Like the poet he will dip for ever into the inexhaustible treasure-house of Nature, instead of coming very soon to an end of his own poor resources."

According to Garrick himself, says First Speaker in this dialogue, an actor who will play Shakespeare to perfection would in Racine feel entwined by serpents round his head, arms, hands, legs and feet. And yet Diderot maintains that to act from the heart is wrong always and everywhere, arguing as though the two distinct styles were one and indivisible.

How fast the theorists bogged themselves in this error becomes clear from William Archer's "Masks or Faces?" This study of the psychology of acting, published in 1888, stays unaware that the romantic actor's meat might be the classical actor's poison. The argument is not which is which, but what is right and what is wrong:

"The emotionalist position is that both actor and audience should yield themselves up to the illusion to a certain extent; the anti-emotionalist position is that the actor will more easily and certainly beget illusion in the audience if he remains entirely free from it himself."

As a statement of the view of acting taken in 1888, "Masks or Faces?" proves invaluable and has lasting worth in the collecting of evidence to show, on the one hand, that "the imagination can in some cases so act on the physical organism as to produce in a more or less acute degree the characteristic symptoms of grief"; while on the other these symptoms may to some extent "be imitated by the direct action of the will upon the muscles, with little or no aid from the imagination".

Yet though he makes no study of the romantic tradition as such, Archer sheds a vivid light upon it merely by referring to Darwin's "Expression of the Emotions". From this he quotes, "He who gives way to violent gestures will increase his rage; he who does not control the signs of fear will experience fear in a greater degree. . . . Even the simulation of an emotion tends to arouse it in our minds."

This seems to be a clue to the frenzies of Mathias in *The Bells*. Otherwise most of the facts amassed by records of acting are of such interest in themselves that they rise like a mist to obscure any clear view of what the exact nature of acting is. All those tales of presence of mind when mishaps occur, of practical jokes played in the midst of make-believe passion, of the ability to take note of humdrum affairs while expressing sublime emotion, signify nothing beyond the usual duality of human personality at all times and in all occupations. As for real tears, why, they are shed alike by the coldly calculating eye and the eye in fine frenzy rolling, and so, as evidence for both sides, wash each other out.

Every actor employs all the methods of simulating emotion that there are. Yet each according to his stamp prefers the one method which gives him that stamp. Kemble and his kind like to contemplate works of art, preferably of the antique in marble, to woo the tragic muse in attitudes of the ideal. The realist, following the mode of his eighteenth-century forbears who visited the padded cells of Bedlam to hear the authentic note for Lear's ravings, copies from the life even to the extent of attending hospitals in order to witness death spasms.

Kean found the rage of Richard Crookback in his own breast; he was an ardent hater all day and every day, particularly when he worked off an ancient grudge for some slight or injury suffered in his rogue-and-vagabond days. While Martin Harvey noted examples from each variety he prided himself on keeping "posts in his brain" to work on what he did in the heat of the moment before the audience. Yet he favoured the theory of emotion remembered in tranquillity, even to the extent of believing that the actor-manager who "shadowed forth the shadow of a king" might draw on his own humiliating experiences of "bad business".

While spontaneity was dangerous with sword and dagger, with cup and saucer it was impossible. Hence the need of "stand-on-the-chalk-mark-and-count-fifteen" methods in drawing-room scenes. Kean would, after rehearsing three different ways of dying, be certain on the night to use none of them; that would not do when a gentleman had to move a chair and a lady to sit on it. Thus the more natural the style the more artificial the means of attaining it, and Mayfair comedies had to be timed like infantry drill.

No sudden mines could be sprung by the warmth of the scene for fear of breaking crockery, a peril from which Iago and his like were immune, because if flagons did fall, by so much was the effect increased. The inspiration of the moment meant much to Martin Harvey. Following Irving's example, he liked to add to and retouch the portraits he painted his life long. He, more than any other actor, made critics and playgoers aware of the romantic tradition, upholding it steadfastly so that it could never be dismissed merely as "costume". Otherwise some such confusion would have resulted from the boom in romance midway through the eighteen-nineties, when all actors wanted to follow the fashion for cloak-and-sword.

Most of them put on romance like a garment. But one actor-manager of the day was a genuine romantic through and through. Beerbohm Tree had a brilliant blue eye—no audience could be conscious of more than one at a time—very mild, pale as a summer sky, of extraordinary dominance. When the part had been suited to it the effect was admirable. In great characters of tragic intensity the effect, on the contrary, was of an urchin's gaze through the eyehole of a Guy Fawkes mask while asking: "How am I doing? All right?"

There was some record of this cerulean iris in the stage-directions of Haddon Chambers's drawing-room drama, *Captain Swift.* Of course, a bushranger who poses as a civil gentleman might exercise such a look, for though it would give him away at once in real life, stage-licence permits behaviour which enables the intelligence of an audience (corresponding, roughly, to that of the dullest person in it) to grasp what on earth a play is all about. But there is no occasion for Hamlet, whose concern is with his own conscience, to supplicate the outward world for its approval; and the timidity in that eye, as though expecting reproof, turned Mark Antony to exquisite burlesque.

Tree first made his mark in farce—the curate who reiterates "I don't like London" in *The Private Secretary*—before downright villains or heroes of doubtful character in drawing-room drama showed not only where his bent but where public taste lay. At last to the Haymarket in the October of 1895 came *Trilby* from America. George du Maurier's novel had, in print and picture, endeared itself like a legend born. Those picturesque figures were, like those of Phiz and Cruikshank, easily represented by costume and make-up in externals.

The risk lay in not being able to make Svengali horrible enough. Tree made him more horrible. The mild eye became baleful, excruciatingly baleful. His hold over Trilby was no mere mesmerist's power but testimony of being, like another Paganini, in league with the Devil. No one put Tree on Irving's level. He was laughed at. Yet here was a performance of incomparable *bravura*. The story, irresistible in its sentimental appeal, was du Maurier's. The character, a revelation of what romantic acting could do in its disdain of any mere interpretative function, was Tree's.

That the public had had enough for the moment of the New at once became evident. Penny plain forthwith gave way to an orgy of twopence coloured in every style from Ancient Rome to modern Balkans. Both the cup-and-saucer comedy and the "problem play" yielded to romance in toga or tunic, chain-mail, lace ruffles or stove-pipe hat—anything rather than swallow-tails and trousers. *The Sign Of The Cross* gave hero and heroine to be eaten by lions to please the masses at the Lyric, with a chorus of praise from pulpits every Sunday to urge them on the right path to the right theatre.

Three days later the St. James's, which was now London's most fashionable theatre, presented a play from Anthony Hope's novel with a setting called Ruritania which made romance possible in the present day. *The Prisoner Of Zenda*, with a prologue of silk knee-breeches and lace ruffles which was outshone by a Balkan or Baltic court radiant with the seismic uniforms of high-velocity hussars, astonished a Mayfair that had barely ceased applauding George Alexander in the impressive gloom of *The Second Mrs. Tanqueray* and the frivolous wit of *The Importance Of Being Earnest*.

Fashionable intellectuals, making some demur at having to descend from the exalted intellectual heights of Pinero, had to yield. Romance occupied fashion's citadel. Why? Woman, with one voice, answered, "But he wears such wonderful clothes." Drama in modern clothes felt the effects of the horrible downfall of one of its leading playwrights.

In the autumn of 1896, romance gained another fillip from the Haymarket where the place of Tree, now building his own theatre opposite, had been taken by Cyril Maude in *Under The Red Robe*, adapted from Stanley Weyman's novel. These three brought dreamers from their hearths, and then from hammocks when companies went on tour. In Paris François Copée contributed *Pour La Couronne*, a fifteenth-century drama of the Balkans with a patriot called upon by duty to kill his father. Forbes Robertson played Constantine Brancomir in *For The Crown* at the Lyceum in the February of 1896, with Mrs. Patrick Campbell as "Militza (a slave)". It had been translated by John Davidson, one of the rare appearances in the theatre of a poet self-dedicated to the drama in vain.

The measure of Irving had never been taken till youth challenged comparison with him in his own limelight. He was ageing. From his fiftieth year the strain of "living on his nerves", which is what romantic acting amounts to, told visibly. Fortune, ebbing from him, left its marks as on the ribbed sea sand. Yet he could safely let his theatre to the best graced of the younger generation.

During his provincial tour in the autumn of 1897, *Hamlet* was staged at the Lyceum by Forbes Robertson, with Mrs. Patrick Campbell as Ophelia. The beauty she had inherited from her Italian mother, besides a passionate temperament and a quick intelligence, made her one of those who begin at the top. One or two seasons on tour as Rosalind and Viola gave her "experience". Three years as Lady Teazle, Rosalind and heroines of Adelphi dramas in Town made her name known; one performance as Paula Tanqueray made her famous, and a portrait by Aubrey Beardsley makes her immortal.

Though Osric at the start, Martin Harvey dropped out in order to play at the Court that October in *Children Of The King*, sample of the fairy-tale vogue then over-riding German theatres. It was a vaguely allegorical elaboration of the babes in the wood, who instead of dying beneath the robins' layer of leaves are mistaken by their rescuers for members of the royal family. Herbert Ross was there as a broom-binder and Isabel Bateman as a witch.

The heroine was a child of the stage equal to anything. Her mother, Marie Loftus, still an idol of the halls, was a serio-comic who sang, "She wore a little safety-pin behind", and was now displaying a shapeliness matured in forty years as principal boy in Christmas pantomime. The daughter also was named Marie, but as she wanted to use the family name without causing confusion she had been Cissie Loftus ever since she sang in her teens on the provincial halls.

Her praises had been sung in the Vienna Café when she first appeared at the Old Oxford close by in 1893, for her "impersonations" of stage celebrities raised mimicry to an art. The Gaiety recruited her at once and there she stayed a year. In New York she played a part in Justin Huntly McCarthy's *The Highwayman*.

Back in London she was the delight of the Old Empire, but ended the engagement when she became (a runaway match it was called) Mrs. McCarthy. Now, with serious thoughts of leaving variety for legitimate, she exchanged the cheers from Leicester Square's garish promenade for the over-awed silence of an audience of children.

John Davidson, called in to revise the English version, interested Harvey more than any of these. Poets were necessary to his theatrical future, and here was one with a moderately successful play and some volumes of fine, virile verse to his credit. Davidson, now forty years of age, had set out from his father's manse at Barrhead, Renfrewshire, for Edinburgh University when his boyhood at the Highlanders Academy, Greenock, was over. It was a very brief boyhood, for at the age of twelve he was working in the laboratory of a sugar-refinery and a year later in the Public Analyst's Office.

He preferred to earn fees as a tutor, since this left him free to write poetic dramas, first in the historical manner and then, daringly, in current settings of everyday. By the time he came to London in 1890, the quality of his verse had been recognized. And now both publishers and managers were aware of him. The door had opened. He had but to prove his worth. "If I ever realize my limitations there will be nothing before me but suicide," said the young poet to the young actor.

But the other side of that door was as queer as the other side of Alice's Looking Glass. The minister's son, resolved on caring for wife and family by his well-earned fees in the profession of authorship, found friends among the lost souls, mentally and physically tormented, of the *fin de siècle*, and became a lost soul himself, doomed to literary drudgery in a world generous with esteem and niggardly with payment.

Suicide haunted his thoughts. Early death from one cause or another gave peace to the romantics, the men accursed, who made a legend of "The Yellow Book". If every number of it had perished at the hands of the people whose feelings it outraged it might be a lurid memory. But plenty of copies are left for innocent girlhood to look at idly, very idly.

"Is this the thing there was all the fuss about?" the child asks. The old exquisite, still with a black ribbon to his monocle and tassel to his cane, feels a stir within him. "It shocked," he says, "people so terribly that at last it shocked itself and died."

"Show me where," commands the child. He turns the pages. She will believe him when he talks of such vanished glories as the Church Parade

in Hyde Park, but "The Yellow Book", alas, has not vanished. It stays—
"rather charming in its old-fashioned way," she says—to make one with
"Sunday At Home" and "Leisure Hour". Since the pages are blameless
even to his historic sense, since Fragonard's swing is nearer the bacchanalian
than anything here, he murmurs something about scandals, about authors
who would not let their names be seen between the same covers as the
drawings of Beardsley, who designed a frontispiece for Davidson's volume
of plays.

"I know," she says, "I lived for a while in a small country village,
but does it matter? I thought this yellow cover was meant to suggest
daffodils."

"Yellow," he meditates, "always indicated some sort of peril."

"That's what comes," she dictates in a firm voice, "of being
hysterical."

Outraged dignity looks like that to the young. All those indignant
waxed moustaches became so ludicrous that the heroes of coming generations made a cult of the effeminate. John Davidson belonged to neither
one scheme nor the other. He contrived to be both a hard-working
father and a "Yellow Book" poet at the same time. Yet the streak of
degeneracy, so-called, linked him with others in a group who hastened
their death.

He was hag-ridden by the idea of suicide. It was not in keeping with
his rugged character, with verse as solid as figured oak compared with
the pretty veneer of contemporary poetry. *Smith*, his "tragic farce", attempts
a self-portrait. Smith, Jones, Brown and Robinson talk blank verse in a
public-house and are served by Topsy:

> SMITH.   You're looking fresh: you've had a holiday?
> TOPSY.   I've had my week.
> SMITH.   Where were you?
> TOPSY.   At the coast.

Smith, who wants to think, goes to a Scottish village with a friend who
wants to write but poisons himself while uttering a soliloquy:

> Death—and the houses nestle at my feet,
> With ruddy human windows here and there
> Piercing the velvet shade—deep in the world,
> Old hedgerows and sweet by-paths through the corn.

Both Smith and the young woman he loves also commit suicide.

To balance this cult of lost souls, both here and abroad a movement began for the recovery of souls. This had a well-defined significance for Martin Harvey. However small his part in the making or marring of Ibsen, however slight his contact with the Dowsons and Beardsleys, he spellbound another ardent community. There was a bewildering lot of separated groups, all intent on wrecking the sorry scheme of things entire while carrying out Omar's reconstruction scheme at one and the same time.

"New" was never so overweighted before. From the way each of its exponents spoke, you might think the whole world obsessed by one vast reforming mission. Each exponent explained it differently; each took a distinct view of it because the mission was not single. In a united resolve to disturb the Old Order, new orders came into existence by the dozen. The prophet of Russia, the dramatist of Norway, the novelist of Wessex, had barely an idea in common, and the iconoclast from Dublin who would use anybody to serve his particular purpose was as unlike again. Before any brain could recover from the dizziness of being whirled round by these, Maëterlinck was discovered by the "souls" as what they understood by "New".

What it meant to be a soul would be hard to explain had none of them left record. Fortunately, A. B. Walkley, a dramatic critic supposedly of a cynical turn of mind, professed his faith fairly clearly in the statement, "Those of us who have had the time can compare their spiritual experiences with M. Maëterlinck's; those of us who have not can still take pleasure in following the adventures of a fellow-man's soul among the mysteries and moralities, and in contemplating the goal to which those adventures have led him."

Another's declaration of faith stated, "The soul has its senses," as the hint of a double life. A third believer delayed his confession until a day of disillusionment. Consequently, Roland Pertwee writes in detachment about his conversion to this sect by a young woman he fell in love with:

"There is something very much akin between a newly hatched soul and anaemia. Both conditions are accompanied by lassitude and a general wasting of the energies. I, myself, was enchanted with the thing and cherished it secretly. I regarded it as a sort of spiritual microscope which revealed and magnified many mysteries. By its aid I discovered esoteric meanings in meaningless objects and phrases. All kinds of closed doors flew open at its command. I dare say, more often than not, they led nowhere, but nothing could have exceeded the joy I felt at being able to enter and have a look round,"

and how this took form in print and upon the stage is reflected in a list of plays by Maurice Maëterlinck, "The Belgian Shakespeare", born at Ghent in 1862:

La Princess Maleine	..	..	1889
L'Intruse ..	..	..	1890
Les Aveugles	..	..	1891
Les Sept Princesses	..	..	1891
Pelléas et Mélisande	..	..	1892
Alladine et Polomides	..	..	1894
Intérieur ..	..	..	1894
La Mort de Tintagiles	..	..	1894
Aglavaine et Sélysette	..	..	1896

Of these, *Pelléas And Mélisande* became the oriflamme, the scapegoat, the spearhead, the living sacrifice, the crowning glory and quite a number of other proverbial things besides.

That part of the theatre which had come under the heading of "sporting and dramatic", ever since real winners raced on the stage and real players went racing, naturally looked at it with the gaze that saw it was not there. The classic actor shook his head; the veteran romantic went back to *The Bells*. But the young romantic saw the light.

"Out of the mists of antiquity, out of the shadows of the Infinite," are Martin Harvey's words. Then the Mrs. Patrick Campbell of Beardsley's exquisite portrait decided on a series of matinées at the Prince of Wales's. To her Mélisande the actor, whose singular poetic wistfulness the theatre had so far wasted, played Pelléas. Forbes Robertson, unconvinced, tackled Golaud.

In her autobiography, "My Life and Some Letters", she gives a strange account of the origin of this project. A demagogue, whose unhappy knack of calling upon heaven to inspire his oratory would one day be the indirect cause of landing him in jail, made it possible. Horatio Bottomley financed Forbes Robertson's management. Funds came from the same pocket, Mrs. Campbell believed, for a tour in Germany. She agreed to play Ophelia, Lady Macbeth and Paula Tanqueray when the company went to Berlin on condition that *Pelléas And Mélisande* would be staged afterwards in London.

Although he agreed, Forbes Robertson thought the play weak and morbid. "Why do you want to make such a damned fool of Forbes?" asked his brother, but she insisted, "warmly supported in my enthusiasm and feeling by Mr. Martin Harvey's full understanding and appreciation of the beauty of the poem". His melancholy face, the curious timbre of voice, his scholar's delight in cadence helped him "to invest the part of Pelléas with an unearthly glamour".

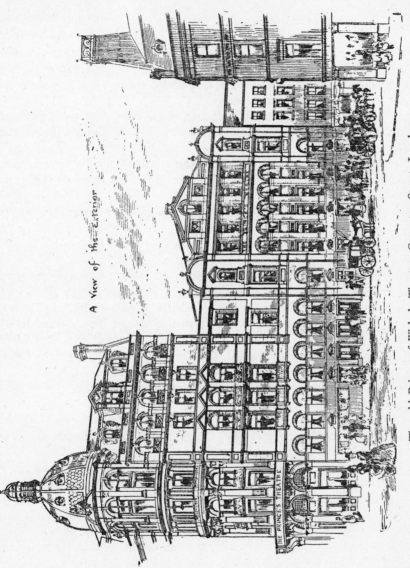

A View of the Exterior

The old Prince of Wales's Theatre, Coventry Street, London
(Opened as the Prince's)

Her account of the story is all the more interesting if it is borne in mind that the word "soul" does not occur in the dialogue:

> "The action of this play takes place in one of those gloomy ancient castles, by the sea, which Maëterlinck has always used as symbolical of what the prison life is to the soul; their ancient impregnable walls, their long tradition of sorrow, crime and tragedy, stand for life in the flesh; and the sea, the illimitable sea, is always there to speak of eternity, and the wild sea birds, of freedom.
>
> "Mélisande's ignorance of her own birth, her sense of exile, her grief by the pool where she has lost her crown, are all symbolic of the soul in life.
>
> "Then comes the contact with man's desire, Golaud's love born of passion; a contact which teaches her nothing; which awakens no love—only fear.
>
> "As the play proceeds, Pelléas and Mélisande draw nearer and nearer, each finding in the other the yearning of their soul's fulfilment, and in their very purity deceiving themselves into the shadow of death."

To-day, when the souls seem funny even to themselves grown-up, there is still no smiling at such a performance as the playgoer at the Prince of Wales's saw. Three of the rarest souls (depriving the word of any period meaning) who ever graced the boards turned a myopic dream to enchantment. The spell of early Maëterlinck lasted more than its hour. Long after he had left that vaguely Provençal, Ossianic, Mabinogion sphere behind, thousands felt the stir of it while ignorant of his name.

By the piano in rows of suburban drawing-rooms young men and maidens, addressing Mélisande in song, told her that her soul must stand alone. Even those who jest in Mr. Pertwee's way let fall a hint of that lingering respect for inexpressible things which belatedly affected the "general public" long after it had been the fad of a few.

These were the ripples lapping with low sounds by the shore. The fountain whose cascade set those circles widening was the play that sent its matinée audiences out, into the raffish air of Leicester Square and Piccadilly, arguing whether they "liked it" or not.

People who attend first performances, as punctiliously as policemen on their beat, always fight against their own enjoyment. *Pelléas And Mélisande* would for years to come be accepted with almost religious fervour as part of Martin Harvey's repertoire. Miss de Silva would be Mélisande. She had her share too in those earlier matinées, for when he "made his clothes act" it was because they were of her designing.

There might be a temptation to say that Pelléas left an imprint on his acting, gave it Maëterlinck's wistfulness. But actor and author had each felt, before they met, that spirit of the age—it likewise expressed itself in myopic paintings which transformed the Tower of London (or some new hotel when its uses were advertisement) into Camelot. There must be this jest at its expense since "if I laugh at any mortal thing 'tis that I may not weep".

The indefinite yearning you felt when Martin Harvey played Pelléas may not come back when you read the play in the expectation of finding it again, but it can catch you unawares when the lark that sings above you drops out of a clear sky, like a stone, into the corn; or when in the darkness of a wood at midsummer, where a stray shaft of sunlight filters through the branches, gaunt clumps of foxgloves stretch four or five feet high to reach its glow—things which, like Maëterlinck's early plays, do not "make sense".

Call it transcendental if you wish or use any other awkward word; whatever term satisfies you must also serve for what those hard-headed Midland and Northern playgoers experienced when they saw Martin Harvey. Nor were they all hard-headed who felt something this side idolatry. A paragraph from Lady Benson's "Mainly Players", concerning a Shakespeare tour of 1897, is expressive of much:

"In Belfast this same year Harcourt Williams came into the Company; quite a boy, with tremendous ambitions, and such was his admiration for Martin Harvey that he would give unconscious imitations of him in his various parts. I remember his telling me with the greatest pride that Marie Corelli had thought him 'exactly like Martin Harvey in face and method of acting'."

That boy of seventeen, coming fresh from the tutorship of Kate Batemen to play the Duke of Bedford in *Henry V*, had had very little time to observe the hero of his worship. By 1897 that hero had had few opportunities to excite such ardent feelings. If he had with such slender chances won a following why did the stage begrudge him even a livelihood? Irving, it was said, "had raised the status" of his profession at his knighthood.

It was an empty phrase, meaning not that Irving had more honour than Garrick, but that knighthood had less. For the general run of talented actors conditions were never worse. In the time of Cooke and Edmund Kean a salaried player might, on his merits, come at last into a blaze of glory. Limelight had changed all that, figuratively and literally. Hitherto, Othello and Iago had fought it out (greatly to the benefit of the acting, for that particular tragedy has never been the same since) who should be in focus, that is to say, whose face should be lit up at the foot-lamps.

By bringing into the theatre the new form of lighting, Charles Kean made sun and moon his servants to follow him upstage while lesser creatures, with their backs to the audience, had to stand and wait downstage. "Limes" then entered into the actor's soul, more particularly Fechter's, for though

I

he had charm enough to challenge allcomers he would get an already beaten rival under contract in order to keep him altogether off the stage.

In his day it became evident that when an actor renounced management he might just as well retire. True, Irving succeeded while on salary, but fate delivered the management into his hands. By the time he did don the purple it was evident that even a second-rater might thrust fame upon himself with that noose of light.

"Let the moon shine on me, Guv'nor," cried the dying Château-Renaud (Terriss) to Irving. "Nature at least is impartial." It was not when commanded by the Joshuas of the stage. The shadows flung by gaslight were soft and heavy. Until every corner should be exposed by battens of electricity the romantic drama would be ruled by "limes".

Never before or since have audiences been so dazzled by spectacle as at the Lyceum in the eighteen-nineties. Visions of light, processions in darkness, midnight of winter, morning in spring, evoked by great artists held in fee, all paid homage to the divine right of him who ordered all—the actor-manager. One by one the juvenile leads of the Lyceum, Château-Renaud, Faust, Lancelot, stepped from that field of the Cloth of Gold to see what glory they could win for themselves on strips of it laid down elsewhere. As actor-managers they all succeeded. It was time for the Dauphin (and Titania) to do likewise.

CHAPTER III

THE DEVIL'S DISCIPLE versus *THE ONLY WAY*

OPPOSITES explain each other. In order to see Martin Harvey clearly, set him by the side of the tall, red-bearded Irishman who also found the conquest of the theatre slow and baffling. While the actor made himself known as a romantic, Bernard Shaw proclaimed himself anti-romantic. He seemed to be the first, although several others had attempted it before. When Fechter shocked Paris by presenting himself as the lover of a consumptive prostitute in the younger Dumas's *La Dame Aux Camélias* realism conquered . . . until the novelty wore off and then, like her crinoline, it became first old-fashioned, then quaint, and then romantic. Other devastatingly truthful masterpieces also lost that penny-plain look as Infant Time got to work on them with his box of paints.

What trick is this that turns our most fearless endeavours to be frank into old wives' tales? Partly it is because fiction, as Solon said, is all lies anyhow. But a better reason must be found since history itself, even to its bare facts, becomes romanticized. The process needs examining. In a certain number of years modes become despised, solely because they are out-of-date and ridiculous—the word used to be "Victorian". That period past, glamour begins very potently indeed at the start. As memory passes into history it looks back in a farewell which stirs in us an uncomfortable sentimentality—the word to excite this became "Victorian" very soon.

In their apple-green-and-gold bindings the plays of George Bernard Shaw already are hallowed. Tender feelings steal over us as pages in turning recall old friendly faces, no matter how sternly the author suppresses the names by not printing casts. Antagonisms blaze no more.

"I am a classic. I have never pretended to be anything else," their author said long ago. "My characters are the familiar harlequin and columbine, clown and pantaloon." Time makes them glow and our hearts at the same time. What *was* the rumpus all about? They are better than other plays. Are they at heart so very different? Why did their author declare himself to be "against" love and lovely heroines?

At the Theatre Royal, South Shields, in 1895, in the midst of these upbraidings, there was acted *Candida*, whose leading lady needs good looks for her rôle of Columbine or Cinderella, filling men with the desire to humble themselves before her. Her clerical husband, the big strong man fooled by the little weak man, must be thankful for small mercies since no butt has been so expertly baited, while she walks in beauty to set her at an advantage over the ugly sister or rather secretary, who is to this play what Katisha is to *The Mikado*.

Now that *Candida* has to be costumed to match its oil-lit evening romance glows there, and the idea that some social moral could be proved by playing, as the author says, "the old game in the old way, on the old chessboard, with the old pieces", is romantic too.

Historic perspective is needed to understand why, when George Bernard Shaw and John Martin Harvey sat down in 1896 to tackle very much the same kind of plot, one should be "pro" and the other "anti". In order of popularity and in order of merit there are decided differences in the play that resulted, but when it comes to a hero of Paris in 1793 who takes another man's place on the scaffold for the sake of the woman he loves, and a hero of New Hampshire in 1777 who takes another man's place on the scaffold to show the Red Coats "we can stand by one another to the death" since that is the force that could make America a nation, there is surely not much to choose between them. Must one be "romantic" and the other not? Since when was a romantic forbidden to be, like William Tell, simply a patriot?

Over thirty years passed before Shaw told how *The Devil's Disciple* originated. The account appeared in the *Observer* as an interview—an example which proves how very valuable this form of journalism can be when authoritative—over the initials of Mr. George W. Bishop. With thoughts of a world tour, Terriss had prepared a scenario for a melodrama of false accusations and narrow escapes.

When asked to write this Shaw put forward his own ideas instead, and gave them form as *The Devil's Disciple*. A reading was arranged and started to take place. A long-drawn snore ended that meeting. The play had its copyright performance (then necessary if an author wished to keep any control over his own work) at the Bijou, Bayswater, on April 17, 1897. In the United States Mansfield played it so successfully that at a congratulatory dinner a senator told him that he ought to thank God for sending him such a play. Mansfield replied, according to the *Observer* interview:

"I do, senator, I do. I go down on my knees at my little bedside every night and thank my Maker for that play. And the last words of my prayer always are: 'But, O God, why did it have to be by Shaw?'"

Shaw's play had the happy ending. Harvey's, like most exceedingly popular plays, had not. The widespread delusion that unhappy endings are unpopular is too promising a chance for a homily to be let slip. It illustrates the fascination of the half-truth. In childhood we are taught that the sun sets in the west, and though no seaman sets his course by taking the setting sun as due west he will laugh if you question it. The surgeon, while his scalpel boils, observes that Lister invented anti-septic surgery, to a patient who may know that "anti-septic" is eighteenth-century and that Lister's word "aseptic" had a distinct meaning, no matter what the great New Oxford Dictionary itself may state.

"If I say a thing three times it must be so" supports not only the brand of truth trotted out for our amusement by Brains Trusts, but also hoodwinks many an expert. Old actors as well as young look you steadily in the eye and tell you that unhappy endings are unlucky. Managers of vast experience which includes highly profitable tours with *East Lynne* tell you the same, no matter how clearly the whole history of the stage proves that the Shakespearean tide in the affairs of actors is a flood of tears.

That must be said in defiance of G.B.S., a dramatic critic expert above all others in intimate knowledge of the stage, who at this time labelled himself anti-romantic and argued:

"The humanist will accept the abandonment of all his minor lies as a bribe for the toleration of the most impudent of all lies. 'I am willing to be redeemed, and even religious,' says the converted romanticist, 'if only the business be managed by a pretty woman who will be left in my arms when the curtain falls.'"

Shaw's argument succeeds until you question what he takes for granted. Is romance primarily concerned with love, redemption by a pretty woman, and happy endings?

Whatever Mr. Shaw had in mind it could not be the repertoire of Irving. Of all the leading romantic actors Fechter alone had the temperament of the lover: even so he rarely enjoyed the combined blessings of redemption and happy endings. Nor will the hat fit Sydney Carton. If the motive of his self-sacrifice differs from Dick Dudgeon's it is none the worse for that; anyhow it is Dick Dudgeon who is at the last moment reprieved, and already Shaw's typewriter had, like Homer's lyre, fallen to the lure of female beauty. Something else about *The Devil's Disciple* besides the costumes is romantic. One cannot be sure whether the hero is not a variant of the man accursed.

Plans for an American tour had inspired Shaw's play, an American manager had made its merits known, and now Terriss was anxious to reconsider it with his eyes open. That was before the night of December 16, 1897. A black figure, rather like an anarchist in burlesque, had been ridiculed by the stage-hands outside the stage-door of the Adelphi. The long cloak passed out of sight as it turned at the end of the alley into Maiden Lane and there by the private door of the theatre it lay in wait.

Terriss arrived, put his key in the lock, stumbled inside and fell dying from the stab of a madman's knife. Other Jolly Jack Tars of real life had exercised their exhilarating energy on the stage before, but there was not one now to fill his place. The romantic drama would take another turn.

For this also we are indebted to America, whose very air seems to give health to the theatre. While in St. Louis, Missouri, with Irving's company, Mrs. Harvey "saw" her husband as Sydney Carton and forthwith entered a bookshop with him to buy "A Tale of Two Cities". In a New York bookshop, very similarly, *The Colleen Bawn* came into being at the picking up of "The Collegians", and while touring the States Wilson Barrett conceived *The Sign Of The Cross*, although not at all pleased when its admirers thought from its resemblance to "Quo Vadis?" that this idea also came from a bookshop. So lucky a trio seems to warrant an addition to the stock of stage superstitions.

Something that is not superstition must be added. Just as the child of the theatre frequently grows into an assured player so the MS. that is nursed in the dressing-room grows into an assured play. Martin Harvey made his play, then looked round to find an author for it. Wills had a brother, the Rev. Freeman Wills, an Army chaplain. In collaboration with another obscure playwright, A. Fitzmaurice King, he once wrote a one-act play, *Rouget De L'Isle*, for a triple-bill toured unprofitably by the Lyceum Vacation Company.

Martin Harvey had it rewritten so as to show the composer of the "Marseillaise" on his death-bed in a garret at the moment that his song becomes immortal, a death-scene sufficiently affecting to oust *Ruy Blas* from the repertoire. This came to mind when the scenario of *Sydney Carton* needed dialogue.

Lieut.-Colonel the Rev. Freeman Wills agreed to provide it with the assistance of a brother parson, who wished to keep the undertaking from the ears of a bishop with strong feelings of disapproval for the theatre. These are queer events to be linked with the chance which had taken W. G. Wills one night nearly twenty years ago to supper with Bateman on the Lyceum's stage, and coincidence is mixed up in it too, for Edward Compton, husband of Bateman's youngest daughter, Virginia, had chosen this very time for putting "A Tale of Two Cities" into a play with the title of *Sydney Carton*.

Dramas of the kind were not customary with the Compton Comedy Company, whose pride lay in Sheridan and Goldsmith, acted in the provinces and in several theatres from the Royal Strand and Opera Comique to Toole's at Charing Cross. No doubt its manager felt the swing of public taste back to romance, which was causing two actors to clash in their desire to swashbuckle in Dumas.

This sudden vogue deserves a paragraph in passing, for it was intense. While Tree prepared *The Three Musketeers* a rival version set out on tour under the management of Lewis Waller, yet another star Miss Wallis had made. He represented the kind of romance which has no use for subtlety. Directly the proscenium loomed in his sight he went for it like a bull at an open gate with a red-flannel petticoat on the other side. Whatever he meant was for the audience; he never played to the gallery—he fixed it, stalls, boxes, dress circle, pit, upper gallery and amphitheatre as well, with his fiery eye.

If the English Army had to be exhorted to do battle he ignored his eighteenpenny supers as men he paid, and attended strictly to the people who paid him. Were the loveliest of actresses waiting at his side to be wooed he would ignore her, and instead of pouring out his honeyed words to one devoted heart addressed them to a palpitating thousand. Critically it was Penny Gaff. Emotionally it was magnificent, not to be coldly withstood, not to be heard without a strong desire to throw hats in the air and cheer.

Responding to that ardour, Clement Scott (no longer "hot favourite" among critics, gazing currycombed out of his box while they champed in their stalls) felt the renewal of Victorian youth. For years he had been addicted to "manly", "fearless" and "generous", not because they had any meaning for him but because he liked the look of them in print. There is a character in Shaw's *The Philanderer* who passes his life amid "scenes of suffering nobly endured and sacrifice willingly rendered by womanly women and manly men". He is a dramatic critic, "the leading representative of manly sentiment in London".

That was Scott. He was conscious of the laughter by the time Waller arrived, but "noble deeds and manly endeavour" simply had to be said. Then, going through his usual vocabulary of a dozen adjectives for the commendation of actors, he added, as he had added to his praise of Irving, "a Shakespearean scholar, a student of dramatic literature".

So great was Waller's popularity that when his Musketeers occupied the Globe, Tree tried to spike their guns by engaging this rival D'Artagnan to be the Duke of Buckingham at Her Majesty's; even so the Globe's version had the longer run. Then the Comedy billed a drama in six compressed tabloids, *The Tree-Dumas-Skiteers*.

And yet with all the stir these made none could challenge the Lyceum's supremacy in public esteem, although a different temperature was now recorded at its box-office. *Madame Sans-Gêne*, written by Sardou for Réjane whose grace reproaches this mere mention, had been adapted by Carr; and Irving had in 1897 played Napoleon "in support" of Ellen Terry. No records were broken.

The time had come to put forth his powers in a masterpiece, such as *Richard II* which he planned. In his own feelings the time was also ripe for encouraging his younger son, who had set aside his career in the diplomatic service. There was a strain of genius in Laurence Irving, but it did not show in *Peter The Great* that January of 1898. The box-office now had to be put first. For the sake of funds *The Medicine Man* came into the bill that May. It proved to be Irving's worst failure, and old pieces had to be revived.

For these Martin Harvey came back because both Irving and Ellen

Terry had need of him. The former never found another Joliquet to equal him in *The Lyons Mail*; the latter often asked him to play Alexander Old-worthy in *Nance Oldfield*.

While *The Medicine Man*, an unconscionable time a-dying, took its last gasp as a Saturday matinée, Mathias and Louis XI jostled with Napoleon for the nightly bills. One evening after the curtain-raiser, as Martin Harvey left the stage free for Ellen Terry to bow before the storm of applause, he saw a newcomer from America, Ethel Barrymore, arriving for *The Bells*.

When he was no longer there to play Joliquet in *The Lyons Mail*, says Gordon Craig, "I do not doubt that Irving was more deeply grieved than if he had lost a couple of thousand pounds; but the most that he said probably resolved itself into: 'Pity the young man wasn't there to-night.'"

In 1899 the young man was resolved on management, for the play Miss de Silva inspired had now come to perfection under her title of *The Only Way*. By chance the theatre had to be the Lyceum. After the contract had been signed the discovery was made that his play might prove harmful to Irving's next play, since both were "Revolutionary". Though Carr called it a "cold-blooded proposition" Harvey stood firm, and with his master's blessing announced the cast. It had a fair sprinkling of players from Irving's company, including Ben Webster, grandson of glorious Ben:

LYCEUM THEATRE
Sole Lessee: HENRY IRVING

Mr. MARTIN HARVEY
Will produce, for the FIRST TIME
On THURSDAY, Feb. 16

THE ONLY WAY,
A TALE OF TWO CITIES

Adapted by Freeman Wills from Charles Dickens's Novel.

Prologue, 1774

Jean Defarge	Mr. HOLBROOK BLINN
Dr. Manette	Mr. FRED EVERILL
Marquis de St. Evremonde .	Mr. ACTON BOND
Vicomte de St. Evremonde .	Mr. NYE CHART
A Peasant	Mr. T. ARTHUR JONES

Play, 1793

Sydney Carton	MR. MARTIN HARVEY
Ernest Defarge	MR. HOLBROOK BLINN
Mr. Lorry	MR. J. G. TAYLOR
Mr. Stryver	MR. SAM JOHNSON
Dr. Manette	MR. FRED EVERILL
Charles Darnay	MR. HERBERT SLEATH
President	MR. F. TYARS
Public Prosecutor	MR. FRANK VERNON
Comte de Fauchet	MR. BEN WEBSTER
M. de Maury	MR. HAVARD ARNOLD
Marquis de Boulainvilliers	MR. E. EARDLEY HOWARD
Gabelle	MR. HENSON
Barsad	MR. HERBERT INNES
1st Citizen	MR. F. POWELL
2nd Citizen	MR. HAWLEY FRANCKS
Lucie Manette	MISS GRACE WARNER
The Vengeance	MISS MARRIOTT
A Citizeness	MISS LIZZIE WEBSTER
Mimi	MISS DE SILVA

Aristocrats, Citizens, Citizenesses, Gaolers, Sans-Culottes, Tricoteuses, Associates, &c.

Synopsis of Scenery:

Prologue—A Loft in an Old House in the vicinity of the Château St. Evremonde (Joseph Harker).

Act I. London. Carton's Chambers (W. Hann).

Act II. London. Dr. Manette's Garden in Soho, 1793 (Hawes Craven).

Act III. Paris. Revolutionary Tribunal (Hawes Craven).

Act IV. Paris. Scene 1—Dr. Manette's Apartments (W. Hann). Scene 2—Cell in the Conciergerie (W. Hann). Scene 3—A Hall in the Conciergerie (Hawes Craven).

Special Music for the production has been composed by MR. HAMILTON CLARKE.

Acting Manager: Mr. Patrick E. Doherty.

Box Office (Mr. J. Hurst) now open daily, ten to five.

Whatever pleasure the new actor-manager felt on reading this seemed small beside the self-congratulatory feelings of his author. Everyone actively engaged in the production had reached a state of mental fever not unlike 'flu, but the Rev. Freeman Wills had never been actively engaged.

On the strength of the theatrical standing of his brother he had turned playwright with unaccustomed ease. By handing Martin Harvey's scenario to "Fitzmaurice King" and handing the latter's dialogue to the former he had achieved the happy state where he had nothing to do but bask. Among playwrights he is unique, for even the idlest usually like a little exercise, even if only with the blue pencil.

No play ever had such an eventful history before it was written. It appeared to exist in public demand for a century. Inklings of it occurred in those performances which dramatized current reports of the fall of the Bastille in the newspapers. Then Lytton and Dumas took up the tale until Watts Phillips' play and Dickens' novel seized it together. Early attempts to put "A Tale of Two Cities" on the stage missed what mattered most. The essential plot, with the addition of the devoted young woman, got told without the Dickens flavour. The seamstress became a leading figure in *Ninon* without the hero, and after that not another mistake remained to be made until Sardou made it. When the time at last was ripe Sydney Carton appeared in duplicate—though Compton gave up his version and eventually revived *All For Her*.

That performance at the Lyceum for the two young players principally concerned passed like a dream. After so much hard work without overwhelming acknowledgment they seemed, in the full glare of the limelight, a little dazed. When the curtain fell on the first act they thought they had at last a chance to recover—only to be shaken at once by a kind of tremor running through the company. One, acting as spokesman, declared they seemed to be tilting direct at one of the theatre's most cherished superstitions.

Was it true that they had not prepared the customary tag-line never spoken at rehearsals and uttered for the first time on the first night? It could not, of course, be the last line of the performance, for the words to be spoken on the scaffold had already been decided upon, so to speak, by Dickens.

But the play proper ended in the prison scene where the dialogue, as things stood, stopped abruptly. Their title (a last-minute inspiration) should, so romantic convention demanded, be pointedly referred to here so that nobody could misunderstand its bearing on the plot. Miss de Silva sat down before the triptych mirror on her dressing-table and then and there, on the back of an old envelope, wrote the tag-lines of the play—"doggerel", she said, to be changed for something better at the first opportunity.

She thought them bad enough to run the risk of disastrous laughter, but when Sydney Carton told Mimi, with that quiet, vibrant earnestness of voice, that this was the only way, the august audience of St. Lyceum was hushed.

The tag-lines never were "but always to be" changed. They were allowed to stand for one year, then for four or five years, then for twenty, thirty years and now, in the printed book of the play, they remain for ever.

Miss Geneviève Ward
(From "The Penny Illustrated Paper", April 18, 1874)

Everybody who reads "A Tale of Two Cities" may recognize which is the most moving episode in the story, and everybody who ever sat inside a theatre will acclaim it as the most theatrically effective. The fact remains that for nearly forty years that episode was omitted when the novel was represented on the stage.

Dickens had put the best words into the mouth of the most fleeting character, one who did not appear under *dramatis personæ* in any revolutionary play—and though Mary Rivers had tried to be her equivalent there was in her words merely the sense of the impending curtain instead of impending death. Dickens gave the seamstress neither a local habitation nor a name. The Harveys bestowed both upon her and a vehicle for themselves to carry them through life.

Their inspiration for *The Only Way* seems to come from one page, even though that page had to change before she could be a stage character capable of standing on her own feet:

"Citizen Evremonde," she said, touching him with her cold hand. "I am a poor little seamstress, who was with you in La Force."

He murmured for answer: "True. I forget what you were accused of?"

"Plots. Though the just Heaven knows I am innocent of any. Is it likely? Who would think of plotting with a poor little weak creature like me?"

The forlorn smile with which she said it, so touched him, that tears started from his eyes.

"I am not afraid to die, Citizen Evremonde, but I have done nothing. I am not unwilling to die, if the Republic which is to do so much good for us poor, will profit by my death; but I do not know how that can be, Citizen Evremonde. Such a poor weak little creature!"

As the last thing on earth that his heart was to warm and soften to, it warmed and softened to this pitiable girl.

"I heard you were released, Citizen Evremonde. I hoped it was true?"

"It was. But I was again taken and condemned."

"If I may ride with you, Citizen Evremonde, will you let me hold your hand? I am not afraid, but I am little and weak, and it will give me more courage." As the patient eyes were lifted to his face, he saw a sudden doubt in them, and then astonishment. He pressed the work-worn, hunger-worn young fingers, and touched his lips.

"Are you dying for him?" she whispered.

"And his wife and child. Hush! Yes."

"Oh, you will let me hold your brave hand, stranger?"

"Hush! Yes, my poor sister; to the last."

Emotion so naked and unashamed struck terror into intellectuals. It was not New. Neither was the actor. He had been known so long that the Town felt towards him too great a familiarity.

How could the venture hope to succeed? Nineteenth-century play-goers always made their feelings plain to any actor known to them man and boy these twenty years.

The whole romantic tradition was based on that. Its actors had to burst upon the Town with the force of novelty. Master Carey, the Pupil of Nature, made himself too well-known in London and had to exile himself in the provinces before he could be acclaimed as a genius under the name of Edmund Kean. His rightful successor, Wallack, stayed in London and found the prejudice so stiff that he preferred the more grateful task of establishing Wallack's in New York as an honoured theatre.

To be French, Italian or Polish, speaking your native tongue to an audience largely ignorant of it, entitled you to canopy and red carpet while John Ryder and his kind trudged through mire to the Bower Saloon. Provincial playgoers, contrarily, liked the mummer to whom they could say, "Ah've known thee, lad, since thou wert so high." The London prodigal too much governed by familiarity to be fêted in his birthplace was not well enough known to be even greeted anywhere else in England.

Neither was the popularity of Dickens at its height at the end of his century. That added to the handicap. People of taste, a united body then, possessed an enormous power of veto in fashionable theatres. Unaware of the transitory nature of "taste", inclined to anger if it were called by its proper name of fashion, undeterred by the swift change of the admired into the detested and back again at the dictates of the calendar, the quidnuncs of culture proclaimed their likes and dislikes solemnly.

Dickens died a Mid-Victorian, and since it was possible to despise his novels in the eighteen-nineties how very reasonable it was to avoid seeing them on the stage.

Aspects of his genius that could not be denied were such as could never be dramatized. He could wring your heart over the sorrows of people like the little seamstress without bothering to explain how or why they belonged to the story. All his plots had been lifted bodily out of his newly-published pages by the blood-and-thunder theatres of the Surreyside and the Bowery, without anything solid or coherent coming of such efforts.

The idea of separating one character, selecting only such incidents as might enhance the colours of the portrait, and shaping these into a coherent self-sufficient plot, came later. The simple idea of taking a character away from the story came first. Lotta, the richest actress in the world, the joy of New York and gold-rush townships alike, bewitched London as the Marchioness.

Bleak House, after many trials and failures, became popular when one part was seen to be greater than the whole: Jennie Lee, after making a hit as a crossing-sweeper in a musical piece, had a new version written especially for her under the title of *Jo*. In the eighteen-seventies she took the Globe in Newcastle Street; during the next twenty years the great globe itself identified that one particular play with that one particular person in Dickens' pages. She came to Drury Lane with it in 1896; only then was the flood of tears ebbing.

Whether the portrait of Sydney Carton at the Lyceum in 1899 had the

THE LAST ROMANTIC

quality—*patine du temps*, perhaps—of later years may reasonably be doubted. Yet even those who shook their heads, in the old playgoer's customary manner, over the play's chances admired it.

To the critical his finest moments were not at the climax but in the scene —taken from a passage in the book he especially admired—where Carton's intentions became plain. Martin Harvey once described his own feelings in the part; though out of modesty, he cited them as the experience of a friend who was "impersonating one of life's failures".

When brought face to face with his successful rival in an affair of love, "The failure" looked long and hard at his rival and said nothing. The pause was involuntary, and the silence puzzling to his creator; he was at a loss to imagine what his creature was thinking about, and it was not until this strange pause had occurred, in many succeeding representations, that it suddenly dawned upon the actor that his creature was realizing "in that long and searching gaze all his own shortcomings in the vivid light which was at that moment thrown upon them by the proximity of his successful rival".

This has its parallel in the annals of acting—a greatly admired effect by Garrick in *Virginia*, a tragedy by the Rev. Crisp. Claudius, the iniquitous tool of the Decemvir, claims Virginia, as a slave born in his house. He pleads his cause before Appius on his tribunal:

"During that time, Garrick representing Virginius, stood on the opposite side of the scene, next to the stage-door, with his arms folded across his breast, his eyes riveted on the ground, like a mute and lifeless statue. Being told at length that the tyrant is willing to hear him, he continued for some time in the same attitude, his countenance expressing a variety of passions, and the spectators fixed in ardent gaze.

"By slow degrees he raised his head; he paused; he turned round in the slowest manner, till his eyes fixed on Claudius; he still remained silent, and after looking eagerly at the impostor, he uttered in a low tone of voice, that spoke the fullness of a broken heart, 'Thou Traitor!'

"The whole audience was electrified; they felt the impression, and a thunder of applause testified their delight."

One all-important difference marked *The Only Way* out of all the many dramatizations of Dickens. It did not merely show you characters from a novel, it brought them closer. With Sydney Carton as he was now acted you became better acquainted; you knew more about him without feeling that he had changed. Such thoughts the performance excited. Surmise at odd moments long afterwards left you wondering whether some traits in him harked back to Irving—the air of vagabondage to Robert Macaire, the sacrificial resolve to Landry, the sardonic humour to Louis XI, the serenity of his farewell to Charles I.

But let there be no mistake about this: what Victorian critics would have called "heterogeneous feelings" could not be separated. Carton, revivified by Martin Harvey out of the novelist's portrait, became a living person a whole nation knew and loved. Great acting is not restricted to great plays. The text of *The Only Way* gives but the barest outline of him. In performance he was vital, compelling. The play was the brass bottle. Out of it we watched that djinn arising—until he floated out of sight away.

Clement Scott shed some of the last drops of his ink in saying the time for young Martin would soon come:

"He has enthusiasm and a persuasive poetic touch, he has the rare gift of modesty, and, like so many more, he is personally popular with his brother players and with the public. Martin Harvey, well trained at the Lyceum, has made a sudden rush to the front, and he will keep his place now that he has won it."

Interest in the French Revolution had not been exhausted. Irving's rival piece, though prosperity never again came his way, was unaffected—Sardou's *Robespierre*, staged at the Lyceum that April with a cast of over fifty and quite considerable crowds, ran for three or four months, then went on tour, first the provinces and then America. The chief scene was where Robespierre discovered he had sent his son to the guillotine. That there was some resemblance to *The Only Way* can be seen in the scene-plot:

Act I.   A Nook in the Forest of Montmorency.
Act II.   1. Courtyard of the Prison of Port-Libre, Paris.
            2. The Place de la Revolution, Paris.
Act III. Sitting-room in Dupluy's house, Paris.
Act IV.   1. Room in the Rue de Matroy, Paris.
            2. Hall in the Conciergerie Prison, Paris.
Act V.   1. Room of the Committee of Public Safety, Paris.
            2. Hall of the National Convention, Paris.

As for *The Devil's Disciple*, though thirty years would pass before Martin Harvey would be responsible for its first full-dress production in London, it was acted before this last year of the century was out. Why it occasioned any misunderstanding can best be understood by reference to the prevailing mania to shock or be shocked. Of course the author had taken a dramatic situation, now almost venerated, and removed what had hitherto been the reason for its persistence.

That alone might not have caused astonishment; for this the author himself was responsible much in the way a music-hall Highlander first raises laughter at "being Scotch" and then rebukes it to get a round of applause. The justly celebrated preface to "Three Plays for Puritans" shows exactly how the New goaded the Old in this very way. That much is frankly admitted:

> "The critics were the victims of the long course of hypnotic suggestion by which G.B.S. the journalist manufactured an unconventional reputation for Bernard Shaw the author."

To laugh and leave it at that would be wiser, but a history of the last romantic must take the first anti-romantic seriously—to point out, for example, that although the devil's disciple himself is not in love, the heroine is; in addition, the niece who more or less deputizes for the little seamstress suffers from a complaint uncommonly like it. Since Shaw objected to the hero who "will do nothing except for the sake of the heroine", it would seem that "what's sauce for the goose" must not apply. But not all his contemporaries were taken in; the play had too shrewd an audience for that. It was staged in 1899 at the Princess of Wales's, Kennington, a theatre which might be termed—because its pit and gallery were filled by the Old Kent Road—Theatre Royal Cockaigne. The novelty of an unmoonstruck hero impressed those playgoers. "Got it," said one the moment he emerged, " 'E don't love 'er—she loves 'im." To this his young woman replied, "I see—*The Other Way*."

As dramatic literature *The Devil's Disciple* endures while *The Only Way* fades. In cold print there is no comparing them, but in performance hack work often demonstrates how fine acting can mean much more than fine words; and if the force of this cannot be felt any longer it is because the tradition which made it manifest is dead. What Martin Harvey had gained by making the Lyceum his house of bondage could be understood by anyone who listened attentively to his voice. Years of small parts meant years of listening, of understanding, just what can be done by inflexion.

"You may know the words," roared an old actor to a cub who boasted of having a photographic memory, and the roar was on a beautiful rising note, "but s'welp-me-bob you will never know the tune." Whether *The Tempest* is a good play or a bad play depends entirely on that, because if Prospero has no sense of "the tune" all he needs is a carafe and tumbler to turn him into a lecturer.

Whether the curtain is to fall on ridicule, torpor or fervour often depends on that rising note, calling no attention to itself when well done, calling down the derision of the gods when ill done and causing the play to be damned for the author's sins when not done at all. If you have heard one Prospero let his soul take flight in his parting with Ariel, and then heard another Prospero giving orders to his batman in those self-same lines, then you may comprehend what Martin Harvey's ascent from the depths to the heights of vocal cords signified when he said, "It is a far, far better thing . . ." *De profundis. In excelsis gloria.*

CHAS A. BUCHEL
1905

"The Breed of the Treshams"
From the poster by CHARLES BUCHELL

[Photo: S. Langfier

Martin Harvey in
The Lowland Wolf

Miss de Silva in
The Last Heir

BOOK IV

CHAPTER I

DON JUAN PURE IN HEART

"DONNING the purple" old players said, when they meant "going into management". You had to think of Ancient Rome before any advancement like it could be imagined. The time would come when the change from actor to actor-manager would mean no more, or even less, than the grand climacteric in other professions. But while the romantic tradition of the stage lasted, the soul in the body, which thus passed from hireling to emperor, felt the sprouting of butterfly wings.

To command sun and moon, to ride the whirlwind and direct the storm, had been Irving's prerogatives at St. Lyceum, and when Forbes Robertson took the theatre these were merely let out, so to speak, on hire. They were again let out when "Jack" became his old chief's tenant. But when *The Only Way* had, in order to make room for *Robespierre*, to be transferred elsewhere, then the newly-fledged purple emperor was in full flight.

Old custom sees some insult in the likening of man to butterfly. But why? Ornamental creatures are not lower in the scale of intelligence than the busy or predatory. The grasshopper makes less pother than the ant and with equal success survives.

Where to move to was a problem, so much depended on finding a theatre with suitable antecedents in those days when playgoers preferred the theatre which kept true to its own particular tradition. The Prince of Wales's in Coventry Street, which was available, had the disadvantage of being fickle. As "the souls" took charge there when Maëterlinck was new, these same playgoers, with or without souls, might be drawn back again.

In its brief history the house had prospered as the birthplace of musical comedy under George Edwardes. Yet despite *In Town* (the very first in 1892) and *A Gaiety Girl* it would not settle down under his direction, and he now sold the lease. It was a wise move, for there was thunder in the air. People were too distracted to pay much attention, even to a play which it was the fashion to see. *The Only Way*, continuing its run there in April without a break, drew many notabilities, including Lord Roberts, without exciting the general public.

There was a weekly loss which bewildered the young management. To the end of his life Martin Harvey never understood why, for an idealist cannot trail his robes through the mire around him. Certainly it is plain from his autobiography that he knew nothing of the widespread depression that deepened month by month throughout 1899.

Theatrical "lives" that burden bookshelves testify to the inability of players to see themselves as part of a whole. Actor-managers, more particularly, must give themselves, mind, body and soul, to what they create. Stage autobiographies naturally become a list of "parts I have played", with some account of holidays in between, and stage biographies follow the pattern. Any such "life" becomes so much like all other such lives that to the lay reader all seem alike. Each, to appear distinct, must be seen against the background of the passing hour.

The early struggles of Martin Harvey's management were severe because they occurred during the upheavals in many private lives caused by the outbreak of the South African War. *The Only Way* stayed in Town through spring and summer until an innings of 167 performances had been knocked up—at an ever-increasing loss.

In the autumn the Martin Harvey Company, up to Lyceum strength with scenic splendour intact, set out in special trains on tour. All the leading cities in the land gave them columns of praise—next to the précis of some Transvaal Blue Book and President Kruger's views on residential qualification for franchise. His demand for the removal of our troops from the frontier was reported. On October 11 the ultimatum expired. There was a state of war.

Civilians like the background of current fighting set to music. In the next few weeks *San Toy*, *Florodora* and *The Rose of Persia* had a fervent welcome. Some popularity remained for comedy and farce, as well as patriotic melodrama, but romance suffered the neglect that was inevitable when heroism suddenly became real. War fever burned intensely through the autumn of 1899 before news of battles had ceased to be exciting, and it was at this very period that Sydney Carton had to present himself to the British people as someone unlike themselves.

Bacon, in "The Advancement of Learning", makes the point clear. The use of romance, or "Fained Historie" as he calls it, "hath beene to give some shadowe of satisfaction to the minde of Man in those points wherein the Nature of things doth denie it". The nature of things, no longer denying it, challenged young men either to be like Carton or to stop humbugging themselves.

Entertainment more to current liking was provided by the music-halls, where songs left over from the recent Spanish-American War immediately took out naturalization papers without changing a word, since "the boys in blue were fighting their noble flag to shield" applied equally to the United States Army in Cuba and the Naval Brigade in Natal. These choruses would ensure a prosperous season for Christmas pantomime, especially when sung by girls in the uniform of the New South Wales Lancers, who had recently passed through England on their roundabout course from one side of the Southern Hemisphere to the other.

But all this excitement hardly encouraged interest in costume drama. Soon there was a change for the worse. During the "black week" of December, three idolized generals suffered defeat, each with the loss of a thousand men. Lapel buttons with these generals' photographs on them might still be worn on schoolboys' Norfolk jackets, but flag-wagging died down as the campaign became recognized as the most dispiriting of all wars. The unprecedented number of two hundred thousand trained men would be under arms to oppose a levy of farmers. Glory favoured the other side.

Idealists must shun actualities. Events of the passing hour had to be ignored by Martin Harvey in order to achieve his aim. As surely and instinctively as the first romantics had insisted on evil so the last romantic insisted on good. In a century the full, unbroken curve of their tradition had risen from crime exultant to virtue triumphant. But while Edmund Kean had found characters for his purpose to hand, Martin Harvey had to search for his.

The first choice had been so eminently right that he expected the next would as aptly express his ardent quest of salvation for the man accursed. Whether the public approved or disapproved is of minor consequence. What his inner self strove for justifies this record of his works. Before it can be studied, more notice must be taken of the actress whom he always acknowledged to be his guiding star.

Angelita Helena Margarita de Silva Ferro had had a lonely childhood in the Spanish Embassy, where her father was First Attaché. The chief event of each day was a drive in the Row, regularly at the same hour in the afternoon. Otherwise she spent her time in being lonely. Sometimes she would be brought from the nursery to stand on the table to amuse her parents' guests at dinner-parties over the dessert. This she resented because she thought she was being "made an exhibition of".

There were no other children and she was without friends. One of the secretaries gave her a half-crown to buy chocolates with; she threw it at his head and later sat on his hat. She was thought to be a backward child until she went to stay with an aunt who taught her in a fortnight to read "Alice in Wonderland", after which she read Hume's "History of England" and every other book she could lay hands on. Grown-ups took trouble to understand her and she found some friends among the Embassy's distinguished visitors.

While on holiday at Sandown she made another. Because the bathing-machine horses seemed to her half-starved she threw stones at the little windows of all those "sentry-boxes on wheels". When nearly every pane was broken she was caught stones-in-hand and might have been handed over to the police had not a stranger paid for the damage and carried her home on his shoulder. She went regularly to his house for tea and sat on the hearthrug while he from his armchair handed her the countless triumphs of his labours as an indefatigable amateur photographer. She found Lewis Carroll the most charming of all adults and his ideas for entertaining a guest the most boring.

She had the gift of friendship. In her years of study, when she was allowed to break the rule of the British Museum by being given a reader's ticket while still a minor, she belonged to a group who shared her interest in the literatures of Latin countries. As a member of the Lyceum company she added to her circle; through Benson she met still more kindred souls; as Mrs. Martin Harvey she became an ardent hostess; as leading lady of their company she entertained celebrities who visited their dressing-rooms, and was an honoured guest at many a dinner-party.

Their constantly growing acquaintance included few friends more welcome than Cunninghame Graham and his wife. Miss de Silva had known them so long that she could not remember when the friendship began. By the time *The Only Way* drew these two visitors regularly, a partnership in ideas was taking shape between player and playgoer.

In many ways Cunninghame Graham was singular. No one else so combined the virtues of Scottish chieftain and Spanish grandee; no other man of any race expressed a passion for democracy in so aristocratic a manner. Love of his own country kept him faithful to a castle in Scotland as his home. In London he was a Member of Parliament, a rider whom crowds would watch in the Row as a model of horsemanship, a writer whose finely tempered style won every author's praise—and an "agitator", a word always uttered with the fervour of an oath, who had been arrested as though responsible for the horrors in Trafalgar Square on "Bloody Sunday", November, 1887, when Household Cavalry in shining armour advanced against unarmed men in rags. In South America he was an explorer, living in the saddle like a gaucho.

In Madrid he devoted his evenings to the theatre at a time when "Spanish drama" meant Calderon and Lope de Vega to English critics, whose general opinion was that with these two the theatre of the Peninsular ended centuries ago. That impression still exists. While every student knows the history of the romantic revival in France, mention is rarely made of its equivalent in Spain. One of the works of this movement held Martin Harvey spellbound as the nineteenth century came to a close.

The mere state of the calendar now caused a change in romance. According to Gilbert's *Foggerty's Fairy*, "Every age is matter-of-fact to those who live in it. Romance died the day before yesterday. To-day will be romantic the day after to-morrow," upon which Foggerty suggests that the fairy might look in again the day after to-morrow. Some such idea inspired the public at midnight on December 31, 1899. Of all the fictions that humanity hugs to its breast as the daily bread of truth the Calendar is the silliest though not the least fateful. Even if the sun lent itself to exact arrangement of days to the year there would still remain the plain fact that the Christian era lost count of itself from the start.

Our system of reckoning was but a make-believe invented for the sake of practical necessity, which meant that the great and awe-inspiring approach of the twentieth century was mere book-keeping. Not that this made any difference. Tankards and glasses emptied themselves down the gullets of the wise and the ignorant alike as "Auld Lang Syne" rang out the Old late-lamented figure in its mass-produced cotton sheet labelled Nineteenth.

A few protesting mathematicians who took their statistics seriously were rather more absurd than the rest. They argued that these celebrations were by twelve months premature, because A.D. ought to date not from January 1 Year 0 but from January 1 Year 1—a protest that had been raised on December 31, 1799, and also on December 31, 1699.

Since still more erudite calculations maintain that the beginning of the whole system is five years out anyway, "Auld Lang Syne" might have been sung at thousands of midnights if it were of any importance to anybody that the dawn of the age of progress should not go unheralded.

After several years of intensive propaganda on behalf of the New, the shine might have been taken out of the rising disc with Twentieth burning upon it. Nobody thought so. Without any tangible cause for rejoicing the ordinary person thought it indeed a glorious thing to assist at the birth of this new epoch. The Queen, having already announced her intention of making a Christmas gift of chocolate to the troops in South Africa, now published a message to them. Lord Roberts and Lord Kitchener were on their way to the Cape. C.I.V.s were being enrolled, though professional soldiers had publicly protested against this impertinence on the part of amateurs.

What it was all about could be left to foreigners to unravel. The ordinary citizen continued to cheer the names of British generals recently defeated at Colenso and Magersfontein with as much enthusiasm as he prophesied better times in store. The plain man did not go in for thinking. He wanted to see Irving in *The Bells* much in the same way that he wanted to see the Chamber of Horrors in Madame Tussaud's.

With all this talk about the future there went a singularly stagnant spirit, unsuited to the launching of fresh enterprise. Over a dozen different ways of being *fin de siècle* had been discovered. Nothing like the same zest went into resolutions for the much-boosted new age.

"War depression" was felt. Jubilee years of prosperity with everybody selling out at a profit had to end in purchase prices too high for anything but a slump. When the prophesy that "this South African business" would be all over by Christmas proved false, fewer people in England had money to burn. On tour *The Only Way* played to enthusiastic critics and absent play-goers, much to the bewilderment of the young actor-manager who never fully grasped what might be happening to the world beyond him.

While still amazed at his plight of piling up debts over a play that pleased everybody, he planned as his next venture a drama of unequivocal romance. It was a way of escape from Joseph Chamberlain's Imperialist dream of turning, as Saki put it, swords into mine shares. But it was unlike any other way of escape found by romantics of that time. Here begins a trend in Martin Harvey's career so distinctive that it must be examined closely in order to be understood whenever it reappears. Spain had already touched his imagination; throughout his life on the stage it would continue to do so. The influence of his wife set him wondering about this undiscovered country.

Out of the many playwrights unknown in London, his fancy lighted on Jose de Zorilla y Moral, who lived from 1817 to 1893; he wrote *Poniard Of The Goth* in 1841 and *Don Juan Tenorio* in 1844. These formed part of the romantic movement which began in Spain with fights in the theatre over *Alvaro*, a play of 1835 written by Angel de Saavedra, whose hero, eloping with his bride, causes the death of her father—an idea that dominates Spanish imagination. It fascinated Mexico where *Don Juan Tenorio* founded the national drama even before Zorilla's arrival. In "The March of Literature" Ford Madox Ford says of him:

"For the greater part of his life he was a politician, and it was only when a pension relieved him of the necessity of thus earning his livelihood that he really took to literature. But his naïve plays, instinct with the sentiments of honour, patriotism and devotion, have sufficed hitherto to secure him a place not merely in the hearts of his fellow citizens but behind the footlights. Certain pure hearts from time to time earn that guerdon not so much of immortality as of alms from oblivion."

Herman Merivale, asked for an English version of *Don Juan Tenorio*, wrote it without a collaborator, though he was one of those playwrights who must ride tandem to make the wheels go round. His MS. came back to him with regrets, he was awarded damages in court, he lampooned the actor, there were more legal proceedings, and in the end he paid damages. *Don Juan's Last Wager* was written by Mrs. Cunninghame Graham instead. It was handsomely mounted at the Prince of Wales's on February 27, 1900.

Ladysmith and Kimberley were being relieved. Newsboys waving pink *Globes*, green *Westminsters*, white *Pall Malls*, *Standards*, *News* and *Stars* from Leicester Square to Piccadilly, shouted themselves hoarse with the excitement of good tidings. There were victories but also rumours that differences between Kitchener and Bobs had proved disastrous to Tommy Atkins. Too many cables home about "overwhelming" defeats of the enemy had caused cynicism, despite all the flag-wagging, and in this somewhat sullen mood the stalls filled on the first night at the Prince of Wales's.

What they had come to see was a spectacle so truly in keeping with Martin Harvey's conception of a world where cynicism could not possibly exist that he might have been the author of it. In boots, hose, trunks and doublet as white as his ruff, Don Juan now demonstrated that process of saving the most damned souls which would be the spirit of the romantic revival's end. "Moved by the utter purity of a young novice, so touched to higher issues by the sheer beauty of a girl's goodness as to revolt from the idea of her betrayal," are his own words to describe the reformed character.

Ever since Byron made of himself a recording angel to set down Don Juan's amorous exploits more in sorrow than in anger, more to be pitied than blamed, a steady improvement in the libertine's morals had been manifest. He had been saved by an angel in Paris. Zorilla had gone farther and let him save himself, with a last scene of repentance in purgatory under the influence of the statue of Soledad de Ulloa—a name chosen by Cunninghame Graham either from excess or dearth of humour.

Don Juan and Soledad headed a cast of thirty, with maskers, gypsies and alguacils as well. There were seven scenes, from an inn to "the undiscovered country". That finale depended for its effect on music and mechanism. Something went wrong and there was no effect. First night nerves being what they are, there rarely is when any kind of apparatus can, as actresses say, "throw a temperament".

Trains telescope. The sharpshooter fires at the flame of one candle, and the flame of another candle goes out. Ordinary doors jam. Electric lights switch themselves off when patient actors have at last left the switch. The wonder is that the curtain ever waits for its cue. Sometimes it does not. Poor plays have been made by mechanism that works, and good plays undone by mechanism that fails when the audience invariably comments, "Bad anyhow."

Desperate remedies were tried at the Prince of Wales's the following May—the result of reading the MS. of a soldier. Captain Basil Hood of the Princess of Wales's Own had first written for the lighter musical stage while still in the Queen's service. When his regiment was ordered to Burma he sent in his papers (no extraordinary thing in the days when commissions were bought and sold) and set himself up as a librettist. The music for his earlier pieces was by Walter Slaughter (conductor at Drury Lane when they first met), whose gift of simple melody set them thinking of children's plays from Hans Andersen.

At Terry's (on the south side of the Strand opposite the Lyceum's bottle-neck pit entrance) Hood and Slaughter formed a programme at Christmas, 1897, of *The Princess And The Swineherd*, *The Emperor's New Clothes*, *The Soldier And The Tinder Box*. Then Hood made a little play of *Ib And Little Christina*, which won the heart of Martin Harvey so completely that despite public distaste for an evening of one-act plays he presented it along with *Rouget De L'Isle* and *A Pantomine Rehearsal*, at the Prince of Wales's in 1900. That venture failed but Hood's play won an enduring reputation as the perfect piece, acclaimed above *Peter Pan*, for children.

Ib kept returning to Martin Harvey's repertoire for many years, an elixir of youth in the message it had for him. He stayed young. Actors of his own age who raced ahead at the start would slow down. Younger actors who strove to pass him would become exhausted. He did not need to exert himself against them since he was plainly destined to survive them all, as the last romantic, until past three score years and ten.

One night in the May of 1900 Ib had just declared, "You bring good news at last" when an era of strict decorum ended in the outburst—long considered shameful though now extolled—which was celebrated by Saki in the lines

> Mother, may I go and maffick,
> Tear around and hinder traffic?

after which the war became very much a matter, for those at home, of charity carnivals with prizes for decorated bicycles, of firework displays, circus processions with wooden gun-barrels amid hay-bags on carts, and bonfire processions with the most up-to-date opponent of the Houses of Parliament.

There were festive occasions in the name of charity for the theatre. Fire had destroyed Ottawa, and a "Canadian Matinée" was arranged at Drury Lane that June. Martin Harvey's, sandwiched between the sextette, "Tell me, pretty maiden", and Tree's first time as Othello, is one of the few solo performances in the list. Another is Richard III to realize a comic man's life-long ambition to play tragedy—the name opposite is Dan Leno. Several ladies promise a Bicycle Lane Ride, Irving brings *A Story Of Waterloo*, and American Zouaves (survival of an 1860 fad) display drill. The Biograph, otherwise known as the Mutoscope, reveals what is happening in the outside world: the Naval Brigade Relief Column entering camp after accompanying Sir Redvers Buller in his Triumphal March through Ladysmith.

Public events get shuffled and reshuffled. Special matinées are the first to be forgotten. The fiercest fires in cities become a tale of local importance. Wars get shut between book-covers. But there will always be a living echo of Dan Leno's desperate desire to be taken seriously. "That gay and tragic genius," Martin Harvey called him and he always thought of him whenever he asked Yorick's skull, "Where be your gibes now, your gambols, your songs, your flashes of merriment?"

Even for the actor, long trained in tragedy, the impulse towards Shakespearean heights might be frustrated. In the first flush of fame, when many a leading lady wished for Martin Harvey to play opposite her, the moment came for him to act, now or never, Romeo. There was a letter with this proposal from Mrs. Brown-Potter, radiantly lovely still though her heyday of holidays at Baden-Baden, in the company of a very exalted personage, had dwindled into a legend. She wished to play Juliet.

Would the Martin Harveys come to her riverside villa in order to discuss it? They took train on a summer's day to a railway platform that fairly exuded pride in being worn by the same shoes as the planks of the Gaiety, and in its courtyard asked for their carriage. It waited with drawn blinds as though for themselves and none other. But inside, lolling at ease with his feet up, was Comyns Carr.

At the other end of the journey they were welcomed by Kyrle Bellew, handsomest of actors, whose good looks were now enhanced by an air of emotional distress. That luncheon party of five had an air of disquiet about it, for a stage romance had ended. Bellew obeyed a command to take Miss de Silva on the river. In her he found a gentle sympathetic nature, though when they spoke nothing was said.

On their return she went to their hostess's "boudoir" to hear a long discourse on money, nothing but money. The atmosphere of the visit was too oppressive. Back at home in Town Martin Harvey barely needed to say what he thought, for it was in both their minds. He wished to play Romeo, knew the moment might never recur. But all the discussion meant to them was the sadness of having to witness the humiliation of a playgoer's idol who had set many a heart wildly beating and now could not still his own.

Mrs. Brown-Potter did not play Juliet. Instead she went on the halls, reclining on a rock while declaiming verse to audiences who did not understand much and cared less but felt somewhat overawed just the same. Martin Harvey doffed the purple for a while when asked to take over H. B. Irving's part in Barrie's *The Wedding Guest* at the Garrick. That was the last time he consented, in Stevenson's phrase, to go "for hire upon the stage", for very many years, and then Barrie would be the reason again.

Shakespeare had been the mainstay of several romantic actors at this time. Tree made stirring spectacles of *King John* and *A Midsummer Night's Dream*. At the Lyceum in February Henry V was impersonated by Benson and in December by Waller. The soldier's rival was Nell Gwynn in the style, naturally, of exceeding virtue. Marie Tempest played her in *English Nell* at the Prince of Wales's that August, to be very soon outplayed by an actress renowned for her Princess Flavia of Zenda, Rosalind and Oberon. Julia Neilson's season opened at the Haymarket a week later with *Sweet Nell Of Old Drury* by an American, Paul Kester.

Her husband, Fred Terry, was Charles II. They had often acted together before; now they set up together in management. At the end of their lease they took Sweet Nell back to her own purlieus by installing their play in Newcastle Street where a housefront, very ordinary except that a canopy covered the pavement as though to shield the hole where the ground-floor had been pushed in, called itself the Globe. There they laid foundations which would long outlast that theatre, for when Sweet Nell set out on a progress through the country she was welcomed by many more thousands than had ever cheered good queens in Nell's own day.

At last the brand-new century excited hopes of a new dawn. Tree in the autumn of 1900 brought out a soul-stirring drama, actually in verse. Though nobody said so aloud there was a general whisper, "Perhaps another Shake-speare." Why not? As the initial effort of a coming man, *Herod* justified hopes little short of wild extravagance. Old and young joined in singing its praises. "Let it at once be said that nothing whatever jars upon the mind most sensitive to the danger of blending sacred things with sublime," said the Victorians. "Mr. Stephen Phillips is not only a poet, and a rare poet, but that still rarer thing, a dramatic poet," said the Edwardians.

There had lately been a Belgian Shakespeare. Ever since the great nose of Coquelin had been dramatized by Rostand in *Cyrano De Bergerac* people also talked of a French Shakespeare. Now they spoke of an English Shake-speare, forgetting we already had one. As for the dramatist himself he made Gilbert a prophet, for in him the last scene of *Patience* came true—the poet who had walked down Piccadilly with a lily in his mediaeval hand became a jolly-Bank-Holiday, matter-of-fact young man. Stephen Phillips, the cathedral precentor's son, lived exactly like that, desiring the pleasures of Bank Holiday all the year round and being religiously matter-of-fact in all things except self-improvement.

When sent a biographical form for the Green Room Book he accounted for his exit from the stage in this way: "took a dislike to touring life, and occupied himself for a short time by taking a position on the tutorial staff of an Army crammer". Poetic inspiration he reduced to "ultimately drifted into the literary profession", as though that would explain the writing of dramas in verse that impressed London's two leading actor-managers.

As a means of livelihood either poetry or drama was precarious enough. Together, as John Davidson still found, these twin torments of Tantalus became a doubly distilled venom of frustration. For over a century the poetic drama's smoulderings had never burned brightly enough to be called un-effectual fires, though fierce enough to burn the fingers of any author, actor or manager who disturbed them. Now the spiritous breath of a poet who asked, like Falstaff, "Shall I not take mine ease in mine inn?" fanned them back to life.

Queen Victoria died on January 22, 1901. Four days later Ellen Terry reported after a visit to Town, "No one in the streets . . . empty buses crawling along. Black boards up at every shop window. All the gas half-mast high as well as the flags. I never saw such a mournful city, but why should they turn the gas down? Thrift, thrift, Horatio." The new century suddenly seemed very uninviting. The rich Victorian felt like the bucca-neering Elizabethan. The Queen was dead. No more conquest. No more enrichment by adventure.

CHAPTER 11

THE NEW ACTOR-MANAGER

WHATEVER Don Juan and other legendary figures meant to Martin Harvey in the pursuit of his own ideals, they meant far less to the public than certain other figures identified solely with him and with no one else. Count Skariatine of Marion Crawford's novel "A Cigarette-Maker's Romance" was the next of these. "The old-world gallantry of the Count, who is taken for a harmless lunatic by the friendly workers in the factory; the devotion of the cigarette girl, Vjera, whose affection for her courtly but rather crazy lover is almost maternal in its tenderness; the curious mental disorder which takes the form of a conviction recurring every Wednesday that his friends will arrive and remind him of his identity, and restore him to his estates, made a very strong appeal to me," Martin Harvey says.

Perhaps this could be regarded as his first venture in character work, but the statement is questionable because there has been no attempt to stabilize the stage meaning of "character". For the sake of clarity let this childlike plan relate styles at a glance:

	Classic	Romantic	Realistic	Naturalistic
Straight				
Character				

From that the fact should be plain that character in romance is to be judged by its own standards in the same way that straight parts in romance must not be judged by other standards. All this might go without saying if it were not for an added complication, caused by the change in the meaning of technical terms.

What "character" stood for at the start of the century can be read in the essays G.B.S. wrote for the *Saturday Review*. Briefly it meant stress laid on outward manifestations of the assumed personality instead of the inward —the approach to Falstaff as contrasted with the study of Hamlet. But a coming generation would gradually insist that any part in a play would be "character" to the player unable to identify himself with it.

Reference to so important a point must be made to "the actor's Bible", now no longer *The Era* but "My Life in Art" by the director of the Moscow Art Theatre. Much of what Stanislavsky offers as the psychology of the actor is the psychology of the amateur. At one of his earliest triumphs he let feelings carry him away and could not remember what had happened. That is not remarkable, for excitement usually has that effect.

The value of "My Life in Art" lies in its record of phases in stage experience that in a professional actor's mind have been forgotten, phases often fundamental. Likewise Stanislavsky, because the theatre was for so long his pleasure rather than his work, is free from that desire which so many stage autobiographies manifest, to talk about something else.

Concerning the reference now in hand, Stanislavsky is so often quoted as having said "all actors must be character actors" that the time has come to add the other half of this half-truth. The sentence cancels itself out with, "of course not in the sense of outer, but of inner, characteristics", so that his meaning is left for the next sentence, "But even outwardly it is best for the actor to leave himself at times."

With all this as justification we might reason that Martin Harvey's peculiar excellences revealed themselves when he was half in and half out of character. The half-wit in Skariatine, like the libertine in Don Juan and the drunkard in Carton, was as unlike the actor as the idealist in each part was like him. As far as popular success went, that was the Martin Harvey formula. In London it rarely succeeded; in the provinces it never failed. Failure in Town was followed, whenever tried, by vast profits on tour.

A Cigarette-Maker's Romance began at the Court on February 11, 1901. It was adapted from Marion Crawford's novel by Charles Hannan, with first and third acts set in the factory and second act in the Count's lodgings. Martin Harvey played Skariatine, and Miss de Silva was the factory girl who interests herself in his helpless state. Anton Skariatine, the cousin who passes as the Count in Russia, was played by an old comrade of the Lyceum Vacation Company.

Such a plot in those days might have been seized as a chance for "doubling" the lawful and unlawful holders of the title. The strange thing is that although the convention had become discredited audiences still lusted after it, and actors loved to gratify that lust. But Count Skariatine had attractions enough without that.

The charm of the part for Martin Harvey was (so he said in a letter to Rudolph de Cordova, published in "Parts I Have Played" in 1909) his mental condition. It is one of suspended memory in consequence of a blow he has received on his head which makes him unable to remember who he is until, at the end, the shock of reading his own name in a most unexpected situation restores the lost balance of his memory:

"This gives great possibilities for the display of half shades of feeling, when transitory recollections come back to the man in strange waves and mental vibrations which pass before he can lay hold of them. The interest of the audience in this mental phenomenon was a great surprise for me, for the mind of the public always seems to be with me while the Count's mind is clear, and yet go off at a tangent when his mind becomes blank again. This identification of the audience with the actor is a great force in the theatre, for it makes actors of the audience, and is one of the psychological results of acting to which few people give heed."

Now the thing happened. Now the interest excited as long ago as *Ruy Blas* spread. Now the embers at last fanned into flame. Praise of "The Martin Harveys" could be heard in the streets. Playgoers in big towns and little cities read the title *The Only Way* under "Prospective Engagements" in programmes and knew what it meant. Where enthusiasm had fired a dozen breasts among scanty audiences on the first tour, thousands now came to see what the few had raved about—or merely affirmed faith in the quiet way that is typical of most parts of England, more particularly where Shakespeare or where his Hotspur lived—Birmingham, Newcastle, Sunderland.

It was the young who swore by Martin Harvey, very much more especially the young men. The happiest phrases ever said of that massed hero-worship belong to a tribute not intended for him, but when this praise of Swinburne was applied to him by Mr. James Agate, middle-aged readers throughout the kingdom nodded their heads in approval:

"To the young men and women of the day he was an intoxication and a passion, awakening half-formed desires, hidden longings and impulses, and secret enthusiasms, and wielding sway more imperiously over heart and sense and soul than any other man of his time did over the intellect or the reason of his disciples."

The intoxication, the passion, the half-formed desires had taken an altogether different turn, but such terms still seem rightly chosen. It was not the spirit of Dickens, for Dickens liked to be practical and definite in the way he moved men to think of the general welfare, but if the author of "A Tale of Two Cities" had witnessed this performance he would have been consoled for all the hurt and injury he had received from seeing his novels hacked about on the stage.

Undoubtedly the new actor-manager stood firmly on that pedestal which makes solid stone of failures as long as there are box-office receipts for mortar. He could please himself in West End theatres as long as he knew that he could fill country theatres as magically as anyone, Irving included. Yet there was no thought in his head, so far, to make a bid for the leadership of the stage.

Irving stood alone, and the only one who thought of challenging his supremacy was equal to it solely in his own wild blue-eye imaginings. Tree was always ready to fill the limelight. Irving cherished his companionship for the sardonic laughter it engendered in him. In "Adventures Among Immortals" Percy Burton tells how Tree suffered from Irving's vitriolic wit.

At the Garrick Club one afternoon Tree remarked, "Next season I intend to do *Hamlet*."

"H'm, *Hamlet*, eh? Very interesting," replied Irving meditatively, as though chewing the cud of Tree's intentions as he reiterated: "Ha! *Hamlet*. Yes! Very interesting indeed."

"Do you think, Irving," retorted Tree, quite obviously nettled, "that you are the only man in England who can play Hamlet?"

"Oh no, my *dear* Tree," snapped Sir Henry, seizing the opening that had been left him. "But I am quite sure you are the only man who can not."

Yet there was no ignoring the bitter truth that while the box-office responded less and less to the knight, it answered more and more to the jester. When the time arrived for a new Lyceum production, the play was rather more apt than tactful. Why did Irving's choice light on *Coriolanus*? There was neither glory nor profit to be won by it. The temporary bitterness that possessed him must have been in Shakespeare when the honeyed pen dipped into such gall as, "the common cry of curs whose breath I hate". Irving chose that particular and unpromising material to please himself.

It pleased his mood. Twenty years earlier Alma Tadema had prepared designs for him; the production had been shelved until this unpropitious moment. The older Irving grew the fewer hints he dropped, and too much may be read into the aptness of so many of the lines he had to utter. Too much attention may be paid to the passage he restored to the text which begins, "As for my country I have shed my blood", as though a reference to his own exhaustion.

Too much may also be made of an accidental comment by Shakespeare upon the altered conditions at the Lyceum, when the lines

> I have been i' the market-place: and, sir, 'tis fit
> You make strong party, or defend yourself
> By calmness, or by absence; all's in anger,

seem to refer to the Lyceum's murmuring shareholders. Too much may be read into the odd chance that the character who says this happens to be named Cominius. After warning ourselves not to jump to conclusions there still seems vibrancy in the words:

> Who deserves greatness
> Deserves your hate; and your affections are
> A sick man's appetite, who desires most that
> Which would increase his evil. He that depends
> Upon your favours, swims with fins of lead,
> And hews down oaks with rushes. Hang ye! Trust ye?
> With every minute you do change a mind,
> And call him noble that was now your hate,
> Him vile, that was your garland.

Even that immortal partnership, Irving and Terry, failed. More credit was won by Benson with Geneviève Ward in *Coriolanus* just before and just after the Lyceum's opening, first at the Comedy and then at His Majesty's. As for Tree himself, he was ostentatiously rehearsing in public to play Count D'Orsay in *The Last Of The Dandies*. In order to establish how thoroughly he was "entering into the skin of a part" he frequently cut his friends in support of the belief that D'Orsay would probably have done so. So Roland Pertwee testifies.

Since nostalgia takes so strong a hold of romance its champions were ever looking backwards. That August of 1901 the thoughts of Martin Harvey turned back to Eugene Aram. He tried again the methods of his first play, worked out the scenario in collaboration with Miss de Silva, and handed the result to Freeman Wills. A certain bishop's displeasure had now no power to intervene. "Fitzmaurice King" had won the right to his own name and *After All* was billed as the work of Freeman Wills and Frederick Langbridge.

Dublin had been dear to players for two centuries or more, and many of them left their bones on the bed of St. George's Channel rather than omit so cherished a Theatre Royal from their itinerary. In the wake of the Keans and Irving, Martin Harvey rooted his sympathies there. Both Charles Kean and Irving found their business managers at Dublin; Martin Harvey did not do likewise, but his life-long guardian was named Frank O'Neill and he did decide to stage new productions at Dublin first. There, in the October of 1901, *After All* began a tour which preceded the London season in the January of 1902 at the Avenue. This theatre stood beneath the girders of Charing Cross railway bridge; these would one day fall and crush the roof so decorated by the wild life of the Thames in 1902 as to earn the name of "The Gull's Retreat".

A retired critic paid *After All* a visit. Though he had but three score years he belonged to the generation which had patted "young Irving" on the head, figuratively, and he seemed like some moral emblem off the Albert Memorial. But since throwing the burden of professional dignity from his shoulders, Clement Scott was as full of enthusiasm as a gallery boy. In a letter intended for the advertisement columns he told the public, "if after all these years they deign to believe me", that *After All* was a fine impressive drama, played to admiration by Martin Harvey:

"I found a prologue which is a play in itself, a miniature tragedy, interesting to pulsation, and acted to perfection. That murder of Daniel Clarke; the three sudden stabs, and then the lifeless, pulseless rag of a man on the floor, the awful silence, the wild look of horror on the face of the just murderer of the seducer of his sister, I am not likely to forget. It took me back to the Paris days of Lemaître and Melingue, when drama was drama, and not curds and whey."

Nobody tried to prove Aram innocent, but each generation had been resolved upon finding him guilty of a better and a better murder.

Following the vindication of blasphemers, murderers and ravishers, it came to François Villon's turn to be ennobled in Justin Huntley McCarthy's *If I Were King*. When first staged in New York it was seen by Irving, who engaged the heroine (Mrs. McCarthy) for his next season at home. When *Faust* returned to London in the spring of 1902 with the unpredictable Cissie Loftus as Margaret, Mephisto saw a changed Lyceum with "Managing Director . . . Mr. J. Comyns Carr" writ large over it. Old princely habits such as "No Fees" and no advertisements had had to go.

The programmes, altogether changed, had doubled in size for the sake of revenue. This adds to their value as relics. The 1902 bowler, all one price three shillings and ninepence, is still the one worn by the original singer of "Tommy, make room for your Uncle", and Greenwich still offers "Recherche fish (whitebait) dinners".

There are riding-schools for cyclists. There is a Roadway Autocar Company selling the 10 h.p. Mors and the 4½ h.p. dog-cart Renault. In the Paris-Berlin race of 1901, the Mors heavy car came first at 47 miles per hour and the Renault Voiturette beat all the light cars at 39 miles per hour. "Coronation Procession Seats from one guinea—Windows from ten guineas" have the top lines.

Again Tree was stealing the limelight. Critics and public alike acclaimed Stephen Phillips' new poetic drama, *Ulysses*, at His Majesty's; the dayspring, after a night of three hundred years, had begun beyond all doubt. The poet, since he had already come into Martin Harvey's life and would come back again and again, must be drawn as full-length as time and circumstances permit.

Despite *Herod*, despite *Paolo And Francesca* and *Ulysses* together, Stephen Phillips always felt the need of money every day of his jolly Bank Holiday life. He lived (according to A. E. W. Mason's life of George Alexander) obscurely in lodgings at seaside resorts, particularly Yarmouth. While at Brighton he used a restaurant in East Street as his address. The Royal Academy invited him to reply to the toast of Literature at its annual banquet. "I should think Phillips is the only author," says Mason, "who ever turned that invitation down."

He had more than an average share of the contemporary hankering after practical jokes. On setting out for Brighton with Tree he sent a wire asking for the train to be met by the police as he had with him a dangerous lunatic who suffered from the delusion that he was Tree. Although the upshot was a scene in the police-station, this was a simple trick compared with what he could manage when aided by Oscar Asche, the young Australian giant from Benson's company who directed rehearsals of *Ulysses*.

To save his voice Asche brought a megaphone to the dress-rehearsal. Tree had a secretary, Lionel Hart, who had been warned by Phillips that

A scene from *Œdipus Rex*

Pizarro at the Princess's

Miss de Silva as
"Emly Jane"

Asche was a drunkard. The rest of the story is told in "Oscar Asche: His Life". Phillips added that when the "drunkard" picked up a megaphone he would next "run amok and destroy things".

The rehearsal reached the Hades scene. Tree, in armour, descended a long flight of steps, past mysterious light and voices. The specially invited audience was stilled to silence, but the lights were wrong, and Asche picked up his megaphone. Phillips warned Hart, who rushed through the pass door on to the stage, let down the iron curtain, seized Tree by the arm, ran him to his dressing-room, locked the door, and fell in a faint.

With a citadel in so commanding a quarter of the town, Tree lorded it over Edwardian romance. Yet he had to win the quidnuncs each time. He could not speak, as Harvey did to his rivals' envied amusement, of "my loyal public". The justness of that adjective all knew who knew England in the days before "Sunday best" had become a playful expression. Those were the days of tours.

By a strange mingling of religious duty and joyous self-indulgence, the Christian millions of Great Britain came out on the first day of the week in all the sartorial splendours they could muster. Hours to be spent in soot-laden, crowded railway carriages deterred nobody who had any wish to be regarded as other than destitute. Through the deserted streets of every town and city, with their heel-taps breaking the death-like Sabbatarian silence, elegant strolling players—who might now be called sauntering players—made their regular journey to the railway station, not furtively like the rogues and vagabonds of old, whose "props" bent their backs, but trailing flounces of glory so that all the faces behind aspidistras and lace-curtains might know the stage was on its way.

"Theatricals" full of pros in frock-coats and silk hats, flowing skirts and picture hats, puffed south from Dundee, Edinburgh, Newcastle, Sunderland and all "small dates" around them, down to Darlington; others from Glasgow, Liverpool and Manchester down to Crewe, while northwards came musical comedies, costume dramas, melodramas and problem plays from Town. Trains of every other kind, except perhaps fish, had precedence of these whose passengers travelled at three-quarter fare with free trucks for scenery thrown in per score, but *eventually*, as the comedian of every company would regularly say, the sidings were reached of the great junctions of entertainments' history.

Nostalgic sentimentalists paint the bright colours of Boulter's Lock on Ascot Sunday. What were all its punts, skiffs, canoes and launches beside the Sunday trains of Crewe or Darlington for cut, style and smartness? "Ships that pass in the night" was the catch-phrase one old friend going north would fling at another going south as they went into the town to spend the two or three hours' wait drinking.

On the more dominant platforms stars of musical comedy might parade their trailing flounces. Behind a stack of milkchurns a knockabout tumbler

L

of the halls might coach his future partner, at this last meeting before "the night" weeks ahead, in the routine of the act. "When you say 'Crewe' to a juvenile nowadays he thinks you mean the boat-race, and when you say 'Darlington' he thinks of Mr. Darlington of the *Telegraph*," the old stager growls.

But all the signs and portents of his world are gone. The *Referee* once littered the whole of those stations with its buff-coloured pages, because it was the Profession's Sunday paper; besides pages of criticism or gossip and columns of theatrical "cards", long lists under the headline "Tours" made it possible to see whom you would be likely to meet that morning in the acrid air. On the bookstalls there were thick piles of *The Era*, still the Actor's Bible after half-a-century or more, and *The Stage*, each copy a substantial wad of satisfying information.

Around these spread the whole field of periodical dramatic literature in a rich variety, which proved its hold not only on players and playgoers but on the whole general public. *The Entr'acte* now had a dying air. Its cartoons, since Alfred Bryan's pen was idle, could not compete with the photographic reproductions of several "glossy illustrateds", with the *Play Pictorial* in the lead. The *Telegraph* had laid itself out to be the actor's Daily with a full page each Thursday of stage articles, flanked by theatrical cards as "small ads."

There was no mistaking, at this zenith of the railroad age when all the famous actor-managers from Irving to Harvey travelled by train to Darlington or Crewe on Sundays with a veritable jam of celebrities in the out-of-town summer season, how very flourishing "legitimate" was. The stage had even been classed by economists among "our industries", which was like their impertinence.

Already the Martin Harveys had taken their place with the younger Irvings in a special category. Sir Max Beerbohm once described the actor-manager as someone with a leading London theatre for his permanent address. That definition would serve for the eighteen-nineties but not for Edward's reign. The rebuilding of provincial theatres on Drury Lane's scale meant that actor-managers could thrive with no permanent address at all.

A dreary existence it seemed. To Irving it was. The cheerless hotels, where he had to keep a tired waiter at his side when he wanted companionship, or put up with some insistent commercial gentleman when he did not, were a purgatory. But to Martin Harvey a hotel was home. This was Miss de Silva's doing. She "travelled" a vast amount of odds and ends that might have been thought unnecessary. Besides dogs (four of them sometimes), there were books (cases of them), photographs in frames and *objets d'art*. When these had been unpacked each or every other Sunday one hotel suite quickly took on a family resemblance to all the others, so that for that week or fortnight it became home.

Perhaps the earnest student of the drama might dismiss this as gossip. Since the time when Addison and Steele founded theatre criticism there has been need of such gossip. The niche Martin Harvey steadily filled in the drama as it existed in the minds of millions rested on that pillar. He stayed in the provinces because the provinces, all of them, were his home. The masters of St. James's and His Majesty's never bestrode England as securely as he. They merely visited where he addressed his own public.

An incident at Blackpool revealed his power. When Sydney Carton took his last farewell of Lucy with a kiss, one in the crowd of Wakes made labial noises which the entire audience copied. Martin Harvey at once had the curtain rung down and told the terrified throng that unless they behaved themselves they would not see Carton die. They did as they were told.

Until now Martin Harvey was the theatre's solitary idealist. The first player with any hint of rivalry in looks, voice and manner was Henry Ainley. At Leeds he presented himself before Benson, and was accepted because he was a bank clerk and somebody had to look after the accounts. At rehearsals for *Henry V* at the Lyceum he was told to play the Duke of Gloucester. In a broadcast many years later Ainley explained:

> "He and the Duke of Bedford are addressed by the king. Together they reply 'We shall, my liege.' That was the full extent of my first speaking part. But one night at Deptford the actor who played Lorenzo in *The Merchant Of Venice* fell ill. Benson had no one available but me."

Alexander was in front with his business-manager, Aubrey Smith—known as Round-the-Corner Smith, the Sussex bowler, in the days before Hollywood was invented. They agreed that here was Il Bello, younger brother of Malatesta (Alexander himself), to love and be loved by that tyrant's wife, and to speak these lines when Paolo looks back towards the towers of Rimini, red in the sunset:

> I have fled from her; have refused the rose,
> Although my brain was reeling at the scent,
> I have come hither as through pains of death;
> I have died, and I am gazing back at life.

Once more the Martin Harveys were in the provinces. That tour included some players of promise, including Leon M. Lion.[1] It was, he says rich in experiences—not all of them completely happy ones—"For, great actor that he was, I did not find the same generous sensitivity towards the young and the aspiring, such as had left such an impression on me with Forbes Robertson. . . . He had inherited what I was told was the Irving tradition that the 'lesser folk without the law' were requested not even to address Mr. Harvey, as he then was, without having been previously spoken to."

[1] With his unfailing generosity Mr. Leon M. Lion gave permission for these sentences to be quoted from his autobiography, "The Surprise of My Life"—in the printers' hands at the same time as the present volume.

Since Leon M. Lion was not gifted with that meekness of spirit which made these conditions very tolerable, there were soon "clashes of temperament in which, as in my schoolboy days, I came off with the bloodier nose". The young player never forgot the "kindly intercessions and generous diplomacy of Lady Martin-Harvey, whose gentle tact achieved a sufficient restraint on both sides, so that I was neither sacked nor gave in my notice".

In his later years Sir John forgot this phase in his own training as manager. How easy it is, past middle-age, to be not only kindly but benevolent towards youth; when we have just emerged from that very state even tolerance is barely possible. While Irving's discipline was then still the model, Benson's iron-rod for absentees from sport was added to it; Mr. Lion remembers how compulsory hockey for every member of the company was "one of those fences at which I shied absolutely". Fortunately, before the dispute reached finality, Martin Harvey himself was hit by a flying ball, "too impetuously driven by one of the young Amazons of the Company, and so nearly brought *hors de combat* that he was persuaded to forgo further participation in hockey matches, and with that, compulsion to the sport became a dead letter".

One extremely healthy thing was bred of such small tyrannies. It provoked in every youngster, says Mr. Lion, an indomitable resolve to have his own ship some day and walk his own quarter deck. Lion learned a very great deal of the "craft" from Harvey's masterly technique, reduced to a rule of rote which never varied. You could have set your watch by his "fractional pauses or the rallentando with which he would bring a scene to its climax". It was also very salutary for young players to be cast for parts they did not want to play:

"I had rather fancied myself as the public prosecutor in *The Only Way*. But when I was cast for the low comedy husband of Akulina in *A Cigarette-Maker's Romance* I strenuously protested, and suffered that curious pain-pleasure combination of having him say to me sardonically after I had been playing the part for a month and he had been watching from the wings, 'You see, Lion, it's just what I said, no one could be better in the part. You're a born low comedian!' Naturally, I didn't know whether to be more angered at his triumph or flattered by his tribute."

Immediate objections will be taken to that phrase "rote which never varied". Many a player who groaned under the ordeal of those constant rehearsals has told how Martin Harvey would say, "Never too late to improve. Take that line like this," after no matter how many years. But contradictory statements do not cancel out; they often "add up".

After the sudden inspiration would come the change at rehearsal, and

when that was effected then the rote would never very—until the next flash
of inspiration. In this fusion of rigid drill with zeal for improvement lay
the secret of long life. Old melodramas might totter round the circuit of
old haunts without a sign that any care had ever been bestowed on them,
but the actor-managers of transatlantic repute prized the oldest "starring
vehicles" in their repertoire more highly than the new.

"Stop-gap" now became frequently used in dramatic criticism. Martin
Harvey had revived *The Only Way* between all his later productions. *Sweet
Nell Of Old Drury* served the same purpose for the Terrys. Most actor-
managers now managed to provide themselves with one. At the Shakespeare
Theatre, Liverpool, on October 2, 1902, Lewis Waller tried out *Monsieur
Beaucaire* by Booth Tarkington and Mrs. E. G. Sutherland, a tale of a
distinguished émigré pretending to be a very humble person in the fashionable
Bath of the eighteenth century.

Before the end of the month it opened at the Comedy where it ran
for a year. When a new home was needed Waller took the Imperial, all
marble and gold within "like a Greek temple", as rebuilt by Mrs. Langtry
to whose Mademoiselle Mars he had played Napoleon there.

Since it was part of Martin Harvey's London that was to become part
of his life, the Imperial comes into this story. Its founder, the daughter of a
Jersey clergyman of ancient family, married to a sportsman whose income
was mainly derived from precarious Irish rents, descended upon London to
capture the most exclusive circles of that very exclusive social system.
Charles Blake Cochran says of her:

> "The romance in the picture of this beautiful young bride, in her
> 'plain frock', attracting crowds of the famous in all sections of society
> to her feet, of people leaping on chairs in the Park to see her pass,
> is familiar social gossip of the period. The power of her beauty was
> admittedly supreme. It captured society."

Even when shining new her Imperial was a doomed theatre, for a
religious body had bought the ground. Though a separate building, it
belonged to the Royal Aquarium—"a sort of Crystal Palace in London
within easy reach of Charing Cross, a covered-in promenade for wet weather,
with the glass cases of live fish thrown in", is how Errol Sherson describes
it in "London's Lost Theatres". Around the space for concerts and variety
shows were stalls for flowers, perfumery and gloves besides side-shows
with freaks and a few fish. As the vast expanse of sooty glass had first to be
removed, the Central Hall would not be completed for many years yet, and
Lewis Waller settled down for a long stay.

Meanwhile Ellen Terry had gone to His Majesty's. To Tree's Falstaff
she played Mistress Page "By the courtesy of Sir Henry Irving". Mrs.
W. H. Kendal, as Mistress Ford, was not to be outdone; she appeared "By

the courtesy of Mr. W. H. Kendal", as though all the world did not know who was sovereign and who consort in that management.

But whenever there were matinées of *The Merchant* at the Lyceum, Ellen Terry was Portia. How evergreen her life stayed already deserved admiration. Her contemporary playwright, whose career went back to the Princes in Oxford Street, was now old. With a fair measure of success behind him Herman Merivale was glad, like other Victorian playwrights, to be given a complimentary matinée. At His Majesty's on June 12, 1902, an imposing array of stars filled the programme—Forbes Robertson in Act II of *Forget-Me-Not*, Irving with Laurence Irving in *Waterloo*, Alexander in Act II of *The Prisoner Of Zenda*, the Kendals in a recent play, Cyril Maude in another, Tree and Lily Brayton in *The Last Of The Dandies*. Merivale died in 1906.

In 1903 the Lyceum was put up for auction—on Shakespeare's birthday of all days—without a reasonable offer. Bram Stoker made it known what kind of bargain the limited liability company had struck when it came into being. According to Brereton's "Life of Irving", it offered him £39,000 to include his twenty years' lease, worth £10,000, and fittings worth £15,000; he had also to give for five years one-fourth of his profits made outside the theatre. As his payment included £12,500 in shares, the real amount he recovered was £26,500 and since then he had paid the shareholders £25,800.

Both the Lyceum and the Princess's remained closed, month after month. Ellen Terry for a season of management chose the Imperial. On April 15, 1903, Gordon Craig staged one of Ibsen's early historical dramas there under the title of *The Vikings*.

These were items of news to the Martin Harveys, for at the end of their provincial tour they sailed for America. Their repertoire of romance was full. Out of it *The Only Way*, *The Children Of Kings*, *A Cigarette-Maker's Romance* (preceded by *Rouget De L'Isle*), *After All* and *Pelléas And Mélisande* were chosen. Their experiences were notable for the discovery that the welcome of Canada was always theirs. No cynicism existed in theatres north of the 49th parallel.

CHAPTER III

FROM NAPOLEON TO HAMLET

"God is in the theatre" still formed Martin Harvey's watchword. The very devil was in it at times. Young actor-managers, returning to the provinces sure of their welcome whenever frustrated, might be philosophical, but the poets who turned dreams into drama felt the vanity of all theatrical wishes. Romance, in urgent, clamorous demand, had no use for verse and turned to the historical novel instead. But all the lasting successes won by costume in the new century's opening years are of less acount than one splendid fancy misbegotten—Irving's *Dante* at Drury Lane.

Thinking of the great actor as a great master of stagecraft, the public anticipated a lavish spectacle—Pisa, Florence and Avignon merely the frame for the Inferno with its flames and ice. The play itself had been written by Sardou, now over seventy years of age, and translated by Laurence Irving. Cain and Charon, Paolo and Francesca, Beatrice and Malatesta—all found a place somewhere.

When the MS. was in that state where the art of the dramatist should begin, the play went into rehearsal. Nobody had a good word for it except Irving. It opened on April 30, 1903, amid every sign of respect, ran for eighty-three performances, celebrated its end with a banquet, went to New York, and had at last to acknowledge failure. But that play will haunt theatrical memory for what it might have been—it is not difficult to see the performance with Irving's eyes and in that way it becomes the resounding climax of his tradition. In actuality he had to fall back on performances, *The Bells* and *The Lyons Mail*, which demanded youthful energy. What exercise, a reporter asked, did he take? "I act."

During the London run of *Dante* Martin Harvey returned from America. He brought back with him a play of St. Helena by Lloyd Osborne and Austin Strong, step-sons of Robert Louis Stevenson. *The Exile* opened at the Royalty in the May of 1903, and whatever its reception it did at least enable the romantic to run true to form by playing Napoleon. Another MS. in his luggage bore the title *The Breed Of The Treshams*. This he tried out at Newcastle in the September and at Kennington in the December. It conformed so exactly to the prevailing taste of Great Britain that the wonder is how John Rutherford, the author, should have been not an English actor but Mrs. E. G. Sutherland and Miss B. M. Dix of Boston, Mass. Such emphatic popularity was won, there was no need for newsprint praise. London critics were at variance with the millions over "costume" generally, and though they could not say that a good thing of its kind was bad, they would not say it was good.

How the difficulty might be overcome may be examined in the following account of the story. Its hero is "The Rat"—Lieutenant Reresby, illegitimate brother of Cornet the Hon. Francis Tresham, traitor to the Royalist cause in 1644. For the sake of the Hon. Margaret Tresham, the "Rat" allows suspicion to fall upon himself. Though the resultant thrill is worth any "unsophisticated playgoer's money", the critic who says this has to make his own sophistication known:

"The hero, it is true, does not lay down his life in the sacred cause of sentiment, as in *The Only Way*, but he is whipped, and stabbed, and burnt for the sake of a young lady who has no further claim upon him than her eyes happen to resemble the eyes of a lady with whom he was once in love. All, let us hasten to add, comes right in the end. The villain is driven from the stage with ignominy, Margaret marries her dear one, and the somewhat battered hero, amid the congratulations of a perfervid house, staggers away to seek for more horrible experiences among far more theatrical people.

"Mr. Martin Harvey scored heavily as 'The Rat'. Up to the torture scene we excused his grotesque mannerisms on the understanding that he was pretending to be slightly intoxicated, and after the torture scene we again excused them on the understanding that he was lacerated. For the rest the representation was quite clever. Miss N. de Silva, as a boy who recked little of death so long as he was allowed to strike attitudes and raise his voice in the presence of his betters, did uncommonly well. Her devotion to 'The Rat', even to the sharing of his proclivity for entering and leaving a room by the window instead of the door, was moving in the extreme."

It must not be overlooked that while Martin Harvey was a disciple of Irving, Miss de Silva was even more so—by a year or two at least. At the Lyceum she had undergone the very special training reserved for young ladies who were required to play boys' parts. Irving insisted that from the first rehearsals they should wear not skirts but breeches in order to grow accustomed to taking long strides and standing with feet well apart.

"What on earth for?" asks the new generation. "Were there no boy actors in those days?" If so, they were ignored. Gentlemen of boyish appearance were preferred whenever the "breeches part" tradition of Nell Gwynn, Peg Woffington and Kitty Clive was set aside. That tradition, otherwise, was sacred from the beginning of the romantic tradition to its end. The "breeches part" survived as a sign of acting for acting's sake, part and parcel of romance.

In the provinces and the suburbs *The Breed Of The Treshams* had become a performance lovers of the theatre swore by. Wild praise did harm; the judicious who came to see Martin Harvey and Miss de Silva for the first time imagined this to be not the extreme limit of their artistic pendulum's swing but their finest achievement. Possibly those who looked upon it as the players' holiday—an interlude between the sincere strivings of the idealist spirit—beheld an entirely different play. They did, if there is anything in the "eye of the beholder" theory. To discriminating and undiscriminating alike, leaving the "trimmers" out, The Rat became the liveliest personage during the heyday of tours.

Tradition was to have a hard fight in order to survive. Its old haunts were doomed. Though the Lyceum still stood, about to undergo major internal operations, old London died on the night of Saturday, July 4, 1903. For three years the London County Council had been buying "Spotted Dogs", "White Harts" and others before abandoning their licences. Holywell Street vanished in the Strand widening.

Now theatres had to go. The Olympic, faced with imminent doom, gave itself up to the services of religion. The Gaiety took its farewell of the public with many of its old players on the stage. Sir Henry Irving spoke, George Edwardes accepted silver candlesticks; glasses filled; everybody murmured "Dear old Gaiety", and reluctantly went outside in the small hours to sing "Auld Lang Syne" and be moved on by the police. St. Lyceum had no such definite and deeply lamented end. That September it merely reopened as a music-hall.

Now came a test of endurance for the *The Only Way*. The French Revolution had been served up afresh with more heads saved from the guillotine—this time for those figures of commanding elegance, Julia Neilson and Fred Terry, as Sir Percy and Lady Blakeney in the Baroness Orczy's "The Scarlet Pimpernel".

The story was originally composed in 1900 under the name of "The Red Carnation", in a setting of the eighteenth century. This, transposed to Russia in the twentieth century, became "The Sign of the Shamrock" in the *Daily Express* during 1903. *The Scarlet Pimpernel,* as a play of the French Revolution with a hero who sacrifices himself as thoroughly as Sydney Carton, first saw the footlights at Nottingham Theatre Royal, October 15, 1903, and went on tour, where it had to avoid confusion with *A Scarlet Flower* and *The Scarlet Woman*, both new. At the urgent request of the gallery Sir Percy designed for himself a happy ending—which must not be read as a desire for happy endings in general (since nobody had ever demanded a reprieve from Martin Harvey) but simply as recognition that *The Scarlet Pimpernel* came under the heading not of romance but adventure.

When acted in frank recognition of this it gave great delight for years. But when brought to the two-year-old New Theatre, St. Martin's Lane, in the January of 1905 its fate, says Julia Neilson, hung in the balance for a whole month. She quotes a critic: "The scarlet pimpernel is a little red flower that opens in the morning and shuts at night. So should the play!"

When C. E. Montague trounced the wholesome play, the popular

successes of Martin Harvey were included. Two of the characters with a
"solid greatest common measure of rough diamondism" were the scapegoat
in *The Only Way* and the scamp in *The Breed Of The Treshams*. He argued
that they show who shall inherit the earth or get clean into heaven—"simply
the you of your vision, the Bayard *manqué*, the Philip Sydney waiting to come
off, the paragon that a man is to himself when he goes fast asleep while a
lady is playing Beethoven, and dreams of the dragons he would slay for
pure chivalry". And yet, having made Bayard, Philip Sydney and Beethoven
as much to blame as Martin Harvey, the critic still found harm in the
identification process which the humble playgoer so thoroughly enjoyed.

That was typical of the Manchester School though the spirit was not
confined to one place. In all countries the tendency was for intellect to be
despised by the urbane and to take on a democratic, everyday, domestic
circle, matter-of-fact, humble-life tone. Brieux, who manifested this to the
world at large, was a carpenter's son. He educated himself zealously, adopted
the cause of social reform and wrote plays for the French equivalent of the
New Drama, informing a not completely convinced world that the road to
hell was paved with bad intentions.

But though his plays may not satisfy the unruly part of our intelligence
which insists that life's problems never by any chance work out in the
way of Euclid, they served a more useful end than most. If read as plays
they seemed sermons, but if read as sermons they seemed to be highly
competent plays.

The audience at King's Hall, Covent Garden, which on less solemn
occasions was the National Sporting Club, came in this spirit on March 4,
1905, to see *The Three Daughters Of Monsieur Dupont*. Julie, victim of a calculating father who chooses for her a repulsive bridegroom in hopes of profit,
was played by the actress formerly known as Birdie and now as Ethel Irving.
Nineteen of her twenty years had been spent in musical pieces: *The Geisha,
San Toy* and *The Babes In The Wood*.

It was fairly well known that these were not the limits of her talent,
but nobody was fully prepared for the moment when she revealed her
electrifying powers. Passive suffering was first the manner of her part.
Suddenly it changed. In a second she became stark, livid; her eyes became
fixed. She let out an unearthly scream. A hint of the gift of Henry Irving
had shown itself not in Henry Irving's sons but in Joseph Henry Irving's
daughter.

But Brieux was for the few, a despised minority ridiculed as "a set of
men with long hair and low collars, women with short hair and low heels".
Those years, as E. F. Benson's novels declare, witnessed a revival of romance.
It could be discerned in Town. It could not be avoided on tour—and the
real glamour of the stage was there.

Year by year the list of travelling companies lengthened. Its titles mostly
began either with *The Girl From*, which meant musical comedy, or with

The Girl Who, which meant real-life melodrama, and their pictorial posters enlivened hoardings in every town and city, though none could boast an expanse of coloured paper to compare with the one which stretched all the way from St. Mary-le-Strand to St. Clement Danes.

There always had been tours from the professional theatre's very beginnings, though it was left to Irving to discover (what Charles Kean barely knew) how the provinces could replenish the treasury. As a rule he let the Lyceum in August in order to visit Birmingham, Manchester and Liverpool, where his financial rewards were such as to enable him to spend very lavishly upon sumptuous productions in Town. The lesson became still more valuable when fashion shunned East Strand with its brick-dust, its disturbance of layer upon layer of the dead's home-life from wallpaper and floor-coverings to holed saucepans and broken kitchen-stoves, its attar of limp cabbages bequeathed by generation after generation of cooks to kitchen stairs now embarrassingly exposed, and its still more noisome horrors.

Vast multitudes of rats, after some midnight conclave of dog-and-vixen-leaders, issued from their drains in broad daylight, and on their way to the river held up the traffic in the Strand where the horses of hansoms, growlers, carters' vans and buses backed to let the legions of the sewers pass. Even without that, the dank smell of cement-mixers would have been enough to form a zareba before the portico of the "dark" Lyceum.

In such drab nights and days, when the solid wilderness that had been the setting of Harvey's education as an actor disintegrated into refuse and rubble, the provinces formed a golden refuge from the grey Strand. Midlanders and Northerners took Irving to their hearts. Long before this Alexander and Tree regularly kept their appointments in the provinces, no matter how rich the run of luck they broke in Town, every summer. To the actor-manager who had no West End theatre of his own the Theatres Royal and Grand in a far-flung circle up the shires were home, and London a place never quite sure whether it liked to be visited.

Even Waller found his West End public hard to please. He failed at the Imperial in the February of 1904 in a version of *Ruy Blas* by John Davidson, called *A Queen's Romance*. Mrs. Patrick Campbell played the queen. When critics complained that the histrionic method of the two lovers was absolutely distinct, she gave as the reason that while she spoke her blank verse to Waller he "addressed his blank verse to the universe".

Ever since John Davidson, writing to her in 1901 from Streatham about *The Second Mrs. Tanqueray*, had likened her Paula to "an opal of many hues and lustres, with stains of life and wounds of passion through which the disastrous fires glow that shatter it in the end", these two had been firm friends. He made a version of Racine's *Phèdre* for her. It was never acted. In Town it might or might not please the critics and nobody else. On tour it was not wanted at all. Let us over-sentimentalize the Edwardians and regret their passing wistfully, without forgetting that as playgoers their taste was childish. The leaders of the theatre sought refuge more and more in the provinces.

In the October of 1904 Martin Harvey played Birmingham at the same time as Irving. They stayed at the same hotel and the faithful disciple went respectfully to listen to his chief's views about what he ought to do and how he ought to do it. People in general were losing the old veneration. How changed life became for Irving when his own temple closed its doors against him can be told from a music-hall comedian's tale.

When Edwin Barwick came behind the scenes at the Broadway, New Cross, to be introduced as the writer of pantomimes, Irving said, "I've heard of Mr. Barwick. How do you do?" This was not "too effusive", so the author thought, as he began to wonder whether his skill in mimicry told against him. The manager, "laughing heartily" while declaring the Governor to be the dearest fellow in the world, explained that one member of the company had asked, "Governor, have you seen a man called Barwick give an imitation of you?" All the tired lion said was, "No, no, I haven't."

As a practical joke—this at a time when Martin Harvey felt such awe for his old chief that he could not speak to him without stammering— other young members of the company were urged to ask the same questio "So you see," said the manager, still laughing heartily, "when the Governor said to you, 'I've heard of Mr. Barwick,' he meant in his queer way that he had heard of nothing else for the last three weeks." The *Entr'acte Annual* published this story in 1905 with an advertisement of George Leyton's engagement to sing "Boys Of The Chelsea School" at the Lyceum.

How strongly the players themselves loved the romantic tradition, how ardently the regular playgoers supported them and how completely London's taste had changed, an ambitious venture at the Adelphi proved. Otho Stuart and Oscar Asche formed a company of Bensonians for *The Prayer Of The Sword*, a poetical drama of mediaeval Italy by J. B. Fagan; *Tristram And Iseult*, by Comyns Carr; and *The Virgin Goddess*, a Greek tragedy by Rudolph Besier.

The last pointed the moral. In his book Asche describes the tumult of applause. When the fireproof curtain was down the audience stayed, "So up it went again, and on we all went for a call, over and over again." At the end the people were discussing it in the street. The Press proclaimed it the greatest play for a century and it ran for five weeks to miserable business. It met the same wild enthusiasm in the provinces, and in Australia, and the same bad houses.

"Heartbreak House" was the name of the theatre for many in those dreary years half-way through Edward's reign when the business of pleasure slumped. Those whose main interest was in profit and loss knew all about *the* depression—none spoke of it as "yet another depression", but out-and-out romantics never interest themselves in the life around them.

Without asking the advice of financial experts (which would be fatal anyway) Martin Harvey chose this time for his first production of *Hamlet*, his first venture into Shakespeare under his own management. Now that the greatest of all dramatic rôles was to come into the same repertoire as The Rat, the opinion of Lamb on this very point deserves special attention :

"I mean no disrespect to any actor, but the sort of pleasure which Shakespeare's plays give in the acting seems to me not at all to differ from that which the audience receive from those of other writers; and *they being in themselves essentially so different from all others*, I must conclude that there is something in the nature of acting which levels all distinctions."

The truth might be that the actor-manager of romantic mould had something of Gilbert's heavy dragoon about him :

Flavour of Hamlet—the Stranger, a touch of him—
Little of Manfred (but not very much of him)—
Beadle of Burlington—Richardson's show—
Mr. Micawber and Madame Tussaud.

That flavour of *Hamlet* was essential. So four actor-managers, coming to Town in the spring of 1905, agreed at once. All that they lacked were those old playgoers whose attitude had been, "Better not see *Hamlet* at all than once or twice."

The new playgoers showed the influence of the argumentative eighteen-nineties when everything cancelled out and nothing added up. If H. B. Irving and Martin Harvey had been prize-fighters there could have been no sterner desire for a decided verdict. The pleasure in the comparison was between the cold, hard, adult mood of the one and the impulsive, emotional adolescence of the other. Twenty Hamlets will not complete *Hamlet*, and the more there are to be seen the greater should be our enjoyment. But as long as the tussle between the old puritans and the new puritans lasted all contrary things would be poison and antidote.

No intelligent person could then admit to liking both Sydney Carton and Dick Dudgeon. Anyone who might say that he did would be classed with unprincipled scoundrels. Consequently those who praised H. B. Irving's Hamlet at the Adelphi in the April of 1905 felt bound to feel critical towards Martin Harvey's at the Lyric towards the end of May.

"He is an emotional Hamlet. His eye is wild, his voice hoarse and his hair untidy," wrote one critic who made it plain that these things excited his disapproval. In his view Stephen Phillips was not an altogether satisfactory ghost. He made his entrances and exits "after the manner of some full-fed modern taking a final stroll round the garden before turning in for the night".

It may be doubted whether the new Hamlet was altogether understood. With this performance began a glimmering that the tragedy was not individual but a play. When such commanding presences as Forbes Robertson's strode through the court of Denmark their plain duty was to put Claudius under close arrest pending trial for regicide. Turn that personal grandeur into wistful youth and then the overwhelming magnitude of his task makes the background alive, credible. The king and queen put on majesty, they assert themselves as characters equally resolved upon fulfilling their own destiny.

The time would come when Claudius and Gertrude, capturing all the sympathy, would convey across the footlight their view of Hamlet as a thoroughly unpleasant, troublesome, peace-destroying step-child in an otherwise well-regulated household. In the London of Edward VII the possibility of acting the play in any such manner had not occurred to anyone, and for most playgoers the new interpretation had already, at its first step, travelled too far from the High Roman manner to be intelligible.

While at Manchester Martin Harvey read the news that the life of his old chief had ended. Of that last performance of Irving's career the episodes have become legendary. How he played Becket unfalteringly to the last line, "Into Thy hands, Oh God, into Thy hands," has often been told. There is one thing more to be added from a hint let fall by Martin Harvey, who had heard in his youth at the Lyceum that Irving as a beginner in London had fallen deeply in love with Nelly Moore.

She was an actress of great charm who joined the Haymarket Company in the eighteen-sixties. At the age of twenty-four she saw her name for the first time in big letters. In the January of 1869 she had begun to play leading parts in one or other of the pieces in the triple bills. Irving arrived at her house one morning with a gift of violets, and heard she had died. Martin Harvey and Miss de Silva believed he thought of her whenever these lines of Tennyson's tragedy were spoken:

> BECKET.   There was a little fair-hair'd Norman maid
> Lived in my mother's house: if Rosamond is
> The world's rose, as her name imports her—she
> Was the world's lily.
> JOHN OF SALISBURY. Ay, and what of her?
> BECKET. She died of leprosy.
> JOHN OF SALISBURY.   I know not why
> You call these old things back again, my lord.
> BECKET. The drowning man, they say, remembers all
> The chances of his life, just ere he dies.

These were among Irving's last words before he dressed, stopped to sign a schoolboy's autograph album at the stage-door, drove to his hotel, sat down in the lobby and there died.

Next Week,

For 6 Nights and Matinee, Saturday, Oct. 21st,

Mr. GEORGE EDWARDES'

COMPANY,

INCLUDING

Miss MARIE STUDHOLME,

As "LADY BETTY."

In the NEW MUSICAL PLAY,

LADY MADCAP

From the Prince of Wales' Theatre, London.

MONDAY & SATURDAY NIGHTS, OCT. 9th & 14th,

THE

MERCHANT OF VENICE.

Shylock .. .. HENRY IRVING.

TUESDAY & FRIDAY NIGHTS OCT. 10th & 13th,

BECKET.

By ALFRED, LORD TENNYSON. Adapted for the Stage by HENRY IRVING

Becket (Chancellor and Archbishop) .. HENRY IRVING

WEDNESDAY NIGHT, OCT. 11th, (Only Time).

LOUIS XI.

By CASIMIR DELAVIGNE.

Adapted and Arranged by DION BOUCICAULT.

Louis XI. .. .. HENRY IRVING

THURSDAY NIGHT, OCT. 12th, (Only Time).

KING RENE'S DAUGHTER

FOLLOWED BY

THE BELLS.

Mathias .. .. HENRY IRVING.

Programme of Theatre Royal, Bradford, the week of Irving's death

There is no moment so significant in the history of the modern theatre. That centuries are fictions and their endings a statistical illusion has already been proved. But when these have been shown to be fit to impress nobody there still remain, as though to impel belief in what the calendar registers, unavoidable signs of great change and decay. Victoria's death had shut history with a thud of gloom. Now there sounded another note of finality.

That profile, as well known throughout the world as any stamped or minted, became in a glance of the newspaper-reader's eye one with the historic past. The measure of Irving's greatness is in his remark when foreseeing his own death—"They will do their duty", meaning that he would be buried in the Abbey. He spoke with assurance which nobody could or would wish to question.

Here was an actor of a stature to be set beside Wellington and Nelson. Such greatness, overruling all argument that like should be likened to like, meant that he ranked above all others whose fame had been won in the immediate past except the most beloved of novelists and poets, Dickens and Tennyson. The arts had come into their own and the theatre among them.

But now the immense achievement was over. There would be other stage knighthoods, but very little likelihood of Abbey burial for any other player. Of that everyone was aware. There was to be one of the last funerals of vast impressiveness. The new age would show itself to be different by refusing to be impressed by funerals. Irving's was not affected.

The tour of *Hamlet* was playing Manchester that October. The Martin Harveys were resolved to attend the service; finding they could not return to the theatre until too late an hour for the curtain to rise on so long a play, they changed the bill to *The Only Way* instead. On the return journey they shared a compartment with Ellen Terry. She seemed wildly elated.

She jumped about, said Miss de Silva, "like a cat on hot bricks", while they were subdued and inclined to have red noses. The pair of unflinching romantics yielded to emotion direct. The actress who became more and more the soul of comedy as she left the Lyceum tradition behind reacted violently against direct expression of emotion. Did they understand one another?

In life the cleft between romance and modern life widened. The next morning Martin Harvey opened his paper to find an article, by a writer of some claim to dignity, which found fault with the change of play for some supposedly artistic reasons, as though people who had to travel from Manchester to London and back in one day had no concern with time. But the motive behind this "attack" indicates something deeper than that. The "Manchester School" of the theatre was very much inclined to elevate the everyday and matter-of-fact at the expense of any player who "dressed up".

Before Irving's inspiring presence leaves this chronicle some more

souvenirs may be snatched from his waste-paper basket. In that wooden box
of relics half-a-dozen scraps of corrected galley-proofs are all that remain
of a speech at the opening of an art exhibition apparently at Toynbee Hall.
Accounts from the *Chiswick Press* reveal how his speeches were prepared:

"October 19, 1904—Printing six copies of Speech made by Sir
Henry Irving at Sunderland. 12 pages f'cap 4to. Printed one side only
with corrections and alterations. Antique laid paper for same. Pressing,
cutting and fastening up in single leaves with plain grey wrapper paper
top and bottom. £2 15s.

"October 25, 1904. Reprinting 50 copies of Sunderland Speech.
12 pages f'cap 4to, printed one side only with antique laid paper for
same, pressing, cutting and fastening up in single leaves (no covers)
16s. 6d."

The builder's bill for work done at the Lyceum in 1904 includes "to
getting out and carting away one load of rubbish from basement", making
cases for packing properties, and rehanging large gate in Burleigh Street.
The ironmonger charges 5s. 6d. for repairing the head of Becket's crozier
to order. A gunsmith claims thirty shillings for revolver and pistol, and a
bookseller four shillings for a copy of "Early English Pronunciation".
Other sums have to be sent to that romantic spot, "The Cottage, Adelphi
Arches", where limelight and coloured fires were provided.

To the present generation the name of Auguste Van Biene conjures
up music-hall memories of an old 'cellist in the sketch called *The Broken
Melody*. A letter in this apple-box reveals him in an ambitious mood. On
the eve of a long tour in South Africa, he asks Bram Stoker, "Now will you
propose to the chief if he will let me do them *The Bells*, *The Lyons Mail*
and *Waterloo*." Sir Henry sent his regrets.

Demands of all kinds are made on his purse. "£10 sent" is written on
Sir Sidney Lee's private appeal on behalf of Shakespeare's Birthplace
Trust. The appeal of a provincial swimming club also appears to have
been successful, and a penniless old playgoer's prayer for passes is marked
"Sent".

Lyceum accounts are complicated enough, but the bulkier packages
are concerned with travel. Railway agents offer to prepare cold food in
hampers on a long journey: they end by telegraphing that a dining-car will
be added to the train at Rugby. In 1904, when there was a transfer from
Hammersmith to Kennington, the Property Bill included drinks to staff
night and morning, "6 clay pipes", "1 oz. Bird's Eye Tobacco", "potatoes
(for farce)", and two lots of Fuller's earth—to be used as snow in *The Bells*.

"Takings" occupy a lot of space with returns from dress circle, pit,
amphitheatre, gallery, and final returns, on the forms of theatres all over
the country. Beneath these are documents of the American tours—plans

M

of cabins, saloon passenger lists, telegrams, and hasty calculations on scraps of paper, followed by supers' salary lists for "Merchant Boys" and "Louis Pages" in Indianapolis, Columbus, Dayton and Toledo.

Insurance policies, appeals to members of the company to be at Euston in good time, the expenses sheets of agents with a passion for cigars, all jumbled together, recall the nervous wear and tear undergone by the faithful Bram Stoker at the time. And among them are notes concerning his blood-and-thunder novel, "Dracula".

Still the bottom layers have yet to be reached. One bundle consists entirely of letters from applicants for tickets of admittance to Westminster Abbey for funeral service. "No" is pencilled on many. One writer's excuse for his request is that he is in London on holiday. Another asks as a brother professional—he is a member of the *Cauliflower Joe* company on tour. And another pleads, "It will be a thing to remember all my life and if I live as long as he did that will be for 56 years longer."

This particular phase must end with a flashback . . . the jingle of a hansom that always passes the Lyceum portico from the stage-door of Drury Lane, the pince-nez of a prematurely-aged face leaning forwards for a fleeting glimpse, the voice of Dante murmuring something about the making of history where the columns in Wellington Street stand; the caustic, bitter, heartbroken comment of surmise about the future of what was his theatre. He never foresaw—a dance-hall.

"I was for fourteen years under him," Sir John wrote in an article which *The Times* published in 1938, "and was never nearer to him in one sense than the veriest boy in the gallery of his theatre. But because, through his art, I was unconsciously brought face to face with his soul, his great enduring, steadfast soul, I adored him.

"For the same reason the English people adored him; and it is for his steadfast soul rather than his rare accomplishments that his name will be imperishable. Though his voice is still, we see proof on every side that his memory is hallowed even more deeply than when he lived. One recalls the words: 'When silence falls on such a voice some everlasting echo still haunts the world.'"

CHAPTER IV

IRVING'S MANTLE

VACUUMS, the armchair scientist tells, exist but to be filled. Actor-managers laboured under the same delusion when the leadership of the stage fell vacant. None would fill Irving's empty place; the very essence of him was that he was unique. But in a world ruled by kings and queens, presidents and prime ministers, commanders-in-chiefs and hereditary grand dukes, greatness always inspired feelings about the divine or democratic right of somebody to step into somebody else's shoes.

That, declared the spiteful, was how Tree got his knighthood, which caused murmurs of disgust at the time though approved by posterity. But however gifted the buffoon, nobody then wanted to see him in the chair of the master. Irving's place could not be filled.

With his mantle there could be some sort of legacy. If too big to be worn by one, it was vast enough to be shared by several. This was how the hereditary principle worked out in the next few years, with rivalry especially vigorous between Martin Harvey and Harry Irving, one with a claim of so many years' service in the temple and the other with the right of blood royal.

They took up the purple where it had fallen—on tour. They had impressive triumphs in the lost leader's old parts. Harvey with the Corsicans and Harry with the Lyonnais, bringing to life in the new century dramas that had been considered dead before the end of the old. It is all very eloquent of the lingering *fin de siècle* spirit which still caused poets to throw their lives away, Phillips by drink and Davidson by drowning, amid the bustle of the brave new world.

Not that the theatrical Irvingites (as distinct from the Irvingites of the apostolic church in Gordon Square, quite another brotherhood) could be considered degenerate by any possible twist of that popular word's meanings. Neither the son nor the disciple clung fervently to the old ways of living. When it came to taking full advantage of what the new ways had to offer, actor-managers under Edward were more enterprising than the rest of the community. While merchant princes still clung to grey toppers and four-in-hands, the emperors of make-believe learnt to handle the steering-wheel.

Martin Harvey one morning entered his home in St. John's Wood with the air of an excited, over-venturesome and rather apprehensive schoolboy. His wife came with him to the door and there saw his first car. From now on, while the Company went by rail, they would go by road.

They joined that ever-increasing band of travellers who were discovering the King's Highway.

"They kicks up a dust and they spoils all the scenery," said others besides the stone-cracker in the song, because it became rapidly plain that the countryside the motorist was so keen to see would not be there long for anyone to see. Old landlords of decaying inns did not want to serve him, farmers claimed compensation every time they could hold up a dead chicken, mothers rushed for their children and screamed, but more wheels and still more wheels rolled over roads that had been deserted ever since the steam locomotive sent out of business the last stage-coach.

The Profession took to "the motor" from the start. Advertising agents, conspiring with picture-postcard photographers, soon made the public aware how many of their idols had taken to driving in emulation of Harry Tate, who was so early an enthusiast that he held for life the registration T8.

To some a new pastime had been invented. When Seymour Hicks, Ellaline Terriss, baby and car posed before the camera together, the picture suggested a jaunt. To the Martin Harveys the new car had its work cut out every Sunday for months. In time the vision of enthusiastic managers perched on high seats in the open air would take its place besides the glimpse of Crummles as he drove his singular ponies. But round about 1905 Phaeton himself possessed no very dissimilar glory to this new brand of gentlemen of the road.

Yet if the manager-motorist had read the signs aright he would have seen in his internal combustion engine a twin of that other reviled machine responsible for "the flicks" and "the movies". In the machine-age veneration for the stage was vanishing. The new outlook on life was taking hold of the provinces even where plays prospered. The old pride in the local theatre had gone.

Think of what the drama had been to the chief cities of Scotland and then read a twentieth-century account of Edinburgh which makes no mention of Lyceum or Royal, unless it is intended in the phrase, "hotels, clubs, warehouses, cafés, picture houses and so forth". Martin Harvey was combating that. Wherever he went the drama again spelt romance—even to that seaside theatre whose foyer was filled, according to Miss de Silva's own lively description, with penny-in-the-slot machines of *What the butler saw* (humble parent of the cinema) and rotating showcases of highly coloured postcards showing large ladies gripped by large crabs behind.

Welcome was assured everywhere. They would sit by the window in the homes Mrs. Harvey made in hotels and look out upon scenes that had all become familiar. At Liverpool they watched, over tea, the queues lengthening. Pittites and galleryites stood two by two far back into the great fun fair. Like children the players at the window marked progress as new arrivals took the tail-end farther back from side-show to side-show. "And now," cried Miss de Silva at last, "they are at the fleas."

They had no fear of (what good showmen fear above fire and flood) empty benches. Their main concern was with Martin Harvey's health. He had constant colds that threatened to develop into pneumonia. "I spent most of my life fighting those colds," says Miss de Silva, "and when a cold was going away, he got gout. Think of those dear little boots, those lovely boots he wore in *A Cigarette-Maker's Romance*. Then imagine what it was to get them on or take them off with gout. Yet he would make light of any physical strain. We were always up at 7.30." The morning was spent in rehearsal. Actors who joined the Company were astonished at the way he worked, and not altogether pleased by it. "Nothing but rehearsals," said those who left.

Although musicial comedy and melodrama predominated on tour with leading ladies and gentlemen who openly boasted of being unknown in the West End and famous everywhere else, romance had several renowned champions. Laurence Irving in his own plays, *Bonnie Dundee* and *Richard Lovelace*, adopted that style for the time being. H. B. Irving toured in 1906 with a repertory including *Paolo And Francesca, Charles I* and *The Lyons Mail*, shipped them to New York, added *The Bells* to them in Chicago, and then resumed his English tour with *Louis XI*.

The Compton Comedy Company held its own. Benson not only did that with a North Company, a South Company, a Mr. and Mrs. Benson Company, but kept giving out shoots; Matheson Lang, in the January of 1907, had won praises for his Othello at Manchester. Rivalry increased each season and yet Martin Harvey remained foremost. When *The Only Way* toured in 1906 the Vengeance was played by Frances Ivor, with whom he had once shared a good notice for their acting in *The Lyons Mail* at the Lyceum. She was with the company when it was at the Camden Theatre in that region where two of Irving's acolytes had walked together every day.

For his season in Town Martin Harvey picked a play by the authors of *The Breed Of The Treshams*. The new work was a farce in costume. As others have discovered at other times, the public will take its romance seriously or not at all. *Boy O'Carrol* was enjoyed more by the actor as a rapparee trooper and his wife as an Irish boy than by their solemn audiences.

But the play has its place in theatrical history, for with this the life of the Imperial came almost to its end. Not that it gave up without a struggle. Half a dozen plays were tried out there in the spring of 1907, mostly at private performances. When Granville-Barker wrote a tragedy of modern life which bore some resemblance to a recent political sensation—a career ruined by the hiss, "sex"—the Lord Chamberlain refused it a licence; the Stage Society presented this work, at the Imperial on the afternoon of November 26, under the title of *Waste*.

So ended Lady de Bathe's handsome new theatre. In Charles B. Cochran's view:

"The ground landlords treated her badly, selling the site over her head to the Wesleyans, and, in spite of the huge sums expended on it, the Imperial Theatre was razed to the ground to make room for the building which now stands on the site. An amusing feature of the negotiation was the resolute refusal of the Wesleyan leader to meet the actress to discuss terms. Perhaps a wholesome fear of her power of persuasion deterred him."

Erroll Sherson thought it likely that the astute finance committee of the Methodists made a good deal. The theatre was sold to the company owning the Royal Albert Music-Hall, Canning Town. Experts took it down carefully, "numbering all the pieces, and re-erected it as the Music-Hall of Dockland".

CHAPTER V

FREAK TOUR

FOR his next Spaniard, Martin Harvey turned to Échegaray. Ten years had passed since he acted with H. B. Irving in *Mariana*, and still the leading dramatist of Madrid was unknown in London though accepted in New York. Shaw held up for praise an author who was a man of the world, a cabinet minister before he became a political exile. This should impress nobody in a country whose dramatic literature includes two works by prime ministers which possess so little merit that in order to keep our self-respect we have done our best to forget them.

Échegaray seems remarkable as plagiarist at first reading. His *Son Of Don Juan*, with a libertine's diseased heir who cries out for the sun, reads like a free rendering from Ibsen. That sets up a suspicious state of mind which observes a resemblance to Maëterlinck's *Monna Vanna* in the Spanish *El Gran Galeoto*. You note that each plot has practically the same *dénouement* and later you learn that the Spanish play precedes the other by nearly twenty years. Both are tales of innocent, chivalrous love, basely wronged by accusation; in one the man responds with "Let nobody touch this woman. She is mine," and in the other the woman says, "Go, you must not take what is mine."

So little has been written about Échegaray that he needs to be introduced. He lived from 1833 to 1916. He wrote his first play in 1877. *El Gran Galeoto* was written in 1881, translated into *The Great Galleoto* for a London publisher in 1895, and adapted by C. F. Nirdlinger for the New York stage in 1908 as *The World And His Wife*.

In the prologue, Don Ernesto, the poet, decides to make the crowd the hero of a drama. He turns to the Inferno, where Paolo and Francesca read how Galleoto was employed as go-between by Lancelot and Guineveve. The gossiping many are Galleoto the Great.

In Act I Ernesto is the cherished friend of Julian and his wife. A slanderer speaks ill of this relationship and is challenged to a duel by the husband. In Act II Teodora visits Ernesto to beg him not to challenge the slanderer. Before she can leave, Julian is brought in wounded. Seeing his wife there, he struggles to his feet in order to strike her, and falls senseless. In Act III Ernesto kills the slanderer and comes to bid Teodora farewell. When everyone makes it plain that they are held guilty, he cries, "Let nobody touch this woman. She is mine."

At the Theatre Royal, Birmingham, in the December of 1908, Martin Harvey played Don Ernesto in Nirdlinger's version, now called *Slander*, with Miss de Silva as the wife and Mary Rorke as the aunt of evil tongue.

With this they challenged that most popular of all our winter entertainments, the Christmas pantomime. And now, since "tours" mean so much in these chapters, the need arises to explain just what they were. Here then is the list which passengers in "theatricals" read in *The Referee* on their way to Crewe or Darlington on Sunday, January 28, 1909; here is the full-blooded national diet of Shakespeare (including three Benson companies), vaudevillized nursery-tales, melodrama, musical comedies (no revues for another year or two), grand opera and a minority that might be termed merely plays:

ON TOUR

Aladdin (Constant). Jan. 25th, O.H., Burnley; Feb. 1st, O.H., Burnley.

Aladdin (Dottridge and Longdon). Feb. 1st, Alexandra, Hull.

Aladdin (Glenville and Osmond). Jan. 25th, Vict., Broughton; Feb. 1st, Royal, Woolwich.

Aladdin (James Kiddie's). Jan. 25th, Royal, Hyde; Feb. 1st, Royal, Leigh.

Aladdin (Thomson's). Jan. 25th, Pontardulais: Abercarn.

Aladdin (Jazon and Nightingale). Feb. 1st, P.O.W., Nuneaton.

At Cripple Creek. Feb. 1st, Prince's, Portsmouth.

At Duty's Call. Jan. 25th, Royal, Leicester; Feb. 1st, Royal, Pontypool.

Babes in the Wood, The (J. Gar Kiddie). Jan. 25th, P.O.W., Grimsby.

Babes in the Wood, The. Jan. 25th, Royal, Dudley.

Babes in the Wood (Levy and Cardwell). Feb. 1st, Royal, Stockport.

Beggar Girl's Wedding, The. Jan. 25th, Metropole, Birmingham.

Benson, F. R. (N.). Jan. 25th, Drill Hall, Durham; Feb. 1st, Grand, West Hartlepool.

Benson, F. R. (S.). Jan. 28th, Pontypridd; Feb. 1st, Maesteg: Treherbert.

Benson, Mr. & Mrs. F. R. Jan. 25th, Royal, Bournemouth; Feb. 1st, Grand, Southampton.

Bondman, The (Croke's). Jan. 25th, Royal, Sth. Shields; Feb. 1st, Metropole, Gateshead.

Brewster's Millions (Hutchison). Jan. 25th, O.H., Southport; Feb. 1st, Grand, Derby.

Broken Heart, A. Jan. 25th, Grand, Radcliffe; Feb. 1st, P.O.W., Salford.

Bulmer, Mr. Jan. 25th, Royal, Leigh.

Butterflies. Jan. 25th, Royal, Bolton; Feb. 1st, O.H., Belfast.

Carl Rosa Opera Co. Jan. 25th, Grand, Derby.

Cassidy, J. Rice. Jan. 25th, Metropole, Abertillery; Feb. 1st, Royal, Aston.

Catch of the Season, The. Feb. 1st, Royal, Bath.

Christian, The (Croke's) (N.). Jan. 25th, Grand, W. Hartlepool; Feb. 1st, Royal, Middlesboro'.

Christian, The (Croke's) (S.). Jan. 25th, Royal, Smethwick; Feb. 1st, Royal, Preston.

Christian, The (Croke's, (M.). Jan 28th, Loughboro'; Feb. 1st, Kidderminster: Stafford.

Cinderella. Jan. 25th, Royal, Seaham Harbour.

Cinderella. Feb. 1st, Royal, Worthing.

Cingalee, The. Feb. 1st, Grand, Swansea.

Claudian. Jan. 25th, Royalty, Barrow; Feb. 1st, Eden, Bishop Auckland.

Compton Comedy. Jan. 25th, Royalty, Chester; Feb. 1st, Lyceum, Sheffield.

Conscience of a Judge. Jan. 25th, Star, Swansea; Feb. 1st, Palace, Bordesley.

Country Girl in London, A. Jan. 25th, P.O.W., Nuneaton; Feb. 1st, Royal, Ilkeston.

Crimes of Paris, The. Feb. 1st, County, Bedford.

Dairymaids, The. Jan. 25th, Grand, Wolverhampton; Feb. 1st, O.H., Cheltenham.

Dairymaids, The (Macdonald's). Jan. 25th, Paisley, Paisley; Feb. 1st, H.M., Barrow.

Dare-Devil Dorothy. Jan. 25th, Royal, Edmonton; Feb. 1st, Pier, Eastbourne.

Diana of Dobson's. Jan. 25th, Royal, Bath; Feb. 1st, Royal, Chatham.

Dick Whittington (Dottridge). Feb. 1st, Castle, Stockton.

D'Oyly Carte Opera. Jan. 25th, Grand, Croydon; Feb. 1st, Royal, Portsmouth.

Early Worm, The. Feb. 1st, Royal, Torquay.

Eve of Her Wedding, The. Jan. 25th, Albert, Brighouse; Feb. 1st, Colosseum, Oldham.

Face at the Window, The. Jan 25th, Royal, Bilston.

Flag Lieutenant, The. Jan. 25th, Norwich; Feb. 1st, Royal, Hanley.

For Love—and the King. Jan. 25th, Grand, Chorley; Feb. 1st, Queen's, Longton.

From Shop Girl to Duchess. Jan. 25th, Lyric, Hammersmith, S.W.

From Slave to Princess. At Cripple Creek. Jan. 25th, Pier, Eastbourne.

Gay Gordons, The (N.). Jan. 25th, Grand, Falkirk; Feb. 1st, Paisley, Paisley.

Gay Gordons, The. Jan. 25th, Royalty, Glasgow.

Geoffrey Langdon's Wife. Jan. 25th, Gaiety, Burnley; Feb. 1st, Royal, Tyldesley.

Girl's Cross Roads, A. Jan. 25th, Osborne, Manchester; Feb. 1st, Junction, Manchester.

Girls of Gottenberg, The (Dance). Jan. 25th, Royal, Portsmouth; Feb. 1st, R., Plymouth.

Girl With the Angel Face, The. Jan. 25th, Prince's, Portsmouth.

Glossop-Harris, Florence, Repertory. Jan 25th, O.H., Londonderry; Feb. 1st, Grand, Lancaster.

Greed of Gold, The. Jan. 25th, Royal, Macclesfield; Feb. 1st, Royal, North Shields.

Havana. Jan. 25th, King's, Glasgow; Feb. 1st, King's, Glasgow.

Her Forbidden Marriage. Feb. 1st, H.M., Dundee.

Her Love Against the World. Jan. 25th, Lyceum, Govan; Feb. 1st, Palace, Newcastle-on-Tyne.

Her Nameless Child (?) Feb. 1st, Lyric, Hammersmith.

His House in Order. Jan. 25th, Royal, Hull.

His Majesty's Guests. Feb. 1st, Lyceum, Govan.

His Sister's Honour. Jan. 25th, Garrick, Hereford; Feb. 1st, Royal, Margate.

Home, Sweet Home. Jan. 25th, Royal, Stockport; Feb. 1st, Hippo., Todmorden.

Humpty Dumpty (Elliston). Feb. 1st, King's, Sunderland.

Idols (Hutchison). Jan. 25th. O.H., Cheltenham.

Jack and the Beanstalk (A. S. Smith). Feb. 1st, Sutton-in-Ashfield.

Jack the Giant Killer. Feb. 1st, Court, Wigan.

Jack the Giant Killer. Jan. 25th, O.H., Leicester; Feb. 1st, O.H., Leicester.

King and Unknown Woman, The. Jan. 25th, Royal, Jarrow; Feb. 1st, Royal, Darlington.

Lady Frederick (Hutchison). Jan. 25th, Grand, Oldham.

Leah Kleschna. Jan. 25th, Colne.

Lighthouse Robbery, The. Feb. 1st, Royal, Batley.

Little Breadwinner, The. Jan. 25th, Mansfield; Feb. 1st, Colosseum, Oldham.

Little Red Riding Hood. Jan. 25th, Colosseum, Leeds.

Love of the Princess, The. Jan. 25th, Alexandra, Hull.

Luck of Roaring Camp, The. Jan. 25th, Star, Liverpool; Feb. 1st, Alexandra Sheffield.

Maclaren's, Ian, Repertory. Jan. 25th, Century, Motherwell.

Man and Wife. Jan. 25th, Queen's, Longton; Feb. 1st, Royal, Wolverhampton.

Married to the Wrong Man. Feb. 1st, Century, Motherwell.

Martin Harvey. Jan. 25th, Lyceum, Sheffield; Feb. 1st, Grand, Hull.

Merry Widow, The. Jan. 25th, Shakespeare, Clapham, S.W.

Message from Mars, A. Jan. 25th, H.M., Dundee; Feb. 1st, Royalty, Glasgow.

Miss Hook of Holland (Dance's). Jan. 25th, Royal, Dewsbury; Feb. 1st, Barrow.

Mollison, William, Repertory. Feb. 1st, H.M., Aberdeen.

Moody-Manners Opera (A). Jan. 25th, O.H., Cork; Feb. 1st, O.H., Cork.

Moody-Manners Opera (B). Jan. 25th, Birkenhead; Feb. 1st, Assembly Rooms Gt. Malvern.

Mother Goose (Pilkington). Jan. 25th, Lyceum, Ipswich.

Mother Goose (Elliston). Feb. 1st, O.H., Southport.

Mrs. Dot (Hutchison). Jan. 28th, Bury St. Edmunds.

My Mimosa Maid. Jan. 25th, Castle Stockton; Feb. 1st, Royal, Bolton.

New Housemaid, The. Jan. 25th, Royal, Belfast.

Nihilist, The. Jan. 25th, Abertillery.

No Wedding Bells for Her. Jan. 25th, Sutton-in-Ashfield; Feb. 1st, Mansfield.

Old Folks at Home, The. Jan. 25th, Metropole, Gateshead; Feb. 1st, Royal, Seaham Harbour.

Old Home, The. Jan. 25th, Royal, Barry Dock; Feb. 1st, Treherbert: Maesteg.

Peter's Mother (Hutchison.) Jan. 25th, Royal, Worcester.

Power of the King, The. Jan. 25th, P.H., Mountain Ash; Feb. 1st, Palace, Ebbw Vale.

Prodigal Son, The (Croke's). Jan. 25th, Royal, Torquay; Feb. 1st, Royal, Exeter.

Prodigal Son, The (Croke's) (M.). Jan. 28th, Newtown: Welshpool.

Prodigal Son, The (Day's). Jan. 25th, Ayr; Feb. 1st, Royal, Coatbridge.

Raffles. Feb. 1st, D.P., Eastbourne.

Robinson Crusoe (Benet's). Jan. 25th, Royalty, Llanelly.

Robinson Crusoe. Jan. 25th, Alhambra, Stourbridge.

Robinson Crusoe (Lintone and Hunter). Feb. 1st, Royal, Crook.

Rollicking Rory. Jan. 25th, O.H., Workington; Feb. 1st, Standard, Hetton.

Royal Divorce, A. Jan. 25th, Royal, Worthing; Feb. 1st, Metropole, Devonport.

Sailor's Wedding, The. Jan. 25th, Royal, Ashton-under-Lyne; Feb. 1st, S., Clapham

Secret Service. Jan. 25th, Royal, Chatham.

Send Him Victorious. Jan. 25th, Royal, Stratford, E.; Feb. 1st, Royal, Edmonton.

Sergeant Brue. Jan. 28th, Stafford; Feb. 1st, Crystal Palace.

Sign of the Cross, The. Jan. 25th, County, Bedford; Feb. 1st, New, Cambridge.

Silver King, The. Jan. 25th, Hippodrome, Todmorden; Feb. 1st, Metropole Glasgow.

Soldier's Honour, A. Jan. 25th, Pavilion, Abertillery; Feb. 1st, Hippo., W. Brom wich.

tarr's, Harry, Repertory. Jan. 25th, Central, Northwich.
unday. Feb. 1st, Royal, Hull.
earle, Edmund, Repertory. Feb. 1st, Alhambra, Stourbridge.
hief, The (Bodkin's). Jan. 28th, Westbury: Warminster: Trowbridge; Feb. 1st, Frome: Wells: Shepton Mallet.
oddles. Jan. 25th, D.P., Eastbourne.
om Jones (Courtneidge). Jan. 25th, Royal, Merthyr Tydvil; Feb. 1st, Grand, Oldham.
urner's, J. W., Opera. Jan. 25th, O.H., Coventry.
wo Lancashire Lasses in London. Jan. 25th, Court, Warrington.
wo Little Drummer Boys. Feb. 1st, Star, Swansea.
wo Little Vagabonds. Jan. 25th, Palace, Newcastle.
yrant, The. Jan. 25th, New, Bargoed; Feb. 1st, Royal, Tonypandy.
ictim of Villainy, A. Jan. 25th, Pardoe's, Middleton; Feb. 1st, Royal, Colne.
illage Blacksmith, The. Jan. 25th, Grand, Doncaster; Feb. 1st, Royal, Barnsley.
altz Dream, A (Edwardes and Frohman's). Jan. 25th, Lyceum, Edinburgh; Feb. 1st, Prince's, Manchester.
ay of the World, The. Jan. 25th, Borough, Heywood.
hat a Woman Did. Jan. 25th, Yarmouth; Feb. 1st, Garrison, Bulford Camp.
hen Knights were Bold. Jan. 25th, Royal, Middlesboro'; Feb. 1st, P.O.W., Grimsby.
ho is She? Jan. 25th, Hippodrome, Salford; Feb. 1st, Grand, Rawtenstall.
ilkie, Allan, Repertory. Jan. 25th, Royal, Castleford; Feb. 1st, Grand, Doncaster.
ith Edged Tools. Feb. 1st, Newport.
oman and Wine. Jan. 25th, Court, Wigan.
oman Pays, The. Jan. 25th, Royal, Consett; Feb. 1st, Cambridge, Spennymoor.
oman's Passion, A. Feb. 1st, Royal, Sunderland.

Next came a spring tour with a mixed bag of all that was most popular
1 the Martin Harveys' repertoire. On their return to the Adelphi for the
ummer the Spanish play, with its title of *The World And His Wife* restored,
vas presented for a series of matinées with Henry Ainley as Don Julian. These
performances made a stir so that provincial managers who came to Town
pecially to see the performance wanted it on their autumn lists.

Whenever a man speaks of himself he often skips, in a sentence, happen-
ngs that to everybody else are astonishing. Of *The World And His Wife* Sir
ohn wrote in his autobiography, "We devoted our entire autumn to it,
iving *Hamlet*, however, on every Saturday night." What memories that
olds of one of the most freakish of all freak tours, the wonder of Darlington,
he incredulous gossip of Crewe, the "theatrical" that bore a small cast for
he burden of seven performances and a positive throng, not only actors but
nusicians as well, including two of the leading harpists of the day, for
aturday nights only.

Everybody in all the many sidings of the northern junctions knew that
he will of Miss de Silva was behind all this. When Échegaray's play proved
ɔ have more of the stuff of popularity in it than Martin Harvey had sur-
nised, he decided that there was nothing for it but to make it the subject of

his tour in order to exploit the benefit of an "entirely new attraction" at dates it had not played before.

There seemed nothing for it but to shelve *Hamlet*. "No," said Miss de Silva, "it is your life's ambition to play *Hamlet*, and play it you shall."

There and then she devised the freak tour, and despite all remonstrances from the business manager the entire production travelled for a single performance each week.

"People called me a mad woman," said Miss de Silva, "but the plan succeeded." It was their business manager's brother who wrote the score which required those harpists. Through composing for Martin Harvey, Norman O'Neill became the foremost composer of incidental music even before *Mary Rose* came his way.

In full measure they reaped the rewards of their enterprise in turning *Hamlet* into a "Saturday night show". These three words usually stood for something of the opposite character at a time when the week ended in an attempt at festival. The stalls were full because the "week-end habit" had not been acquired, and the bars were full because nobody feared "a head" when the next morning was a day of rest.

Drink flowed in such quantities as coming generations would never know. The supply was unlimited and the cost small. Pockets were full on Saturday night and audiences warmed themselves up as the hours passed. Musical comedy suited this mood and now *Hamlet* did also.

There might be gloom upon the stage but there was cheerfulness behind the scenes. And then they were reminded by the morning's paper of the shadow ever likely to fall over those who thought less of gain than taking risks in art. John Davidson had drunk his bitter cup. This rugged Scot, so unlike the pallid poets he had been numbered with, was a family man. He took his wife and children to Penzance for a summer holiday He disappeared.

Newlyn fishing-boats took his body from the sea a few days later. He had left a note, "This will be my last book", with the MS. of some poems. "He expressed a wish in writing," Mrs. Patrick Campbell wrote, "that no work of his should ever be presented again. I do not think he realized his gifts— or perhaps he did—and others did not."

.   .   .   .

Now exultant evil was to be Martin Harvey's theme. He was to put himself side by side with Edmund Kean. He would play Richard III. Out of the policy he set himself he gave the first performance at Dublin in the April of 1910 though Irish psychology seemed, so he discovered, to jib at the orgy of bloodshed. The problem can be left to ethnologists or anybody else. The peculiarities of the new Crookback are more pertinent, since they complete a circle in the tradition of romantic acting which began with Richard III as conceived by disorder and genius, wild imagination and drunkenness.

What would their spiritual heir make of it, this descendant of theirs who completely reversed the way they headed romance? "I revelled in every shade of Richard's diabolical villainy," he said. Villainy it was, not crime—the poetry of evil, not the near presence of it. You never shuddered over Martin Harvey's murderous intent. It was concerned in the picturesque mood of a mediaeval ogre who lopped a rose from its stalk as one of the Princes passed into the Tower, and lopped off another rose as the door closed on the other.

Even the diabolical can be idealized. Milton demonstrated that with Satan for all time. Martin Harvey dealt similarly with Richard for his own day. It was inspired by the colour, the mystery, the glamour of legend. It was a bright dream of horror rather than the grim horror itself, an illuminated page of history, not a costumed episode of the Newgate Calendar.

If one comma in Shakespeare's lines may be twisted very slightly it was

> To entertain these fair well-spoken days
> I am determined to prove a villain
> And hate the idle pleasures of these days.
> Plots have I laid, inductions dangerous,
> By drunken prophecies, libels and dreams.

Harvey wore his villainy with a difference, more debonair than other Richards, more decorative in his ferocity, more picturesque than deformed. The true, the essential romantic, came out when he stood by the footlights at the end of a soliloquy and roared. It was an added embroidery upon Shakespeare, like Fechter's solitary laugh.

Yet another endeavour was made to acclimatize the Spanish drama in England. This, which was to be Martin Harvey's last, impressed its audiences; but what lasting effect all these efforts together had may be gathered from the prevailing ignorance which still exists in this country about the plays, the playwrights and the theatres of Spain. We can but quote Sir John's statement: "On February 15 of the following spring, 1911, we produced for the first time at the Opera House, Leicester, a version by two American gentlemen (Messrs. Marburg and Gillpatrick) of the Spanish adaptation by Échegaray of Angel Guimera's Catalonian play, *Terra Baja*."

The theatre of the early twentieth century meant intellectual awakening for thousands of Londoners; they discovered America, France, Holland, Belgium, Russia, Italy, Scandinavia, Germany, Austria and Hungary. But Martin Harvey alone interpreted what Spain had to say, and even he did not bring *Terra Baja* as far as the West End (which by and large had no idea that Spain contained more than one language).

The new play, like *Mariana* and *El Gran Galeoto*, was still about love, unchastity, jealousy and consequent murder, like grand opera without the music. The distinction lay in its portrait of the goatherd beguiled by a master whose nature prompted the English title of *The Lowland Wolf*.

The innocent, trustful mountaineer might have been written especially for Martin Harvey. The reader of the typescript hears the tones of his voice when Manelich tells the villagers how he had prayed for a good wife while they laugh. At first he enjoys their merriment, but now he orders, "Don't laugh at that, friends!" When they continue he shouts, "There's nothing to laugh at in that", and at last, "The next man who laughs will get something that'll stop his laughing for a week."

With good humour restored he describes how three mules with three riders came upon him in the mist:

"I had only just time to prepare a kid and put it in the pot to broil, and there they were! Well—when we'd finished eating the master called me on one side, and he said, 'Are you content to be a shepherd, Manelich?' and I said, 'Why of course! It's what I've always been!' And he said, 'Wouldn't you rather be a miller and have a mill of your own?' I said, 'I don't know.' And he said, 'Wouldn't you like to marry a pretty girl?'

"He made me feel—you don't know how it made me feel! 'Well,' I said, 'if she liked me and if she was pretty!' And the Master said, 'You see Marta there? I took her and her father in, and gave them the mill next to my house; now the father is dead—and the place needs a miller. Look well at Marta and see if you would like to marry her! If you do I'll pay all the expenses of the wedding.' Then I had a sly look at Marta, and she pleased me I can tell you. So I said, 'Good, I'll marry her!' (All laugh.)"

That portrait is the play. There is less originality, less force, in the soul-stirrings of Marta. Manelich forgives her, tells his master, Sebastian, he is going back to the mountains, and adds, "Marta's coming with me." When Sebastian strikes him, Manelich submits—"He is the master." Marta says: "He is the man—do you understand? The man!" He rushes at Sebastian. The villagers drag him away.

In the last act Sebastian comes to fetch Marta and offers her violence. Manelich strangles him. That is the expected end. The surprise is all in Act I, when the goatherd reveals a new stage personality.

.   .   .   .   .

Here ends another book. With all the accomplishment of these twelve years of management, its courage can be regarded as "preparation". If Martin Harvey and Miss de Silva had left the stage in 1911 we could appreciate what they had then achieved for its own sake. But since in the next twelve years they achieved greater things, all that went before becomes of relative importance. The two players took heart anew from the signs—aviation, wireless, Russian ballet, and (if you wish) Reform of the Lords—that the long expected New Age at length was here.

Those last years of Edward VII had been Tree's. He had tried to maintain the glory of the Victorian Shakespeare though he had often succeeded only in burlesquing it. A solitary scrap of "business" will show what his influence amounted to. Shylock's return to the deserted house was introduced by Irving. He gave one knock and the curtain descended. He did so for the last time in London at Drury Lane in the May of 1905.

As Shylock at the Garrick that October, Bourchier gave two knocks. Tree at His Majesty's in 1908 gave three, and then, to quote a critic, "broke into the house and had some sort of a seizure". Another young actor broke all records with six before the whole theatrical profession decided as one man that this kind of thing must stop. Irving had carried his tradition as far as it would go.

In one of Lady Martin-Harvey's liveliest recollections of visits to His Majesty's there is a moving picture of Tree in characteristic style. He was playing Micawber. "At supper," she says, "he took a large bite at a herring, or it might have been whiting, and went on speaking. Whenever he tried to be pompous the bones got in the way and could not be pulled out of his mouth quickly enough. Directly he began to pontificate afresh yet another bone obstructed him and had to be removed, not without a lot of fuss and difficulty."

Tree was a romantic, but not without an effort. That rich personality of his had to be kept up. What work this required becomes evident when the story is told of the efforts made to bring under his notice the play that suited his ample notions. It was *Kismet*. While he was breakfasting in the Dome the MS. was read to him. He interrupted by raising a boiled egg and tapping it with his spoon. "I'll crack an egg with you any day," was the jest he had thought of.

When Knoblauch tried vainly to interest Tree in one play, another work of his had attracted William Faversham, a Londoner, who found his feet on the New York stage and kept them there until he was seventy. In 1911, when *Kismet* was successfully presented by Oscar Asche and Lily Brayton in London, *The Faun* was appreciated by New York—and brought to London two years later by Martin Harvey.

In those sumptuous productions of Stephen Phillips' poetic dramas at His Majesty's, Isabel Bateman made some of her last appearances on the stage. Then she took the veil. She became the Mother Superior of a convent in one of the busiest thoroughfares on the outskirts of London, where playgoers passed on their way to the King's, Hammersmith, to see old Lyceum plays acted by Martin Harvey and still older plays, such as *Richelieu*, revived by Isabel Bateman's brother-in-law, Edward Compton.

Some attention must be paid to other Lyceum leading ladies. After celebrating her stage jubilee one year, Ellen Terry married the next. Bride and bridegroom appeared together in *Captain Brassbound's Conversion* at the Coronet, Notting Hill. "Blithe and bonny" somehow came into your head at any of her frequent smiles with the springing well of happiness that glinted in her eyes, a sparkle no camera ever caught.

It was sad when she took to lecturing instead of acting. That she should ever grow old—the thought of it happening at any future time made you catch your breath. It was altogether different with Geneviève Ward: that she should grow older and older filled you with a relished prospect of time's polished grandeur.

Meanwhile Comyns Carr had become one of Tree's playwrights— adapting *Oliver Twist* and writing a new *Faust* in collaboration with Stephen Phillips. Once you get used to the idea that life is rather untidy with its plots, these are characters, scenes and situations as flamboyant as any in stage romance. And it is not simply because he took the final curtain call that Martin Harvey became the best clue to the shadowy story. His idealism does wind it up and give it significance.

Martin Harvey as "Satan" in *Armageddon*

[Photo: A. Corbett
Martin Harvey as
"Everyman"

[Photo: A. Corbett
Miss de Silva as
"St. Joan"

CHAPTER VI

EXULTANT VIRTUE

At the risk of exciting the rude guffaw, the statement must be made that stage ideas of what "success' and "failure" mean must be revised before we survey Martin Harvey's achievements. Anyhow the folly of going by length of run must be apparent, for this is no criterion even of profit and loss. "Weather always tops the bill," says the music-hall performer, who knows how differently his performances fare under different conditions.

Box-office figures are interesting in themselves but only an expert can expound them, they are eloquent of so many other things besides merit in a play; and if the actual "takings" depend on sun and rain, strikes and jubilees, "floating populations" and depressions, what is to be said of the London triumph which merely means that an inexpensive cast can be maintained at some pocket playhouse without loss as long as people dropped in for shelter on wet nights?

Added to the usual crop of arguments on this subject there is the plain fact that the failures of Martin Harvey sometimes paid more in royalties than the successes of other actor-managers. That merely clears the ground. The important fact here is the acting, more especially what was acted. When his whole career is regarded these failures of his are seen to have one striking quality in common.

Don Juan Tenorio clearly aimed at spiritual conflict. Carl Rossler's *Great Possessions*, which he presented at the Adelphi in 1907, had a similar purpose. The impression may be left that Martin Harvey was attempting the impossible, but that is where his opponent will find himself in strict agreement with his champion.

At regular intervals throughout his life Martin Harvey would valiantly strive to make the theatre serve to express a religious ideal. He tried to strip bare his soul. Town scoffed. Country applauded. Acting passed. Empty typescript remains. Futility? Perhaps. But the plain record of those vain beatings of his imagination's wings against prisons of bricks and mortar should justify this book. Whatever the public response to this new production, he did succeed in expressing what was in him as the wealthy youth filled with a resolve to soar without knowing which way or to what end.

Great Possessions is a New Testament story, concerned with the household of Asarja, a Hebrew usurer, reeking with the lust of greed and thrift. Nathaniel, his son, naturally inclined to revolt, listens to two voices. One is the distant preaching, "Give all thou hast to feed the poor." The other is the hedonism of a Greek who once attracted the usurer's wife so strongly that he might be the youth's actual father.

"Better be joyful with the jocund grape" is the way this sybarite argues against the amassing of riches. Nathaniel is betrothed to Ruth, his brother's widow, who wants life to be one unending festival. Asarja's revengeful brother appears and strikes the usurer, who places all his possessions (thinking he is dying) into Nathaniel's hands. In Act II, while the Greek talks of life's pleasures, the Messiah approaches. In Act III Nathaniel has decided to give all he has to the poor. Ruth rebels. "Longing is naught. Fulfilment is all," she says as she drags him into the house.

Arguing that as money is a curse to the rich it will also be a curse to the poor, he attempts to bear the family treasure-chest to the lake. Asarja's hired assassin puts a stop to such nonsense, whereupon the Greek comments: "Here lieth one who went astray. He never found the path for he searched too diligently," and sets out for Rome with Ruth.

For *Great Possessions* an unfortunate evening was chosen. However vast London might be it still lacked space for more than one new play a night. When two clashed the one the newspapers favoured overlaid the other at birth. This season, more than any other, the Irish Players had won the public ear; they were "news" now they had ceased to be an experiment; they had found in J. M. Synge a playwright who inspired reverence except among the Irish.

Even the leaders of the Irish National Theatre could not keep their hands off his masterpiece; they cut its "bad language" at rehearsals, but even so there was a week's rioting in Dublin (for reasons no Anglo-Saxon could understand) when it had first been played at the Abbey Theatre. At that time Martin Harvey had accepted *The Playboy* and put it into rehearsal until one morning he remarked, "I'm not going to do it." As they were going to Dublin they had to scrap it.

Now Synge's masterpiece found London playgoers like children on Christmas Eve: that this would be one of the most memorable of first nights everybody knew in advance. It occurred at the Royalty on June 10, 1907. The actor-manager so unworldly as to present a play about martyrdom for righteousness sake could hardly be expected to be aware of competition as worldly as that.

As *Great Possessions* was put on only for a week the number of inveterate playgoers who did not see it came to a formidable percentage. This is a pity, because they are the chroniclers and this play had special claims to be chronicled, to be faithfully recorded to show the effect on its audience. It marks an extreme in that tradition which began at the other extreme—at its birth the devil, at its end a saint.

From the disorder of Edmund Kean, riotous in private life, demonic in public performance, romance had gradually but steadfastly changed to the repentant, conscience-ridden mood of Irving; and now Martin Harvey had begun at the expiatory scaffold where his beloved master left off, and aiming at the direct opposite of what Kean had stood for, linked exultant evil at last to exultant virtue.

Meanwhile the Lyceum, a little way farther along the Strand, had returned to the drama in 1907 with Walter Howard's *Her Love Against The World*. Another piece by the same author, *The Midnight Wedding*, followed in June, and as this had come from a venerable blood-tub in Paddington's market-place, Irving's temple seemed to have come down in the world. It was rescued by the Manx Shakespeare, Hall Caine, foremost of the world's authors as far as royalties went, for he was worth a quarter of a million pounds.

By adopting the Isle of Man and by wearing Shakespeare's beard he had undoubtedly advertised his goods sufficiently, but that was not all. He knew how to tell a story and he was very sepulchral about sex. The heart of one of his Manxmen "was a wasted field of volcanic action, with ashes and scoriae of infernal blackness on the surface, but the wholesome soil underneath". As the heroine who was "necessary to his resurrection" belonged to another, his soul became prematurely white—" 'Study', said the world, and it bowed its head the lower."

In the theatre Hall Caine's rôle was peculiar. Whether his idea of drama might be considered good, bad or indifferent, in one respect it could never be challenged. He stood alone as a re-dramatizer, for as each of his plays grew old enough for the rag-bag he turned it into an exposition of some burning question, preferably the Woman Question, of the day, and then turned it back again when the question stopped burning. Two old-fashioned melodramas of the Victorian era thus started fighting at the outposts of thought late in the reign of Edward. Their success was such that the Lyceum found, as "the Popular Theatre", its new place in London life.

Although the long runs of *The Christian* and *Pete* added to the renown of the author some notice must be given to the actor. Matheson Lang, caught when boyhood and manhood exerted their spell together, when glory of youth and first fruits of experience joined, bore the wily old Manxman back into the limelight. Lang was secured for *The Devil's Disciple* in a repertory season at the Savoy, but the Lyceum management held on to their magnet for two years. When his success as Romeo led to Hamlet he was well on his way to become another actor-manager of note in the style of romance.

In the last years of Edward VII the wraith of Irving seemed to visit the stage. The public, in a fickle mood that evidenced a decided distaste for plays which might have appealed to him had he been living, crowded to see those whose titles he had made famous. Both Martin Harvey and H. B. Irving experienced this when they maintained the Lyceum style so faithfully as to share the master's mantle. Copyright restricted performance of some plays in that famous repertoire but not *The Corsican Brothers*, which had been adapted to suit the requirements of many theatres; there were so many versions that a cartoonist spread the vogue with Corsican negroes (one rising out of the ground beside the other) and Corsican cows (one coming out of the grass the other is nibbling).

Martin Harvey decided to have the dialogue revised. Though he believed that people "spoke like that" when the play was new—"*vide* much in Jane Austen", he argued—the old stilted stuff invited ridicule:

> "I remember a choice phrase in a copy of the old *Corsican Brothers*, when Fabian was describing to the young French gentleman the operation to which the twins were subjected: 'Fortunately a surgeon's scalpel separated us, but the moral adhesion still subsists.' "

He had his copy of the play "very much worked over" with fresh material from a copy of the original novel by Dumas. Canon Langbridge's daughter wrote fresh passages in a pastiche. "You could not," said Harvey, "see the joints."

There was enough enthusiasm to astonish him, but the way he contrasted the two brothers put fresh life into the story. As the Parisian he bore the look of idealism, wide-eyed innocence almost, which is always asking for trouble and defenceless against evil. As the other he showed a fearlessness when challenging his tall opponent which Irving's height and reach made less astonishing; Irving was an avenging fate, Harvey the ardent brother; one advanced like doom, the other fought like a young tiger.

In the autumn *The Corsican Brothers* opened a new season at the Adelphi. Another Irving character followed. Once more Edgar Ravenswood returned to the stage, this time in *The Last Heir* by Stephen Phillips. After three weeks it gave way to *The Only Way* and at Christmas *The Corsican Brothers* returned.

In the repertoire of the Martin Harvey company *The Last Heir* cannot claim a foremost place. Yet it is not the least interesting. It attracts for two contradictory reasons. On the one hand it wins respect for upholding the long Ravenswood stage tradition, and on the other hand for flouting it. The way Stephen Phillips dramatized *The Bride Of Lammermoor* is at first confusing; you barely recognize the story and decide that he has indulged in excessive stage licence.

When each detail is taken separately you are surprised to find far greater fidelity to the original than versions of Merivale and others possess. Since incidents and speeches are reproduced exactly, what then has changed? The answer is: the whole spirit of the thing. The poet had decided that the Master of Ravenswood is not the hub of the wheel. There is much to be said for his view, since Andrew Lang had pointed out how much the character lacked when set beside others romantically accursed from Hamlet downwards.

Leaving fine theories unquoted the one simple fact obtrudes that what the Master says or does barely affects the issue. Finding such a protagonist unemployable Phillips gave him all the plot he was entitled to and then, by inserting that part of the story which was too much for Scott's masculine muse, made of *The Last Heir* a stirring drama by inventing for its *scène-à-faire* a woman-to-woman contest between mother and daughter, with the old witch as a good third.

So this, we learn at last, is precisely how the Scottish Juliet was borne down by weight of other women's crafts and will-power. The consequence was that Martin Harvey found himself crowded out of Act II, Scene i, and three quarters of Act IV, Scene i. He might almost have been regarded as prologue and epilogue.

The action consists of Lucy's combat with Lady Ashton who is aided by the hag Gourlay—Mary Rorke played first one part and then t'other—as well as Bucklaw. All these characters have long speeches. Lucy's, to Lady Ashton, ends:

(*Goes back to steps. Throws herself on steps by pillar.*)
And—woman, for no mother are you to me now—this is not the worst, that I must spend my life with one whose voice is a blow, whose touch is a sting, whose look is an injury, but that I must endure all this with the added torment of happiness forbidden (*rises up again*) with the sight of paradise added to the couch of hell (*going down to R*). I forget now that you brought me into the world. I let that pass. I ask you as woman to woman, who gave you leave to inflict all this on me? Answer me. Answer me.

There is a grand climax almost in the manner of Lady Macbeth:

(*The stately opening dance is concluded when the two bridesmaids are seen waiting at the door. Lady Ashton points them out to Bucklaw. Immediately an arch of swords is formed under which Bucklaw passes out with shouts of acclamation. The dance now takes on a wilder and wilder character and the music becomes shriller and shriller, but suddenly a shriek is heard from above.*)
BRIDESMAID (*coming down stairs C*). She has murdered him.
(*All stand silent and motionless as the white face of Lucy Ashton peers, as it were anxiously, round the staircase. She comes slowly in her nightdress with bare feet, in one hand she carries a dagger covered with blood.*)

In the last scene Ravenswood rides to the Kelpies Flow. In the final tableau three hags point to his hat and feather on the moonlit sands.

By popular acclaim H. B. Irving was now walking away with the laurels in Town. As Barrie's castaway butler in *The Admirable Crichton* he established his place in up-to-date plays, and left critics wondering how far he would go if he left romantic drama behind to develop the genius for comedy which always seemed to lurk behind his immovable solemnity.

He disappointed all such expectations by cherishing the spirit of the Lyceum and cherishing it very successfully; in fact, his father's belief in fustian was astonishingly vindicated at the Shaftesbury in the autumn of 1908. On October 15, Harry Irving's revival of *The Lyons Mail* excited the new generation with the twin portraits of Lesurques and Dubosc.

The old play, passing its century for the first time in its English history, totalled 128 performances. To follow this in the spring of 1909 he put on

Hamlet, *Charles I* and *Louis XI*. At the Queen's in Shaftesbury Avenue he opened his autumn season with *The Bells*. There seemed no doubt that he thought of making a bid for his father's title. Even Robert Macaire a year or so later would not be the end of the attempt, for *A Story Of Waterloo* was to serve him as a sketch on the halls.

Not just one kind of audience existed for "tours". Birmingham, Manchester, Liverpool, Leeds, Bradford and Edinburgh meant six weeks. Planets of the theatrical heavens, who closed His Majesty's and the St. James's during the dog days, wanted no more. Stars who swung round in their orbits in or out of season needed engagements in all cities. Cardiff, Swansea, Leicester, Derby, Middlesbrough, Sunderland, Dundee, Glasgow and Aberdeen were all "big dates".

The background is unaltered. There is still a working-day atmosphere, usually industrial at that, and in this you might discern a desire for romance after eight hours or more at desks, benches or looms. Martin Harvey found the greatest eagerness in such surroundings; he appealed to the same hunger which creates oases of music in an unmusical land. He could sound the depths.

There was another country for Fred Terry and Julia Neilson. They packed those pavilions and other architectural singularities which decorate old England's southern shore. *Sweet Nell Of Old Drury* and *The Scarlet Pimpernel* played here to packed houses at raised prices. New plays went wrong, but with two "stopgaps" they could always recuperate. They would spend six months in Town at the New Theatre and the rest of their working year on tour. Even pieces that they regarded as failures, such as *Dorothy O'The Hall* in 1906, stayed alive in public memory.

Two years later they found a third stopgap in *Henry Of Navarre*, by William Devereux. When it was tried out that November at Newcastle-on-Tyne, Julia Neilson was ill and Marguerite de Valois was played by her understudy, Queen Elizabeth in the other piece. Here was an actress of the forthright romantic stamp. Miriam Lewes, born at Starie in Russia, brought to England in childhood and trained as a dancer, first acted in *Driven From Home*. For eight years on tour she played all manner of parts from Kate Hardcastle and Lady Sneerwell to Ouida's *vivandière* Cigarette, love's martyr in *Under Two Flags*. She began to make an impression on the public. She made an even deeper impression on players who took their calling seriously.

Stage reputations are made either by critics' cold print or by playgoers' word of mouth, not always in agreement with one another. There is a third brand of praise: Green Room gossip, still surviving despite the abolition of Green Rooms, occasionally bestows an unwritten diploma. Laurence Irving, for one, stood higher in professional esteem than elsewhere, for those who acted at his side accredited him with genius. Another to win these rare laurels was Miriam Lewes. She drew our notice just when romance had such popularity in the provinces that "people of taste" in Town would have none of it.

BOOK V

CHAPTER I

ŒDIPUS AND EM'LY JANE

DENIALS that any man by taking thought shall add a cubit unto his stature form another of those half truths. As long as stature meant feet and inches the statement passed unchallenged; to-day we still accept it, although the reference is to prestige. The change turns ancient wisdom to nonsense, especially in the theatre. What else should an actor do but strive to add to his stature and how shall he strive without taking thought?

By doing so Martin Harvey rose cubit by cubit. One he added by turning actor-manager, and another by assuming Greek grandeur—at a time when box-office managers were set in the opinion that a masterpiece on the subject of incest was, in performance, about as alien to modern life as the burning of heretics. There never has been such a shaking up of hidebound rules and conventions as when this wild-cat scheme—so many people called it—burgeoned from something mooted into something afoot.

Greek tragedy added to Martin Harvey's height, for he strapped on his feet the gilded buskins of a hero's elevated life. The stilted walk might have made many a player afraid of ridicule, that last-but-one infirmity of noble minds, but he had a soul fit for lofty demeanour. Before he wore them he was one romantic among many; afterwards he had his place alone.

There may be some argument about this. Some playgoers hold a player's stature to be what he is by nature, without reference to what opportunities he seizes or is granted by circumstances. You will never disabuse the human mind of a hankering after things as they ought to be, and this is a sample of it. But if we think in the way of a detective who will not rest content until he has all the clues imaginable, the question of histrionic stature is not going to be dismissed as easily as all that.

Parade before the inward eye all the romantics among Martin Harvey's contemporaries, who might have wrested from him the title which is the title of this book. In that splendid array of rich personalities, bearing their renown in their glance, we can pick out a full dozen who had powers worthy to be crowned. Had they but taken the proverbial thought the extra cubit would not be in doubt. Waller's fancy could not soar much higher than Henry V. Godfrey Tearle gained summits and came down again. Julia Neilson, in her own gracious confessions, contented herself with what she called "little plays", though her devoted servants by the thousand were prepared to swear that she could take just whatever she chose by putting out her hand.

No one could accuse Martin Harvey of resting content. Year by year his records show how he strove and what he strove for. Shakespeare formed part of his stage life, melodrama in costume another. If his grasp had never exceeded his reach he would have been far wealthier and more highly respected by those who can respect nothing more highly than material success. That he demanded more of life and of himself those Spanish plays in his repertoire had already proved. Critics questioned the wisdom of his choice. But whatever it was in him that made him walk these unbeaten tracks was also what made him constantly stride into undiscovered country— undiscovered, that is, by the contemporary theatre.

When he first spoke of Œdipus there was a start of surprise as though moral horror had no place on the modern stage, as though it would be tolerable only to people who basked in accustomed sunlight, who sat at their ease in high galleries of marble theatres in Mediterranean air. In the scooped-out hillside of Taormina, with the sea around and Etna offering its smoke indolently to gracious skies, the fear of malignant fates above could trouble no one unbearably. But if the Greek spirit did not belong to our murky picture stage, which needed the glow of romance as it needed artificial light to keep it alive, there had at all times been some attempt or other to represent it there.

Early in the twentieth century Professor Gilbert Murray's English version of *The Bacchae*, said Shaw, "came into our dramatic literature with all the impulsive power of an original work". In Granville-Barker's repertory season at the Court in 1907 the first play was *Hippolytus* and the second *John Bull's Other Island*. Out of the thirty-odd plays that established repertory for three years, eleven were by Shaw, three by Euripides and two by Ibsen.

Thus Martin Harvey's project was characteristic of a queer period. A cosmopolitan drama, unrestricted by time or space, was at loggerheads with a minutely localized view of it. Even London, struggling hard to keep itself to itself, began to yield after the rest of the civilized world had become interested in both tendencies. But the strength of London's resistance must not be underestimated, since the effects of it are still apparent to-day in our ignorance of great continental dramatists whose genius was quickly recognized everywhere else. In the smug, self-complacent atmosphere of Edward's capital intellectual enterprise was smothered in cotton wool. Many of the fresh impulses that stirred the theatre in the eighteen-nineties went to the country.

What had happened to the drama in the twenty-five years before George V ascended the throne is common knowledge. Irving versus Ibsen sums it up. The theatre of the actor, with its centuries-old tradition, had been assailed from 1885 to 1910 by the theatre of the author with its brand-new intellectual passion. Granville-Barker's championship of Shaw, Ibsen, Galsworthy and Greek tragedy at the Savoy meant that they ranked as West End entertainments, that they could even break records for long runs, that Victorian actor-managers wondered whether they might not exploit the New Drama to their own advantage. Granville-Barker even included the plays of Shakespeare as work whose authorship should be respected. What had long been made to serve each actor-manager's own ends now won as much respect as though written by Pinero.

No study of the twentieth-century stage can ignore Miss Horniman. She was born in Forest Hill, where her father built a pleasant little museum out of profits from packets of tea. Wealthy enough to choose her own kind of life, she became private secretary to W. B. Yeats. In 1894 she "backed" Shaw's *Arms And The Man* at the Avenue, and the Irish plays sponsored by Yeats and others at Dublin's Abbey Theatre.

At Manchester her enterprises were under her own name, and there the Gaiety, belying its name as so many theatres do, made "repertory" synonymous with unflinching realism. Between 1908 and 1912 she put on nearly a hundred new plays and some seventy old ones. "I used to go into the bar where young men were speaking their minds and challenge them. If any of them would write a play I would produce it. I gave my promise to do so no matter what it was like. Several young men took me at my word and the results were most satisfactory."

So she said years later, when the Manchester School had created, not only its own playwrights with their own manner taken direct from everyday life, mainly Lancashire and Ulster, but had trained a considerable school of acting to match it. "Repertory" sprang up in big provincial centres with a business-like resolve to take over the entire drama. You can still see the new attitude in photographic "groups". Miss Horniman's young men and maidens dress well but like people with work to do. Other theatrical groups, even in the still life of a time exposure, contrive to swagger. Vast arrays of faces (with a word underneath to explain that the rest could not come) still convey the excitement of a musical comedy "First Tour" and a hint of what the effect of its arrival in Manchester at a rival theatre would be on Miss Horniman's box-office.

What a variety of unlike things the word "stage" now conveyed to ordinary pleasure-seekers. The romantic drama seemed lost in the main contest, which was between town and country. While Leicester Square and the Strand sent their show-girls to the provinces, the provinces returned the compliment by sending *Bunty Pulls The Strings* to break records at the Haymarket in 1911. From Manchester, *Hindle Wakes* would soon be on its way to the Playhouse.

Some plays from abroad were as much localized as these, but the true cosmopolitan spirit expressed itself in lavish productions which could hold any playgoer spellbound whether he understood the language or not.

In opera houses the music of Richard Strauss compelled fashionable admiration for the poetic dramas, *Elektra* and *Der Rosenkavalier*, of Hugo von Hofsmannsthal; in the circus buildings of Berlin the scenic effects of Reinhardt made the quidnuncs rush to see Hofmannsthal's *Odipus Und Die Sphinx* (written in 1896), as a sensationally new thing. Not everybody was impressed. In Elsie Fogerty's eyes, Mounet-Sully reached great heights by simpler means:

> "Even Mounet's first word, 'Enfants,' as he stood before the lofty temple of Thebes, seemed to include the vast audience in the crowd of plague-stricken wretches who cried out to him. Reinhardt made of the same opening a spectacle of tensely waving arms, rigid in a cubist design, etched upwards to a tiny distant figure without dignity or pathos. It was a thousand times more expensive and complicated than the actor's voice. Did it move one as much?"

Nor were London crowds in 1911 interested yet. The first display of Reinhardt's power of setting before your eyes a spectacle that held the astonishment of supernatural vision was ignored at first by the multitude. The magnificence of *The Miracle*, an idea from Charles B. Cochran's teeming brain which he engaged Reinhardt to materialize in the arena of Olympia, would have vanished unseen had it not been presented by the greatest living showman and boosted by the most popular newspaper of the day. After that Reinhardt's name stirred the slow-moving mass, but not until he had become slightly involved in a fantastic episode farther removed from "real life" than any to be found in the kind of fiction which relies on verisimilitude for its appeal.

Whether life itself will ever give up being romantic may be left to the Brains Trust to say, but it most certainly had not at this particular moment. Allowing once more for reality's inveterate untidiness when it comes to plot, what could be more Gothic, rococo, arabesque, decadent and barbaric than the story Martin Harvey had to tell concerning how Reinhardt's scheme came into his hands?

The English rights had been acquired by the Great Lafayette, misanthropic magician more highly coloured and monstrous than anything in the pages of the de Goncourts. "The more I see of men, the more I love my dog," he emblazoned over his ostentatious home in a Bloomsbury square like a family motto, and while he worshipped his pets he treated his captive wild beasts with a callous brutality no modern audience would tolerate. "Illusionists" must always travel; otherwise their magic would grow stale. They are ever the most up to date in knowledge of what is happening to the music-halls, the palaces of variety, the winter gardens and the circus buildings of the world. The Great Lafayette saw one of his old haunts in the grip of the classics, observed, moreover, that it was packed out as never before.

What was this that people went out for to see more eagerly than any vanishing lions or tight-rope elephants? The throng round the box-office in Berlin was enough for him, whatever he thought of the showmanship of Sophocles. He bought Reinhardt's London rights and thought of Tree, and the most modern thing in ancient art seemed destined for His Majesty's.

ŒDipus and the Sphinx
A page from the programmes at the Royal Opera House, Covent Garden, January 15, 1912

Then the most worshipped of dogs died and was embalmed. As though part of the funeral rites, the Edinburgh Hippodrome took fire, possibly from the torch flourished to make a wretched lion leap in frenzy against the bars of its cage—and it is not entirely out of keeping with the Great Lafayette's character that he might have wished for so monstrous a pyre. As a last masterstroke of the macabre, the body of Lafayette, recovered with difficulty, proved to be not his but that of his "double", though Lafayette had perished there too.

Because of these events the English rights of the Berlin production came into Martin Harvey's possession. At an earlier date he had obtained a drama of the whole life of ŒDipus—written according to the romantic model with no incidents related but all enacted—from W. L. Courtney, one of the finest minds in the realm where stage and study met. His version of *Œdipus* was not a translation, but so free a handling of the fable as to be reckoned a new and original play.

As such it inspired no awe in the Reader of Plays, who knew a forbidden subject when he saw it and withheld the Lord Chamberlain's licence. In places where people found it possible to admit that they were literate, there was surprise not unmixed with ridicule and unpatriotic references to darkest England. Whether the ban would have been lifted is, unfortunately, merely a matter for surmise, since the problem solved itself when, with Courtney's full agreement, the new English play was withdrawn in favour of Professor Gilbert Murray's translation, a bold, original poetic drama but still a translation, or at least so classified. The Reader of Plays was fully authorized to licence Greek tragedy, even in English, for this would come under the heading of educational even without the advantage of having been written by a professor, and the morals of His Majesty's subjects could take the consequences.

Any wary playwright who knocks at the door beneath that modest portico in St. James's, to discover in advance what he may safely dramatize, will worry officials with his questions and bewilder himself. The Commandments of State authorship consist of endless repetitions of "Thou Shalt Not" followed by blanks to be filled in when the sins have been committed, not before. Some plays have been banned because they were moral, some because they were immoral. The powers of this veto are without limits.

The Lord Chamberlain was officially described as a dictator in the days when the word had not such a very bad taste in our mouths. In theatreland his word is law, and willingly accepted as such because the alternative, possible interference by the police as in New York, is inconvenient to theatre managers. The playwright's feelings are not worth considering, not even to the extent of drawing up a list of subjects which are *verboten*.

Where theatres are concerned the Lord Chamberlain inherits the Tudor office of Master of the Revels, ruler of all London actors who are still, in effect, His Majesty's Servants. Whatever may displease His Majesty, if only in theory, must not be put upon the stage. Consequently, although no directions have ever got as far as official print, the parents or grandparents of the reigning sovereign must not be impersonated, flatteringly or unflatteringly; even great-grandparents or members of still remoter royal families must be treated with care.

With religion, of course, you never know where you are; once there was an idea that any representation of the Deity was rigidly taboo, but ever since a mediaeval morality was revived with each Person of the Holy Trinity among the *dramatis personae*, the rule was sufficiently relaxed for the appearance of the Lord in the form of a negro preacher. Farther back there were such queer instances as the banning of *The Mikado* for fear of annoying a Japanese embassy, and the outlawing of Jack Sheppard until he and all his associates had changed their names, though not their nature.

Martin Harvey had been thwarted once before by this unwritten law. Miss de Silva wished to accept a promising play by the wife of that popular Irish journalist and politician, T. P. O'Connor. It was about Parnell and had the title (adopted years later for quite another Parnell play) of *The Lost Leader*. It has always been understood that living persons must not be impersonated in plays; as the leading characters in this had the names of persons who were dead, some hope remained that the tragedy of a great idealist was fit for the footlights if sympathetically treated. But this is the most uncertain ground of all, for at any moment the Lord Chamberlain's Office may introduce the equivalent of what barristers call "new law". Mrs. T. P. O'Connor's play was not licensed. A playwright of the future would seize her lost chance.

Any Ancient Greek writer could "get past on his name", like a reporter at a football match, and the way was clear for Martin Harvey to grapple with the greatest of all classic rôles. In order to indicate how much he sacrificed when turning from Shakespeare to Sophocles, there must be an explicit statement of what is meant by the classic style. When critics agree that Hamlet has been acted in this manner there ought to be a clear reservation that Shakespeare's major characters are classic only in being of accepted greatness. No part in the English drama is classic in the other sense, even though he may be acted in such a manner.

So much becomes unmistakable directly you note how the heroes of Ancient Greece deport themselves according to the stagecraft of Athens. These figures are static by comparison with those of the English stage. "Enter" and "Exit" almost set the limits of the space they traverse. From the zenith of power to the depths of disaster they pass undivested of dignity, upright.

The most majestic of Hamlets cannot stalk on buskins; his feet must be on the ground and his mind on earthly matters; yet his bouts with words in the churchyard and with foils in the palace place no classic actor at a disadvantage; these romantic clashes are easily treated by John Philip Kemble and by Forbes Robertson with exalted condescension. The Greek hero is not so adaptable; when deciding to present *Œdipus*, not as a new and original work by Courtney but as a translation faithful to the spirit of the original, Martin Harvey vowed to respect proprieties which tended to freeze his face into a mask and stiffen his legs into stilts. He would respect them, but without blind obedience.

Now consider all the accomplishments that gave Martin Harvey his prestige as an actor. Much of his popularity had been won by personages concerned half in, half out of, "character". Such technique is inconceivable in classic drama whose outlines are as clear-cut as statuary. Think of Rat Reresby's pipe, his camp-fire behaviour with it, his gallows-humour when he drew a chuckling comfort from it at the moment of imminent death, the puff of tobacco smoke which floated into sight before he made his deliberate appearance, barely able to exert self-control, after torture. Think of the ingenuity, the excitement-tickling sensibility, the precision-timing in the change-over from thrills to jest and back again, which had been developed year by year in such an adventurous atmosphere as this. Think of Sydney Carton's sardonic turn of mind, able in a moment to check the flood of sentiment by an alcoholic breath or sardonic raising of an eyebrow which you will not find in the pages of "A Tale of Two Cities"—a quality which would-be detractors dubbed "improving on Dickens" only to find themselves giving praise when they meant to sneer.

Dig deeper into the psychology of these contrasted styles of acting. Whatever romance may signify, what becomes of it when your Kean tries to do what your Kemble does superlatively well? Neither his frenzy nor Irving's remorse fits in with the Hellenic scheme of things. Similarly that spiritual appeal which Martin Harvey had made his own had no existence there. "The appeal of the under-dog" it was called in everyday life. The fullest expression of it can be found in the Sermon on the Mount or the Epistle to the Corinthians—and there perhaps some affinity may be discovered. Œdipus Tyrannus mildly anticipates the teaching of "Greater love hath no man" when set beside the ideas proverbially associated with his rank and title. A tyrant who sacrifices himself is to the unlettered a contradiction in terms.

But Reinhardt's methods were far from classic. Surging crowds are not in accordance with the classic tradition. They are a rival means of expressing what the Greek Chorus has to say in the set forms proscribed for it. Forests of arms and emotional outcry are not only romantic in style, but they have always been in accordance with the romantic tradition. Reinhardt may have found new ways of exploiting the stage-management of the circus drama which combined parterre and stage; he probably invented the rush of supers through the aisles of stalls; but the massed effect of hands held aloft in unison had been exploited by Charles Kean at the Princess's—as a woodcut of his revival of *Pizarro* shows.

That suited Martin Harvey's mood. Consciously or unconsciously he approached the part as the most exalted conception of the man accursed known to the stage. Justification for this statement can be read in his book where he declares that interest in Œdipus stays alive because "his disaster is largely the result of his own weakness". What he is reading into the verse is another and a greater portrait of *l'homme fatal*. He saw Ravenswood, Eugene Aram, Don Juan not altogether dissimilarly. A whole century of romantics had tried to make the man accursed guilty of a sin while at heart nobly and purely innocent, and Martin Harvey had obeyed the impulse more strongly than any of them since Nature had cut him out for the

dealist's task. And here, by one of those twists of history which make non-
ense of critical theorizing, was the idea in classical perfection from a remote
past. The actor's aim, according to an account he left among his papers,
was to unite past and present:

"If the story were merely one to demonstrate the irresistible power
of a malignant fate, of the ineffectual efforts of poor mortals to avert
their doom, or the spectacle of humanity struggling in the grasp of an
inscrutable god, it could never arrest and hold the attention of a modern
audience as it does, for we of to-day hold that ' 'Tis in ourselves that
we are thus or thus.' What gradually evolved from a long study of the
part was the essential humanity of the man, as living and actual as a
character from Ibsen or any modern dramatists of them all.

"Passionate to the verge of hysteria—look at his unreasonable
scene with Creon, in which he behaves like a spoilt child—arrogant,
precipitate to resent a fancied slight, or blindly rushing on to unwarrant-
able conclusions, idealistic, even near to mysticism—remember the
accusation to his eyes before he blinded himself:

> Ye looked on lives, whose like earth never bore,
> Ye knew not those my spirits thirsted for,
> Therefore be dark for ever.

"I read in this a hunger for spiritual perfection, and a capacity
for self-sacrifice in his cry to the taunts of Teiresias:

> I have saved this land and care not if I die.

"Every Greek would have known that the gods had marked him
for destruction after that wild burst of fey self-glorification and fancied
security as he rushes to his fate."

So thorough a romantic could never escape romance. If there can
be any doubt about the colouring Martin Harvey gave to the play it goes
when he wonders whether he could, in his remote ancestry, ever have been
Greek. This inspired the feeling "which possessed me in the playing of
that part, and which almost persuaded me that I *was* a Greek". But there
is a definite difference between what he thought of the part and what it
was according to the classic mind, as interpreted by Professor Gilbert
Murray:

"It is important to realize that at the beginning of the play he is
prepared for an oracle commanding him to die for his people. And
he never thinks of refusing that 'task' any more than he tries to elude

the doom that actually comes, or to conceal any fact that tells against
him. If Œdipus had been an ordinary man, the play would have been
a very different and a much poorer thing."

To stand in awe of him as the Earth-born rival of Apollo required,
from a romantic, too great an effort. There was enough earth in him to
make him some remote ancestor, however far excelling in grandeur, of
Sydney Carton. This time the King of Thebes was not far off, but near
enough for us to identify ourselves with him. From the hill-top seats of a
Greek theatre, in the drowsy heat of the sun under a blue sky, mountain-
tops and Mediterranean beyond, the mask of Œdipus never appeared so
unremote. For deep tragic enjoyment our seat must be in that sun-drenched
marble-lined hillside confronting the cool stone stage. Inside Covent
Garden tragedy cannot be classic to the exclusion of all other styles, because
audiences are not ancient enough. So it was an Œdipus in tune with our
modern mood—the "ordinary man" of realism would be too poor a thing
—that Martin Harvey brought to life on the night of January 15, 1912.

What Tree would have made of it can be dimly surmised by thinking
of his crowd-compelling Mark Antony. But if his Hamlet could be funny
without being vulgar, the mischances of Œdipus are enough to shudder at.
Its contact with modern life is never felicitous. "This is a beastly play" were
the words that came to Martin Harvey's ears from Granville-Barker's
box; and the Greater London matron who had seen the performance,
passing Covent Garden with another who had not, provided enlightenment
with, "Married to his own mother without knowing a thing about it, but
then I always did say a man should marry a woman younger than himself."

How deep that performance was rooted in the romantic tradition can
be judged from the record of each member of the cast. Louis Calvert the
Creon, H. A. Saintsbury the Teiresias and Hubert Carter the Leader of the
Chorus all had their training in the wars between virtue and vice where
Irving won his spurs. The Jocasta was Lillah McCarthy, who had so identified herself with the heroines of Shaw, Ibsen, Schnitzler, Galsworthy and
Masefield as to seem the head on the currency of modern thought; but
before that she had been Wilson Barrett's leading lady in the masterpieces
of Caine, Shakespeare and Barrett himself.

The Messenger from the Palace must be given closer attention, because
he stayed with the Martin Harvey Company throughout its period of
triumph. Franklin Dyall began at the St. James's in a series including *The
Importance Of Being Earnest* and *The Prisoner Of Zenda*. Next he was with
Forbes Robertson's company at the same time as Martin Harvey; after
that with Waller in *Henry V*, *Monsieur Beaucaire* and *The Duke's Motto*, and
then in three Ibsen revivals. He played the name part in *The Lowland Wolf*,
among other parts in the Martin Harvey repertory. "The best Golaud
you could possibly imagine," Miss de Silva said of him.

The Ghost at Elsinore: *Hamlet* at His Majesty's, 1916

[Photo: M. Arbuthnot

Martin Harvey as
"Hamlet"

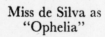

Miss de Silva as
"Ophelia"

That the performance should have a quality that might be called *vibrato* was, therefore, not surprising. There was a consistent feeling of violence under restraint, of emotion in leash. The Greek sense of Nemesis, of fate overtaking mortals incapable of resistance, wavered under the influence of minds accustomed to action. Nobody not attuned to this would be aware of it, because playgoers prefer to believe what they hear than make themselves receptive to undertones. But to judge such acting by the classical standard is to quarrel with it—as some critics did.

The epicure at the play must be as versatile in his appreciations as the epicure over a glass. Our delight in Beethoven never debars us from enjoyment of a great conductor's new values. Greek tragedy in line with Lyceum tradition, adapted to the horseshoe of Royal Opera and drilled into massed effects after the manner brought into being in circus buildings, was not Sophocles pure and simple. But then what setting is the indoor equivalent of things seen in the light of a blazing sun?

That year became notable for scenic innovation, so Baughan (immortalized by *Fanny's First Play* as "Vaughan") reported in the next *Stage Year Book*. Of *Œdipus* he wrote:

"The whole production was an attempt to underline the horror of Sophocles' tragedy. The black columns of the palace, the blood-stained altar, the dim lights and rushing crowds achieved this, but destroyed the dignity of the tragedy. It was a veritable hocus-pocus of stage art. Mr. Granville-Barker imitated this style of production in *Iphigenia In Tauris*. The temple was blood-red this time, and everything was done to create a scene of horror, in spite of the fact that Euripides' play is full of hopefulness and open air. However, *Iphigenia* was well-acted, and when Mr. Barker took the production to the Greek Theatre at Bradfield College one was able to appreciate the fact that apart from its trappings the performance of the play was excellent."

Even without this very broad hint good reason exists for supposing that half the audiences of that date could not take their mind off scenic innovation. Shakespeare either amid black curtains or else in front of perspectives that aimed at dwindling Versailles by comparison into a tennis court had been accepted, but anything in between was "istic".

. . . . . .

Since the crossword clue for achievement is "ways and means", Œdipus must acknowledge as a near relation a twentieth-century cockney, Em'ly Jane. While Martin Harvey was dreaming of Œdipus in imposing surroundings, Mrs. Martin Harvey was fixing up a suburban and provincial contract to play *An Idyll Of Seven Dials*, duologue by Rosina Filippi, round the halls.

O

Of course these were the days when Bernhardt, Tree, Alexander and other leading lights of the West End gladly named their price for going on the halls. One of them wrote an article and, having come to the theatre by way of the O.U.D.S., he signed it "Arthur Bourchier, M.A.", upon which Seymour Hicks published a reply which stated that he wanted the same letters after his name as he, too, was "a music-hall artiste". The accent was on art, and eminent actors were as much entitled to the label as any sensational "living statues" in white fleshings instead of neck-to-ankle clothes.

The trouble was that while audiences at sumptuous palaces of variety were prepared to put up with art, as Mrs. Brown-Potter had more or less made clear, the less submissive industrialized North was not going to be patronized by it. Galleryites were not only rude; they also instinctively threw things. Miss de Silva was warned, but having decided how the trouble always came about she knew she could take the risk in comfort.

Her tour was not only successful but enjoyable. She liked the life. It had a freedom that the theatre, with all its kindliness, rarely knows. "Cast" is often spelt "caste" because protagonists live in a rarefied atmosphere compared with the chorus, whether in Athens or Leicester Square. Turns in a programme, on the other hand, can all be equal between shows, no matter how violently they might squabble about where each should be placed by rights on the bill.

The leading lady of the Martin Harvey Company felt proud when Albert Chevalier, the Coster's Laureate, beloved singer about Bank Holidays when in pearlies he looked "every inch a bart", roundly declared that as Em'ly Jane in *An Idyll Of Seven Dials* she was the best cockney he had ever seen. For a fortnight he took the other part in the sketch. Afterwards she played it in the lowest halls of rowdy seaports and to her great delight found crowds waiting for her at stage-doors, where her hands were clasped by brawny fisher-girls and she was hugged. Some dates had not been played when the theatre called her back again.

At a later season, with only a few weeks to spare, she fulfilled her contract by rushing round from hall to hall, four a night towards the end of the tour, with the aim of honouring all obligations and be at Liverpool just in time to catch the boat.

CHAPTER II

DISASTER IN THE ST. LAWRENCE RIVER

How continually the old order was giving place to the new, theatrical events faithfully reflected. Changes that had been expected ten years before, and then despaired of because so long delayed, became visible in the first years of the new reign. George V ascended the throne amid no fanfare of great expectations. Yet the twentieth century, which the general public then regarded as an overrated swindle, at once revealed itself as a dynamic force out of control.

Simple old people on benches in the park, as well as such prophets as H. G. Wells and experts on the atomic theory, speculated concerning what it would all come to. Processions demanded more Dreadnoughts, touring companies gave warning of the next war in *An Englishman's Home*, and posters advertising some new *feuilleton* foretold how Nelson's Column would topple and lie across Trafalgar Square like a broken sugar-stick during the War in the Air.

Meanwhile *The Only Way* had taken the place of *The Bells* as a play everybody had to see, as necessary a part of human experience in England as a visit to the Tower or the Abbey. When it continued past the 1,500th performance there seemed to be no reason why it should ever stop. Nor was there any immediate prospect that Sydney Carton, fifty years of age at this time, would grow old. The latest tribute to his standing as a household word was paid him when The Follies at the Apollo decided to give a potted version of *The Only Way* with their own M(orris) Harvey as a hero on the scaffold who says, "It is a far, far better thing", while counting heads in the stalls and summing up, "Two more than last night."

There was the obvious temptation of resting in middle-aged comfort on laurels already won. "Our faithful country audiences", as Martin Harvey called them, encouraged that state of mind. That England which was to become labelled "pre-war" contained many millions who were all the more determinedly settled in their taste because of the many attempts to unsettle it. Enterprise atrophied in the breasts of many of their stage favourites.

Why worry over keeping abreast of the times while *A Royal Divorce* still played big dates? W. W. Kelly ranked with Tree among the leading lights of the Touring Managers' Association with its 120 members. This must not be confused with the Travelling Theatre Managers' Association, formed in 1907, "among managers and proprietors of portable theatres" —a reminder that the word "travel" has a meaning of its own in stage language. To travel anything from a husband to a dog is to take it with you. To travel a theatre might mean a booth or gaff, but usually meant the boards and the curtain, with floats and limes as well as scenery and costumes, to be erected in any hall licensed for plays.

Facts for importance to both Associations alike were published in *The Stage Year Book* for 1913, which reported that new regulations concerning the railway travelling of theatrical companies and parties of music-hall artistes, adopted by the Clearing House, had come into force on July 1, 1912. These concerned the truck privileges and the prices of trucks, "the three-quarter fare concession which *The Stage* obtained for theatrical companies in 1896 happily remaining unaltered". To a generation that has acquired a taste for surrealist poetry these regulations should have a certain charm and period atmosphere:

1 to 9 passengers.—No free truck. 6*d*. per mile for a truck exceeding 21 ft. in length, but not exceeding 45 ft.

10 to 20 passengers.—No free truck. 3*d*. per mile for a truck exceeding 21 ft. in length but not exceeding 45 ft. in length.

21 to 33 passengers.—One truck not exceeding 21 ft. in length free.

34 to 66 passengers.—Two trucks not exceeding 21 ft. in length free.

67 to 100 passengers.—Three trucks not exceeding 21 ft. in length free.

101 to 133 passengers.—Four trucks not exceeding 21 ft. in length free.

134 to 166 passengers.—Five trucks not exceeding 21 ft. in length free.

167 to 200 passengers.—Six trucks not exceeding 21 ft. in length free.

3*d*. per mile for each additional truck not exceeding 21 ft. in length; maximum load, 50 cwts.; minimum charge, 5*s*.

6*d*. per mile for each additional truck exceeding 21 ft., but not exceeding 45 ft. in length; maximum load, 5 tons; minimum charge, 10*s*.

9*d*. per mile for each additional truck exceeding 45 ft.; maximum load, 5 tons; minimum charge, 15*s*.

Each passenger, whether first or third class, to be counted as one passenger in reckoning the allowance of free trucks.

Regulation governing guard trucks and runners cancelled so far as theatrical scenery is concerned.

To pay some attention to all that is worth while. It will serve from time to time as a reminder that theatrical companies, like armies, cannot be whisked from spot to spot, but have to be transported with varying amounts—two not unimportant words—of bag and baggage.

In the realm affected by such news as this, a realm where *East Lynne* still thrived, where *The Belle Of New York* still had a modish air, Martin Harvey, almost alone, felt the stir of the New Age. Perhaps other romantics of Crewe and Darlington had become aware of the inadequacy of Edwardian "costume" to match the new habits that life was rapidly acquiring. Yet he won all the fervour of those of the new generation who did not want Shaw or Ibsen but yet found cloak and sword not enough.

In Town fustian was under notice to quit, chiefly owing to the popularity of Gerald du Maurier's success in making new entertainment out
of *Diplomacy* by flattening out all its thrills. H. B. Irving had tried unsuccess-
fully to repeat his *Lyons Mail* success with a new *Dr. Jekyll And Mr. Hyde*
by Comyns Carr. Most London romantics swore by Laurence Irving, who
infused the new intellectual passion into old tradition.

The difference between father and son hinted at some magical metem-
psychosis. There was in both the same eloquence of legs, explaining why
Ellen Terry saw in their length a surprising beauty while others noted
nothing save oddity, even ungainliness, of walk. Each had height and
seemed even taller than he was. Each peered, though the direct, piercing
gaze of Henry became in Laurence a far-away look towards immensity.

One was the Victorian man of mystery, the other the intellectual product
of the New Age, a type who lived by sweetness of reason and revealed
something unsuspected in the English character—all the more to be loved
by John Bull's normal offspring who lived by letting their feelings run
away with them. The outward differences might be taken for granted but
they are worth mentioning—cropped hair instead of locks; panama instead
of majestic silk hat, wide-brimmed or hard felt; cigarette (in holder) instead
of cigar; lounge suit instead of frock-coat; hands in pockets instead of
wielding an imposing cane.

H. B. Irving was different altogether. There was some slight suggestion of the masterful female about him even in *The Lyons Mail*, where his
Lesurques was a *grande dame* and his Dubosc a Bloomsbury landlady—if you
cared to see him that way, in which case you foresaw his triumph in comedy.
Neither should have attempted, if he wished to scale artistic heights, to
step into his father's shoes, even though Harry made a box-office success
of it.

Laurence, at the other extreme, acted those plays of Ibsen which the
stoutest Ibsenites considered impossible. He dramatized *Crime And Punishment* while Dostoievsky was a cult among the very few. His kinship was
with dawn as his father's had been with sunset.

That is how things were in a year—1913—which held the promise
of spring for the theatre. On his way from Hull to London by way of
Glasgow and Edinburgh, Martin Harvey perfected the liveliest revival of
The Taming Of The Shrew seen in our day, with Christopher Sly—played by
Charles Glenney, constant companion since early Lyceum days—seated
in the orchestra, back to the audience, keeping his place in the picture to
the end.

Such a plan, consistently followed in the way the scenery was changed
in everybody's sight, showed the story as an entertainment arranged by
a Lord as a hoax upon the drunken tinker. Since it was thus removed
from reality, whatever Petruchio might do would be excusable. Even the
most ardent suffragettes of 1913 could hardly have objected even to a

wife-beating in what made little more pretence to verisimilitude than a harlequinade.

Yet having found full excuse for a wild display of mock brutality, Martin Harvey went to the other extreme. This was where idealism triumphed over the traditional exercise of horseplay. When the old Shakespeareans said "comedy" they used a peculiar emphasis that made the spoken word unlike anything which can be put into print. We who read it as the fingerpost to thoughtful laughter, as defined by Meredith's authoritative essay, note the vast difference when it is uttered as "Ah! You mean COMEDY" in a way which shows that Sly's "Is not a commonty a Christmas gambol or a tumbling-trick?" has a lot of good sense behind it.

That was the spirit of *Twelfth Night* at His Majesty's, where Tree exhibited what comic could mean in romantic as distinct from natural acting. The two styles were never wider apart than in the distance between Tree and Hawtrey, for even when the former wore modern dress and the latter costumed himself as Applejack the Pirate, the contrast was still there —one acting the whole time for all he was worth, the other so relaxed that to innocent eyes he was merely being himself, not acting at all.

There was no doubt that Katherina and Petruchio at the Prince of Wales's were romantics, no doubt of that whatever, for both revelled in the art of physical movement. They were not ashamed of their young Elizabethan author's love of a frolic. But they were idealists, too. They would have none of the whip-cracking, the insistence on horseplay which the lovers of fustian observed as faithfully as sacred ritual.

With all his "inherited traditions" (as Sir Nigel Playfair said about him on another occasion), Martin Harvey had not lost touch with the younger generation as Tree had done. But that is not the last word to explain the essence of this Petruchio. Idealism went much farther than that. Martin Harvey gave us the essence of it when he said, "As for my conception of Petruchio, I see in him one of the greatest gentlemen Shakespeare ever drew."

But they were on their way to a distracted London: once more a son of Irving had taken the wind out of their sails. Cities, even the biggest cities, rarely have room for more than one stage sensation at a time. Before they had brought their new idea in production to Town, Laurence Irving had caused libraries and box-office to be besieged by thousands eager to see him. In *Typhoon* at the Haymarket he had at last excited the general public, as well as pleasing the critics and inspiring something like awe among younger players. It was a drama of Japanese stoicism at a time when the Anglo-Japanese Alliance was acclaimed as a Good Thing (by all except the righteous, who murmured that no good could come of an agreement between Christians and "heathens").

As the unco' guid never went near the theatre anyway except to ask "What doest thou here, Elisha?" to nervous young men in pit queues or to display banners with warnings about hell fire to *décolletée* women on their way to the stalls, this minority did not matter. Laurence triumphed in his passion of patriotic devotion at white-heat. He also found a place among accepted playwrights, even though he had adapted the piece from the Hungarian.

It was somewhat strange to get such dramatic intensity from Budapest with its doll's playhouses (apart from the sombre national theatre for classics) which regularly inspired the lightest of the world's light comedies, like those of Ferenc Molnar. No matter whence it came, no matter whether this was the Far East merely as Central Europe saw it, the result caught London's fancy so fast that playgoers forgot nearly all else.

In the Prince of Wales's, a theatre where even *The Only Way* had not paid, lively hopes changed immediately to a blank bewilderment that would have been crushing disappointment to a management less schooled in the ways of the great Capital. Despite all the intelligent care bestowed upon *The Shrew*, all the high spirits of fine swashbuckling acting, and all the convincing praise of reputable critics, the production had to be docked until the next tour. Its place was taken in June by *The Faun*, whose success some years before in America had put Edward Knoblauch on his feet. It had been written at the same time as *Kismet*, which Knoblauch had, after some exasperating experiences with Tree, placed with Oscar Asche.

At the Garrick in 1911 the burly giant's heartfelt cry of "Alms, for the love of Allah, alms" had raised such unintended mirth that he had "played for the laugh". Humour had lightened the burden of Arabian Nights splendour, there was a run of over three hundred performances, and the author was now in a position to lay down the law. He wanted a voice in the choosing of the cast, he wanted exactly the right type for each part, which means that every player should look off the stage like the character he has to represent on the stage, and this meant that a girl at the very start of her career was engaged for the heroine.

When Miss de Silva yielded her rightful place as leading lady of the company in *The Faun*, the romantic tradition acknowledged the new system of organizing the theatre. Its nineteenth-century constitution had previously held that stars played star parts whether matched or not; children played bereaved mothers, mothers played abducted children, buxom brides played boys, matrons played Romeo. No justification had to be pleaded. The more unsuitable the rôle, the more acting would be called for, and if the acting were excellent who cared one straw about verisimilitude? Unless you can accept that you might just as well make no further attempt to understand the romantic tradition.

Your perceptions have atrophied by being exercised in a theatre where there is nothing but "casting to type". Suppose that an ancient Greek is wanted: go to Greece and engage an old man (trusting that he is not a model from Chelsea). That is the method of "the pictures", and it became the method of the legitimate drama when Miss de Silva gracefully made way for what our elders called "the juvenile".

Not that it made any difference. *The Faun* was one of the many blends of actuality and fantasy which Londoners reject angrily. In America they succeed even when they are bad. In England they fail even when they are brilliant. Martin Harvey, as Prince Silvani, skilfully made himself into a civilized personage with traces of blood-relationship to other species of other worlds in his pointed ears and eerily glinting eyes. He moved over chairs and squatted on tables as though tree-stumps came more naturally to him than household furniture, but all in vain. "Doesn't make sense to me," said the gallery as it went downstairs. It was yet another "failure in Town", though welcomed in the country before they set out for Canada, whither Laurence Irving, too, had gone.

Fate, at a last meeting between them, exerted itself so grimly that the memory of it would for ever bring a pang to the survivors' hearts. They had been friends for twenty years or more. Laurence wrote his first play, *Godefroi And Yolande*, for Martin Harvey, though someone else played the hero instead. When *The Only Way* first went into rehearsal he volunteered for Defarge.

Now they travelled parallel roads, though their fortunes were opposite. Where one prospered the other lost. In Canada, Laurence Irving never excited the warmth of feelings that welcomed Martin Harvey from coast to coast. So at the extremes of twentieth-century romance these two cherished an old, mature friendship, gladly comparing notes which revealed one as the complement of the other.

Laurence, frankly homesick, angry at the neglect he had brought upon himself by his outspoken resentment of criticism, resolved upon an early return to London. He wanted to sail with his old friends on the *Empress of Ireland*, but every berth was taken. Martin Harvey changed his plans, owing to a wish first to see whether there was a theatre available for Œdipus in New York and then to make for Munich to see a poet's work that appeared to be destined for him.

Directly Laurence heard of this he asked whether the bookings could be kept for him. Mrs. Martin Harvey agreed to sail with the company on the maiden voyage of the *Calgarian* and the transfer was arranged. In Quebec, that May of 1914, she met Laurence and his wife, Mabel Hackney, just before they went aboard. The two liners sailed within a few hours of each other. They passed in a dense fog and spoke each other at parting. *Calgarian* gave warning against speed, and then her skipper hove to until the pea-souper lifted.

After forty-eight hours a calm sea and clear visibility enabled them to head for the Atlantic in confidence. At Liverpool they heard the dreadful news, all the more incredible because, since the loss of the *Titanic*, all voyagers knew that extra safeguards had been taken against loss of life at sea. There had been a growing faith that disasters so appalling occurred but once. But *The Empress of Ireland*, where the St. Lawrence widened to the North Atlantic, gaped wide open when rammed by a tramp steamer in that terrible fog.

She sank so rapidly that the number of passengers who went down with her was greater than the number who perished in the slow doom of the vast liner in mid-ocean. The last glimpse of Laurence Irving and Mabel Hackney was a heartrending picture of a terror-stricken woman with her arms tightly clasped round her husband's knees so that he stood helpless, unable to save her, until those in the boat could wait no longer by the plunging wreck. Those two were named in the list of over a thousand dead, raised in the derelict, brought ashore and laid in long rows on land, where they stayed to be identified.

"But for my change of plans he would be living to-day," was the thought that haunted Martin Harvey on his way to Munich. This mood matched his errand. What he saw was no ordinary play. The theatre was turned, for him, into a cathedral by a poet's drama of religious significance which chimed with his mood. It was a new version of *Everyman*—Hofmannsthal's *Jedermann*—and the idealist of the English theatre at once decided to transport the spectacle, with the scenery and costumes he saw, to London that autumn—a bold venture, for the Austrian poet, despite *Elektra* and *Der Rosenkavalier*, was very little known in England.

The English read foreign novels reluctantly, foreign plays only under compulsion, foreign poetry not if they can help it, and foreign poetic plays not at all. Yet there had been one previous link between the player and the author of this play. When Hengler's old circus was transformed into the Palladium in 1910 the management's ambitious policy not only netted Martin Harvey in *The Conspiracy*, but also a wordless play to exploit the success at the Coliseum of Reinhardt's *Sumurum* in its compressed form. In the November of 1911 Hugo von Hofmannsthal's *Das Fremd Madchen* (The Strange Girl), a wordless play with music by Hannes Rich, was in the Palladium bill.

Poetry again proved a magnet. Once more Martin Harvey purposed to risk his all in order to bring it back to the stage. So many thousands remember him because of *The Only Way* and *The Breed Of The Treshams* that his biographer must stress how much more of his energy, as distinct from length of days, went into the performance of works not only of dead poets but of living ones. He aimed not only at keeping poetry but poets alive; it would be hard to name many other managers who have held this aim so constantly in mind. Certainly Tree had given Stephen Phillips his first public acclaim, but they were far apart now when the author of *Herod* came back to the playbills merely for having adapted Walter Browne's spectacle, *Everywoman*, for Drury Lane.

The dramatist favoured at His Majesty's was Louis Napoleon Parker, the pageant-master whose alfresco displays of local antiquarianism broke out in highly-coloured blotches all over England like a noisy epidemic. More than a word must be said of him. He was born in Calvados, France, in 1852; educated at Freiburg and the Royal Academy of Music; first engaged as "director of music" at Sherbourne School, Dorset; and for nineteen years he composed cantatas.

When he succeeded in getting three of his plays acted in 1890 he devoted his life to the stage and kept up an average of three a year. He adapted *Magda* for Mrs. Patrick Campbell at the Lyceum, wrote *Harlequin King* for Waller at the Imperial, turned W. W. Jacobs' "Beauty and the Barge" into a play about society people for Cyril Maude at the New, and made a romance about Disraeli and the Suez Canal, which was first acted at Montreal in 1911 and later seen by the entire world either on stage or screen.

For His Majesty's in 1912 he wrote *Drake*, which inspired a note in the lively observations upon life of Beachcomber in the *Daily Express*. While noting the leisurely fashion in which plays begin nowadays, he recalled how the curtain used to rise on costume dramas, citing Mr. Parker's work, though he seems to be recalling William Devereux's *Sir Walter Raleigh* at the Lyric in 1909:

"A sailor was saying, 'And the Spaniard lay dead at my feet.' I prefer that to the silent entry of a maid who dusts the room until a bell rings. 'That'll be 'er,' says the maid, and the good-humoured audience rewards her with a nervous laugh. My favourite beginning in fiction is the cry 'Marked cards!' in *Under The Red Robe*.

"Quiller-Couch quotes somewhere a stage direction to this effect: 'Enter slowly seven soldiers on their way back from the Thirty Years' War.'"

When the long run of his Elizabethan adventure (without Tree in the cast) at last ended, another drama from Parker's pen took its place for the autumn of 1913. In two ways *Joseph And His Brethren* was designed to set people agog. It was full of real animals. It was puffed as being the first Biblical play to pass the censor.

DRAKE, THE DYNASTS, ARMAGEDDON

THAT spring of 1914 fulfilled the promise of a new romance in the Theatre. To the joy of youth the fug of the old century at last eddied away. Pure colour came like sunlight upon the stage to displace *décor* which made gardens or forests look like upholstery. The statement may be unfair to the old school of scene-painters, but that is how we felt when the Russian Ballet influenced Shakespeare. Granville-Barker's Savoy revival of *A Midsummer Night's Dream* in the February caused only the fusty to scoff at golden Asiatic fairies. The rest of us, old and young alike, vowed we would have no other Shakespeare than this. Then in the April came Tree and Mrs. Pat in *Pygmalion*.

In his adverse comments upon that production, Mr. Shaw was one against many. The story went that at rehearsals Mrs. Pat retorted with, "One day, Mr. Shaw, you'll eat a rump steak and then God help us poor women." But young and old again agreed that just as the new manner was good for Shakespeare, the old was good for Shaw. To some of us who doted over it in the grand manner, *Pygmalion* has never exerted so powerful a spell since. It was, no matter what the author wanted it to be, romance. There was a swagger about the acting. Old tradition had mated with the brand-new intellect.

As spring ripened into summer the most incredulous, fantastic, utterly preposterous, speculative, horrible absurdity insisted upon being first possible and then imminent. The crowds who clung to the railings of Buckingham Palace found relief for their bemused thoughts in singing the music-hall chorus of *Sons Of The Sea*—"but they can't build the boys of the bulldog breed that made old England's name".

The most advanced of poets wrote verses to try to comprehend how the soldier he talked to one day might be dead on a battlefield in the near future—"Back, hound, back to your kennel," he said to this not-to-be-tolerated thought. Friends told each other that in a month or two battleships would be sending each other to the bottom, told each other this because they could not believe it.

Postal orders were given as change when you sorrowfully parted with a gold coin; you had been told sovereigns were being called in and you suspected that despite all this talk of Treasury pound-notes, money would shortly give out altogether, and where would you be for food and drink then? In short, the world was simply not used to it. As for the theatre or art, or anything of the sort, any man who had heard or read what the intellectuals were saying wanted no more of that.

Romance made a brave attempt to serve the country—to uphold, as the War Office would say, civilian morale. Tree led the way by reviving *Drake* on August 19. The usual first-nighters, who filled the stalls of His Majesty's in evening dress according to the new watchword of "Business as usual", showed in their conduct the prevailing bewilderment concerning how to change from peace to war. They listened to the overture with a little more respect than usual because it consisted of the Allied National Anthems. When the turn came of "La Marseillaise" a young long-haired Fabian stood while nearly everybody else sat.

When "God The All Terrible" followed, everybody else stood and he slumped down again, muttering, "If you won't stand for the Republic, I won't for your Tsar"—omitting the Trafalgar Square adjective, however, as proof of respect for their feelings. There was still the old glamour about those great figures of Armada days, more especially as Elizabeth herself gained considerably in appearance through being played by Phyllis Neilson-Terry, tall, lovely and consciously belonging to the aristocracy of the stage.

Undoubtedly Drake was stirring. But the public, like all animals, when driven one way runs another. It declined, very casually, to be stirred. That August it left for its usual seaside holidays. At Brighton, Margate, Broadstairs, Bournemouth, Blackpool and all the rest of those chosen scraps of old England's shores which turn human beings into flies, vast swarms took their pleasure as usual, though one evening's news bulletins on boards along the promenade put the words "holocaust" and "decimated" into every mouth—our own losses at Mons.

Pleasure was resumed. Why not? Young men who seemed to invite the white feather knew quite well that since no training establishment had room for them there was no need to rush. Pre-war ways of life were lived as long as possible and pre-war kinds of entertainments were in demand. While other companies precipitately disbanded, Martin Harvey kept his together; it was difficult while the short, sharp shock lasted, and then *The Breed Of The Treshams* revealed itself as exactly what the public wanted—with appeals for recruits thrown in.

With that the gauntlet was flung down. Had romance any part in modern war? Martin Harvey, like the Ruperts who took command of the British Army, was quite convinced it had. Bearing the badge of a recruiting sergeant on his coat, he gave "War Lectures" in the theatre every night for two years until they became what he called "a last prayer for voluntary service in order to avoid the threatened conscription". The idealist saw "voluntary service" as an array of Galahads, all stalwart or at least fully grown and able-bodied, and "conscription" as a chain-gang of miserable, cowardly galley-slaves.

So begins that sweet-scented manuscript of war which ends with a dashing cavalry onslaught, and people would still cling to it for years to come, though the folly of viewing bloodshed romantically had been shown as far back as Omdurman. *Arms And The Man* tried to dispel it, but Shaw was too far ahead of his time. Instead of indicating exactly what would happen when cavaliers tried to ride down machine-guns, he paid us the compliment of thinking we could grasp this fact and passed on to the next step, which warned the War Office what would happen if the gunners who grinned at the squadrons were badly served by ordnance. Another of his warnings was against romance as poison, and there again he was fully justified by events in 1914.

The test had come. Romantics more in touch with everyday life than an idealist who had succeeded in getting above its dust and grime were anxious now to throw off their old allegiance. Nothing but the starkest realism could survive. So any close observer might well have reasoned while looking on the darker side of the call to heroism. Lovely young actresses offered their lips to "anyone ready to join". They looked less alluring to the harassed woman with a husband and son already in arms and a child, barely out of the nursery to her, not to be restrained by her pleading to wait until he was old enough. Romance undoubtedly had failed. The ordinary workers could see that. The recruits themselves were well, very well, aware of it, though the worst was yet to come.

Looking back on those days no one can feel great sympathy for the virtuous impulse which made middle age require self-sacrifice from youth. The younger the boys were the more quickly they responded, and the foul military mind, a curse to other countries besides Germany, sent these children out to be butchered before they could bear arms or learn to take cover.

So far no orator has denounced the day when he volunteered to make recruiting speeches. One of those who excelled as the mouthpiece of the heavenly hosts qualified for a distinguished place in the rogues' gallery; many others tried shamelessly in public courts to avoid military service when the age limit was raised to make them liable; more than one celebrity would eat dirt as though he liked it rather than do what he had once told others to do. The chilled spectator could but reflect that the very virtue of idealists inclined them more readily than other men to this defect of judgment.

Happily the chance to risk his own life under shellfire did come Martin Harvey's way for him to prove his own eagerness to share the peril. In addition, both Miss de Silva and he worked indefatigably for the wounded, and when the public at large had grown less sensitive to horrors they never slackened in their efforts.

War correspondents still described, after all "Haig's Hammer Blows", how the cavalry rode into the blue and left history to tell belatedly what happened to them there. Romance now had to be defined as wearing rose-coloured glasses in real life and looking at rose-coloured spectacles on the stage. Champions for *The Breed Of The Treshams* bluntly maintained that romance was a luxury pure and simple, arguing that it served the purpose of relaxation in time of war rather more intelligently than "leg shows".

Too much should not be demanded of it. Works of art are a burdensome responsibility in a house on fire, and in that predicament the greatest master-piece on earth is of less value than a hose. Going to the theatre, anyway, was now on a par with getting slightly drunk—apart, of course, from such inveterately realistic plays as *Damaged Goods*, which had to be forced upon the troops, like blackjack, whether they liked it or not.

The debate, vital in 1914, still has significance, though nobody then thought of realism as food and romance as drink. Analogies never take us very far, but this one will serve if it suggests the folly of first demanding too much of any one thing and then condemning it as a failure all round. In matters of the spirit we misuse all we have. There is no greater blasphemy than our oath to tell the whole truth. Who could ask that of any man? Why expect it from any actor?

Garrick, the most universal and catholic of them, embraced the whole range of drama—the whole range, that is, of his own day. He never attempt-ed what Martin Harvey perfected, and what fault has been found with him in the foregoing pages on account of his Sunday night war lectures in the theatre springs from a desire to define not merely a personality but a whole philosophy by indicating certain limitations. Unless you paint shadows you cannot reveal the light.

Remember they were difficult days. The greater the brain, the greater the error. Mr. Shaw's defence of his pamphlet, "Commonsense About The War", made it indefensible, for while man may be vindicated for his desire to serve the cause of truth, he must be judged by results when he swears he wrote for the cause of propaganda. The realism of that pamphlet was more poisonous than romance. But could anybody who tried to think do right by any other light than the one within him?

The noblest attempt by anyone belonging to the stage occurred in the November of 1914 when Granville-Barker adapted Hardy's *The Dynasts* to the stage. Once the thing happened there was nothing remarkable, in the eyes of the matter-of-fact, about it; but before it happened it was, so to speak, not to be thought of. With a theatre the size of the little Kingsway the project, even when in rehearsal, was still something to smile at. "Just a series of odd scenes with Henry Ainley as Reader to supply a voice for Fates and Destiny"—so word went round.

Yet here was the quarter-deck of *Victory* with Nelson, here house-fronts at Brussels with English people watching the troops on the march out of sight below, and a girl breaking her heart as her partner at last night's ball rides out of sight, here the field of Waterloo, with Wellington and Napoleon—nothing but the distance between P. and O.P. to separate triumph from disaster, but that was enough. Here was one of those nights that justify a lifetime's expenditure of hope upon the theatre. The public stayed away.

With all the opportunities we have had it is somewhat amiss that modern science has not diagnosed war fever in every minute particular. Perhaps it is merely a protracted kind of intoxication (with a protracted hangover), but under its influence the ordinary mind does achieve a state of exaltation.

The war plays of 1914–15 will serve as symptoms. Barrie wrote a minor monstrosity called *Der Tag*, which may prove nothing more than that he had no very strong head. Pinero wrote a music-hall sketch called *Mr. Livermore's Dream* to encourage war savings. Shaw wrote *Augustus Does His Bit*, informing the wide-eyed innocent who is now writing this book that he was falling into line with other playwrights. This evidence points to what we find on looking into ourselves, namely that war fever, as inspiration to literary endeavour, is not worth much.

Yet under an influence which caused most civilians to make nuisances of themselves with useless offers of war effort, Stephen Phillips resolved to harness dramatic poetry to immediate national needs. That last effort of the theatrical marvel of 1901 should stir the heart. Of all his old crowd of friends there were a few left. Martin Harvey and Miss de Silva had never failed him. There was a typist who would, at the end of her own day's work, labour as his devoted secretary every evening without fail. There was also Irving Taylor, a journalist from Ulster of the staunchest friendship.

While himself engaged on an epic greater in length than "Paradise Lost", he yet had energy left over from strenuous hours of reporting for the *Standard* to assist Phillips in his labours. He awoke the interest of all and sundry in the imminent masterpiece. Whenever a bleary-eyed critic, roused from his morning slumbers, tried to enter the swing doors which formed the last barrier between himself and full awakening, Milton's successor would rise as though from a paving-slab and shamelessly buttonhole him. For Irving Taylor, public-houses held no interest. He saw to it that they had none for Phillips either. *Armageddon* got finished.

What is more it was joyously, enthusiastically accepted as the drama's third attempt to be apt to history in the making. The Martin Harveys saw to that. The year 1915 held a glorious First of June for Stephen Phillips, for the loyal, unflinching typist, and for Irving Taylor, whose joy was greater than any his friend, the dramatic critic, could buy with his last golden sovereign.

It was a memorable first night. Martin Harvey became the very spit of Milton's devil—fallen archangel with sable wings, Satan himself, unlike Mephisto as conceived by all the great romantic actors before him. Next he changed into the Abbé of Rheims and then into an English general meditating beneath the portrait of Joan of Arc. That vision was brought to life by Miss de Silva in armour, a vision so admirable that Martin Harvey kept photographs of this Joan in a wallet next his heart all the rest of his life.

From the public he expected little, and certainly, to use his own words, got less. The noblest expression which the drama had contributed to the all-absorbing question of the hour had to give place to *The Corsican Brothers*. Late that season the public found what it wanted in *A Little Bit of Fluff* elsewhere—under another management, of course.

As *Armageddon* went into the Company's repertoire for the autumn tour, prospects seemed brighter for the author, though the utter, unequivocal failure had shattered what was left of his spirit. Six months later, with no worldly possessions above the value of a fiver, he died rich in the love of what friends he had left.

The cause was 'flu, though, if the authorities would have allowed it, the word on the certificate should have been "despair". The stage, proverbially fickle but actually stable wherever time, space and war give it a chance, had forgotten him. His funeral was a family affair. Miss de Silva was the only player-mourner, for her husband was ill. "They put me into a carriage with the relations who mistook me for the secretary who had helped to give the poet his last acquaintance with fame"—the last of his lifetime, that is, for in twenty years' time an invention which persuaded people to listen would restore Ainley his youth, permit him to stand before our inward eyes as Paolo again and send him again down the white road to Rimini. The poet will not die.

In those years "the loveliest and the best" vanished fast. Basil Hallam, *jeune premier* of *The Faun*, had won a wild ardour of admiration the next April in *The Passing Show*, a blaze of colour at the Palace. Before the crowds that loved him had stopped singing the chorus of his "Gilbert the Filbert", his blithe spirit took its farewell of the world from an observation balloon dropping to earth in flames.

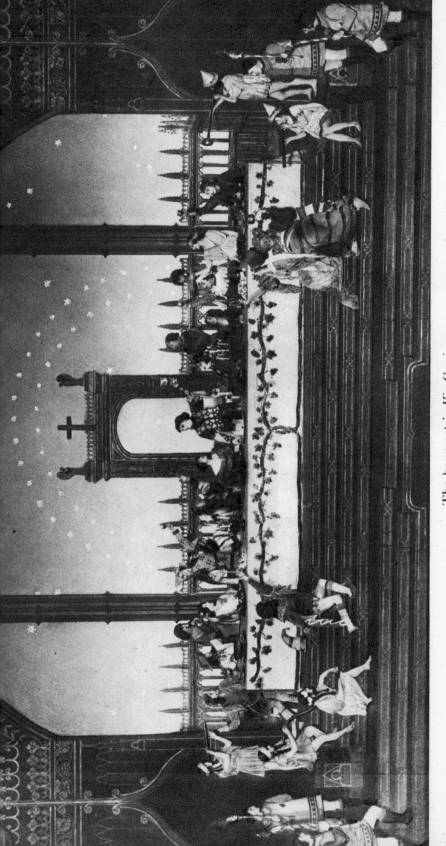

The banquet in *Via Crucis*

Martin Harvey as
"Blanco Posnet"

[Photo: F. W. Schmidt

Miss de Silva as
"Feemy"

BOOK VI

CHAPTER I

THE STILL SMALL VOICE OF WAR

JUST how Martin Harvey came to take His Majesty's for the spring season of 1916 troubles no one now. Shakespeare's Tercentenary, the desire to raise funds for the Red Cross, and Tree's appointment with Macbeth in Hollywood, all helped to create this opportunity. Such whys and wherefores make interesting gossip for an autobiography, but all that memory holds dear are the vivid glimpses which resulted of full blossoming genius.

Nothing seen of Martin Harvey before had prepared Londoners for this true marriage of the arts of actor and *metteur-en-scène*. According to his own account one production was in the manner of Reinhardt, another Elizabethan and another makeshift. That is how he saw them at first rehearsal. In performance there were no contrasts to break the series. It was a sequence of settings by and for Martin Harvey. Nothing seen since on the stage can blur the image of them.

St. George's Day was the date for remembering the death of Shakespeare. Drury Lane chose May 2 for an all-star performance of *Julius Caesar*, memorable because Benson had no sooner died before the Capitol than his presence was commanded in the ante-chamber of the royal box, where, with a sword hastily fetched from the nearest theatrical costumier, he was knighted. Otherwise the most impressive part of any all-star performance is the audience. Who played who and how at that Tercentenary has inspired no eloquently fervent pen.

On the other hand, Martin Harvey's acting six days later moved several leading critics, including S. R. Littlewood and Arthur Machen, to fine words of praise. Walkley alone was disdainful, but then he never forgot this, his pet vendetta. In all else he was one of the best-equipped critics the theatre ever attracted. But as Martin Harvey and Arnold Bennett both discovered, he was waspish. His virtues are forgotten and that vice remembered. Alas, the fragrance of inspired criticism may be as transitory as the insubstantial pageant it criticizes.

Derisive references to "The little stage Frenchman who sat in the stalls" take the place of the delighted laughter over his wit. But when this addled, in his notice of the greatest Hamlet of the war, to spite over the actor's "duck of a bonnet", the poison went the way of the poison on Laertes' foil. What threw him off his balance directly he saw Martin Harvey never became clear. "Blood group did not call to blood group," a bright neo-Freudian might say; in other words, the romantic temperament was not his. In London any number of others lacked it, and still more would lack it as cynicism increased.

The rest of us, with eyes to see, could not but marvel. There have been many Hamlets since, in many settings from modern dress to a revival of Kemble's stance with the skull against a brilliantly star-lit sky, but none of these formed pictures so easy to recall as the Hamlet in a dip of the ground looking upwards to the skyline where Ophelia's coffin was borne towards the slanting tombstones around a gnarled, wind-swept tree in the fading light.

Perhaps no one noticed in this triumphant vindication of modern stage-management and lighting one fond link with Irving. That tree had been brought from the Island. They had noted it at Bonchurch, marked its stage-struck, wizened look, and recognized its affinity with their old master's pet "prop". Miss de Silva said at once, "That is our Fate Tree," and what she meant can be understood by reference to Ellen Terry's recollections of the old Lyceum. The dark, overhanging branch of the cedar suggested to Irving the cruel outstretched hand of Fate. He called it the Fate Tree, and used it in *Hamlet* and *Romeo And Juliet*. In *Eugene Aram* it drooped low over the grave where Irving lay in a black cloak. "Not until a moon-beam struck the dark mass," says Ellen Terry, "did you see it was a man."

That fate tree symbolized the upholding of Irving's tradition under all the trials of a season of five weeks, with a change of bill every Monday in a strange theatre, which meant problems of new-fangled scenery for an unfamiliar staff. In a normal London of regular playgoers, of normal interest at peaceful breakfast tables, in long theatre notices in full-sized newspapers, besides full-page critiques in weekly reviews, Martin Harvey would then and there have been acknowledged as the one actor-manager with some of the glamour of greatness about him.

How clearly this Hamlet stands out from all others becomes ever clearer as the playgoer makes more and more comparisons. Many a Hamlet of the past fades into the memory of a face in soliloquy. Most are of that kind first and foremost. Martin Harvey's is remembered otherwise. He had proved himself as Œdipus under uncharacteristic restraint. Now he triumphed in his own style.

In great romantic rôles he lived and breathed and had his being in full freedom of movement. By his side in recollection all others seem to be static—sable figures frozen in horror against battlements, deep in thought on X chairs, prone on a rug intent on watchfulness or posed around a skull. But against that vast illimitable sky, behind the toppling gravestones on the cliff edge of Elsinore, the sweet prince borrows nothing from classic stillness.

He is that paragon, man, refusing to submit to the coming night until he has first asserted his own minute will. He does not passively endure, is not overcome with Irvingesque horrors and remorse; he is valiant in every trenchant limb. And so, after all, was Shakespeare's Hamlet—so much so that earlier and later romantics easily raised him to "a melodram". In this Tercentenary wartime performance one extreme was as safely avoided as the other. It was, to repeat a word, the blossoming of romance.

To compare him in the part with Sir Johnston Forbes-Robertson is to gain fuller understanding of both. The merits of what we literally *saw* three years earlier when the tall figure, with face so deeply furrowed as to indicate how little he had used the muscles of it, inspired very little descriptive writing. We remember that last moment when he passed his hands before his unseeing eyes to make "The rest is silence" signify also "The rest is darkness."

We remember how he stood behind Ophelia at their parting and lifted his trembling fingers over her tresses—that usual "bus." of self-sacrificing heroes which Irving loved. The blemish did not matter. We no more heeded it than we heeded property trees, like those of toy theatres, in the King's orchard. We had come to see Forbes-Robertson, and having seen him, all we wanted was to listen.

Later in life he occasionally recited Shakespeare in concert-halls. He sat the whole time, made no gestures, and his face was expressionless. You would watch him and be aware of this effortless passivity; and yet how the words lived, how exciting they were! "As fine as a performance of the play," said hearers, stirred to capacity. If he could, when approaching three score years and ten, move us so deeply while speaking from his chair on the bare platform, how much of his spell as an actor had been created by his voice alone?

Golden voices were not so rare at the zenith of his career, but his was the noblest utterance of them all. To G.B.S. it suggested a clarionet in A, played only in the chalumeau register, "but then the chalumeau, sympathetically sounded, has a richly melancholy and noble effect".

That Martin Harvey spoke in tones less "richly melancholy" need not be disputed, but the mere timbre of his voice, as many noted, expressed some quality purely his own, more potent than any other's to conjure up the magic of Shakespeare's unexpected turn of phrase. Great speakers of verse may enchant us anew with the most familiar lines, but this Hamlet made us hear, as though we had never heard these before, such oddities as "unpregnant of my cause" and "sense to ecstasy was ne'er so thralled". He did not excel in making the plain image plainer still but in creating from the less obtrusive thought a glow of mysticism. Dull ears might easily have missed what the attentive did not always note until this Hamlet had been heard a second or even a third time. And even for the pleasure his voice gave simply as sound Martin Harvey had virtue enough to brave comparison with an actor of resonant sonority whom he engaged for the Ghost.

When she first acted with Stephen Phillips, Miss de Silva had met Herbert Ross, stocky in appearance and unlikely off the stage to make anyone think of a wraith, but his voice had an organ roll in it. Now he joined the Company as the most impressive of Ghosts. The fearfulness of encountering a disembodied spirit conveyed itself not in any make-believe to be looked at by a world sceptical of spooks, but in ear-haunting cadence.

A comprehensive history of the English stage for forty years past might have been written at first hand by that experienced company. With a nation-wide renown as a musical comedy rajah at Daly's, Rutland Barrington had already made Polonius his own with "Forbie", and now he took charge of that part at His Majesty's. To Horatio, A. B. Imeson brought a sense of stagecraft acquired, like Irving's early training, in melodrama; and Franklin Dyall, who had rejoined the company as the Shade of Atilla in *Armageddon*, put enough virility into Laertes now to have walked away with the play had there been a less magnetic spirit in the lead.

"N. de Silva" stirred old admiration afresh as Ophelia. Hamlet, watching her in the wings, could not but applaud with the audience as the scene ended. Some feel strongly about Ophelia. Others may see in her nothing but a decorative effect, deliberately designed as such so as not to upset the groundlings' sympathy with Hamlet, and not to be raised into a major person of the play by any study of her character. Martin Harvey, who held the orthodox view, had seen many Ophelias; he preferred Miss de Silva's above all, Ellen Terry's included.

The next week *The Taming Of The Shrew* was revived. The third bill was *Richard III*, without any innovations apart from an almost shamefaced order to keep the lights off the old scenery and "concentrate it on the centre of the stage". The results pleased the critics "to our amused amazement", but the fact may as well be mentioned that more than one of those who marvelled at the effect had been fully informed beforehand.

After three weeks the first-night audience had adopted a feeling of friendship for the management with a tinge of the old Lyceum's academic interest in it. There were learned discussions, Stage *versus* Press, in the intervals. Quite a lot of sound learning and wide knowledge was aired, though the one argument whose living accents still linger on the ear was the championship by Miriam Lewes (rehearsing for the next bill) of Martin Harvey's wordless roar when all had been said and done.

This brisk symposium did, for once, respect the curtain. There were so many brief performances not to be missed. Harcourt Williams, under the banner of the idol of his youth, spoke Clarence's lines that seem to have strayed from *The Tempest*. The Princes were lovely sisters, Eileen Glover, destined to die soon, and Dorothy Glover, who would leave the stage and return as a dress designer. The programme excites its chief interest on the distaff side. N. de Silva was Lady Anne, and the cursing had two very notable exponents. Nancy Price, vampire in Drury Lane's sporting dramas, spoke the most vicious of all.

> Therefore take with thee my most heavy curse
> Which in the day of battle tire thee more
> Than all the complete armour that thou wear'st.

Above all, Geneviève Ward came back to the stage to play Margaret.

Just before that revival of *Richard III* she was interviewed. As the reporter came into her drawing-room by Regent's Park she strode from her background of world-tour relics with, "You remind me of Harry Ainley," which was the finest compliment any young man could be paid. She said she had long passed three score years and ten, declared that she still enjoyed her daily exercise and laughed because the gardeners in the Park called her Johnny Walker.

About Queen Margaret she said: "I can play that part because I can curse. I always did know how to curse." To remove any wrong impression she added, "on the stage." What a pity she had never acted a full-length Queen Margaret, a character doomed rarely to be impersonated except by young women at elocution schools! Shakespeare spread one of his greatest heroines over four plays, and though the three parts of *Henry VI* are sometimes telescoped such "vandalism" has never been designed for her especial benefit.

There have been many Ophelias and Desdemonas, poor creatures beside her. She has been played only by one actress in the category of Lady Macbeths—and so Geneviève Ward played her, after the High Roman manner, in Martin Harvey's revival of *Richard III* at His Majesty's. How strangely enthralling it was to see the marble classic spirit take the stage for a brief spell from volatile romance, to set our eyes on that unassailable figure, unshaked of motion, deathless we thought her, so rightly cast for that queen who was a resurgence from earlier history—how enthralling it was as she, with passion so sublimated as to have nothing of frail blood or tissue in it, brought down the very elements themselves to the footlights with

> Earth gapes, hell burns, fiends roar, saints pray
> To have him suddenly convey'd from hence.
> Cancel his bond of life, dear God, I pray,
> That I may live to say, THE DOG IS DEAD.

So it would be, the hushed playgoer felt, were Roscius to come back to the boards by a miracle greater only in measurement of years, not in the quick sensation of a golden age blessing a sparsely endowed present. Geneviève Ward—her name suddenly stills the tongue of this babbler as if she spoke again and he afraid to lose a word.

The fourth week brought *Henry V*. It was "in the Elizabethan manner", one of the manager's grave, unconscious jokes. There rarely was anything done more in the Harvey manner—with that altogether admirable trick of making the scenery act. Said the slight, boyish Hal, born leader, majestic in eyebrow and nostril, so ready to spur men on with the look he had used to quell unruly audiences that rant never intruded:

> Cheerly to sea; the signs of war advance;
> No King of England if not King of France,

and the great gate of embarkation swung open to reveal on a blazing backcloth the English Fleet in being. The sight moved us to applaud with its sudden shock. That was the main piece of "production".

Was it Elizabethan? At the moment we would have agreed to anything, we were so won over with patriotic delight. When the magic dimmed, long, long afterwards, we recognized it as Christmas pantomime—the transformation scene put to legitimate dramatic effect. Shakespeare had never thought of it. If he turned in his grave it would have been to wish he had.

Once more Miss de Silva and other stalwarts of the Company took their share, but the manager again asserted his sense of showmanship. There was in his casting one thrill of surprise. What Miriam Lewes made of Chorus has never been approached by any of the gifted lovers of this epicure's part. That flash of the eye and that joyous tongue like a steel whip to strike sparks out of stone hearts proved for once that there could be an answer to her prayer, "O for a Muse of fire."

Into a programme of that season a critic, with no thought of ever being called upon to chronicle it in future, slipped a letter, dated June 9, 1916, which had been handed to him with the comment, "If that's a fair sample of stage manners from the provinces better send all your —— actors there." This was its characteristic style, in contrast to the publicity paragraphs usual from manager's offices:

"Dear Sir,

"The production of *Hamlet* was so recent that I can scarcely expect to have the pleasure of a visit from your dramatic representative on Monday. But I should be extremely grateful to you if you could find a corner in which to mention that the new presentation of the tragedy was so enthusiastically received during the week of May 8th that we are giving a further week's representations, beginning next Monday, as the final item of our programme of Shakespeare Tercentenary performances.

"I am, dear Sir,

"Yours faithfully,

"J. MARTIN HARVEY."

A caricature of Martin Harvey

That spring of 1916 marks the Company's zenith. Through no fault of their own it was short-lived. Trucks were no longer to be had, free or costly, for heavy scenery. "Little plays," said Miss de Silva, "must be had instead," as she thought of those Wyndham had made popular in what was to the new public a remote past. The gayest and most volatile star of comedy now haunted the foyers of his theatres, a sad ghost of a man, still attractive to any eye capable of seeing grace even in age when listlessness makes known the fading mind.

David Garrick, which he had played during the eighteen-eighties in a version said to be his own, now needed another habitation and a name. *Rosemary*, which took its place at the Criterion a decade later, was by Louis N. Parker and Murray Carson. Pictures by Dendy Sadler and Marcus Stone of the England of Victoria's girlhood were its inspiration. Runaways to Gretna Green, a breakdown, breakfast at a wayside hostelry, overtaking parents, peace-making by a very fine old English gentleman, a frustrated romance between the bride and the all-too-perfectly mannered host in his well-appointed house—all these familiar blooms, arranged by a deft play-wright and a good actor, exhaled the old-world rose garden perfume, and Wyndham, when saying good-bye to his long-retained youth, had charmed again as the fine old—but not too old—English gentleman.

Such a delicate pair of costume dramas could be called old-fashioned and survive. The grace of Martin Harvey might be less volatile, more grave, farther from laughter, nearer to sentiment. The faithful in towns and cities from north to south approved his choice. To many the new Garrick and new Sir Jasper became associated with those middle war years; to a number they were experiences never to be forgotten.

That journalist of many parts, Gordon Stowell, who edits encyclopædias, takes dozens of subjects from art to radio in his stride, besides adding to the usual qualifications of dramatic critic the unusual one of being a leading man of amateur theatricals, is among this number. He recalls the Christmas of 1916 when he was the typical lonely soldier, stranded in London, turned out of barracks to enjoy himself, far from home, barred from the house he had been invited to because 'flu had got there first, and with just enough money to get away to friends the next morning.

But how on earth was he to spend Christmas Eve? With barely a shilling to spare he turned to the Shakespeare Hut, a Bloomsbury sanctuary built by the Y.M.C.A. on the site purchased for the National Theatre (though it would grow into the School of Tropical Medicine instead). Private Stowell, after he had made sure of a bed and something for supper just slightly more filling than a bun (for he had qualms about the morrow's fare) found himself on the general free-list for a play.

He looked at the stage in the hall and decided, "Anyone who could act on that could act on a tea-tray" and then set his incredulous eyes on the notice-board which announced the personal appearance of Martin Harvey in *David Garrick*. In his tired, outcast-at-Christmas mood, he sat without any great expectations until the visitor appeared. Still he was unimpressed.

"Those little ferrety eyes in that great ham of a face revolted me," expresses his first feelings. "Then," he adds, "they riveted me." In all fairness that performance ought to be on the record of the National Theatre, upon whose soil it undoubtedly took place. Lady Martin-Harvey remembers it because they played by candle-light. That suited *David Garrick* perfectly.

Not that Christmas but the last one of the *David Garrick* tour impressed tself most on Martin Harvey's mind. They were at Torquay, packing the

Pavilion by the sea. There was to be a Christmas party with the dinner of greatly honoured custom in all its glory. Every member of the staff was at table, with the head carpenter on one side of Mrs. Martin Harvey and the wardrobe-mistress on the other.

The scene was set for the entrance of the turkey. It missed its cue. What came on looked like a very inexperienced understudy—mixed grill. The head waiter said the course was being served as ordered. There was a lot of explaining to be done, but it led nowhere until Rutland Barrington volunteered the information that he had thought fit, on the strength of his unquestioned standing as a gourmet, to alter the arrangements for both food and wine.

The Company, who knew their Rutland Barrington, saw the funny side of it. The staff could not. He is one more to be added to the list of actors who have become hypnotized by their parts. He had played the Rajah of Bhong far, far too often. Poetic justice overtook him in *Rosemary* when he played the old professor who has been invited for two nights and has stayed several years, for everybody agreed he had been perfectly cast.

The postilion, always the apple of Marcus Stone's eye whenever he thought of Gretna Green, brought back to the footlights a red-headed, jockey-built, galvanic marionette, with an alert sensitiveness to comedy that made us marvel—Jimmy Welch, one of the little geniuses of the stage, forgotten by the public at large but cherished by inherited theatrical memory. Few people are interested in the painters of miniatures. Megalomania biases our ideas of fame. But before we have finished with the stage of 1914-18 some respect will have to be paid, anyhow, to "little" plays.

In these middle years more and more of Martin Harvey's energy was given to unrewarded services. Since idealism was an integral part of his nature he did not weary in well-doing like the majority who rushed in 1914 to offer their spare time for the good of the cause and revelled for ever after. His enthusiasm was so unflagging that it inspired a story which may be untrue to life as far as facts go, but does for all that convey a sense of the atmosphere in which he lived.

While at Leeds he agreed to lecture one afternoon at both Bradford and Huddersfield. One invitation came from some ancient order of staunch virtue and the other from "the troops". To a man in a hurry one wad of script looks exactly like any other wad of script that has come from the same typewriter. Some local wag (as the word was still in use presumably the species it denoted was also) made this the peg on which to hang some fantastic report how rows upon rows of snow-white whiskers waggled when told

> Get the bloody guns out,
> Have some bloody sense,
> Prepare for bloody wars, boys,
> And self-de-bloody-fence!

and how some two or three hours later rows of khaki figures, under the baleful eye of the sergeant-major, heard themselves extolled for their long years of unswerving devotion to the cause of total abstinence and regular contributions to the local maternity hospital.

On top of which he was, to an extent that would justify any such story, other-worldly. Concerning some soldiers who were singing in a railway train, plaintive, almost ghostly, and very quietly, he wrote, "They seemed 'fey'; they seemed the wraiths of men", and a great longing came over him to be one of them in a world which had "removed them from everything which we on our side of the water counted as real and worth while". In the Y.M.C.A. uniform of "a Christian Soldier" he set out on the pilgrim's progress described in some typescript among his papers:

"Night is falling and the packet-boat is filling up. No one smiles as in the old days when sailing from this port meant a pleasant adventure in a foreign land. Men are either set, determined, quiet, or laugh over-much with the false and reckless note of those who know this voyage may easily be their last. Not a lifebelt is worn, however, though the prudent see that they are in a handy place. The packet is cast off and we drop down with the placid tide.

"A naval officer plays a lament on the bagpipes, as he paces the quay besides which a warship is dry-docked. It sounds bizarre, out of place, depressing. Night has fallen: every glimmer of light in the ship is cloaked; even the small glow of a cigarette brings a sharp reprimand from the First Officer and instantly it is stamped out.

"A line of shadow over the stern—our unpolluted England—is swallowed up in the blackness, and a shadow of another shape—our escort—steals up over our bows, the hand of Britain which protects its voyagers by the way of the sea."

So far the romantic had immersed himself without knowing it in realism —and realism of a kind that no playwright or novelist, nor even liars who write history, will ever be able to paint in pleasant colours. Martin Harvey's integrity stood the test. He never lied about that tour under shellfire. Irving's tradition was never meant to be brought so near the unquestionable shape of physical pain; but can anything of the mind survive it? The realist laughs at that eager little figure, filled with the Shakespearean faith of the value of words at the very moment when many a ditch is to be filled up with our English dead. But the realist would be less useful. The mind that has lost all wish to think, and has good reason for losing it, may find a way of escape in romance even when it hankers after song-and-dance—but it abhors realism.

The mood of *Drake*, of *The Dynasts* and *Armageddon* had been left behind, like a railway station our express had started from. In the fourth year of war no dispute could continue whether the theatre should be ruled by actor, author or producer. It had been given over to the function of amusement with Oscar Asche, "swelling wisibly" to an enormous size, the presiding genius as Chu Chin Chow in his own Ali-Baba musical at His Majesty's.

No war play in the grand manner could be set up as a rival side-show, in this new Vanity Fair, to such good fun as that. But what blaring spectacle could not hope to do might be achieved by the still small voice. So Granville-Barker decided, when he read Maëterlinck's *The Burgomaster Of Stilemonde*. He passed it, with a strong recommendation, to Martin Harvey, who at once agreed that it was a "noble work", but felt strongly inclined towards the conventional phrase about not seeing himself in the part.

For nearly forty years, apart from such preliminary frolics as the Pickwickian Fat Boy at St. Lyceum, he had been "straight". In his own eyes that had been his way, and he had never departed from it. Granville-Barker, on the other hand, had noted all those leanings towards "character" Martin Harvey had displayed even in parts with which he had supposedly identified himself.

In the belief that "acting is a matter of muscles", Martin Harvey had consistently varied his manner, his grimace, his stance, his walk. These had been elaborations of himself—the kind of man he would have been had he lived that kind of life. Now there was a further demand. What had been decoration had to become, crudely put, camouflage. He had not to adorn his own personality but conceal it. Just as a scrubby beard would alter the look of his face, so a plain directness would blot out his natural flamboyance. The soul of the man, said Granville-Barker, was all that mattered. There the player and the part were one. No other actor then known had that simple faith.

This is to be wise after the event. At the time "Martin Harvey in a beard" suggested all the misgivings that were in his own mind, which persisted after the first night at the Lyceum, Edinburgh, on October 4, 1918. His confession has some bearing on our modern way of risking the whole life of a play on the verdict of one audience. From that time onwards the deep affinity between the actor of flesh and blood and the burgomaster of fiction created an impression unlike that left by any other play.

Where were all the conflicts of earth and hell in stirring dramatic references to British naval and military history? Where were all your patriotic speeches now when that very foreign personage, a burgomaster, in the remote predicament of possessing a son-in-law able and willing to take some share in his execution, spoke for us and all our kind? Both he and the heroine, Miss de Silva as the Belgian wife of a Junker and about to bear his child, told of a life more closely related to what we had read in the newspapers than our own lives. Yet it moved us as no other war play had done as an experience which should become part of our own existence.

In order to dwell apart there is no need to find waste places. While constantly in full view of thousands of faces Martin Harvey lived in the serene

isolation of an anchorite, as an idealist must do if such figments as his
Burgomaster are to stir our souls. How little he saw beneath the surface of
what went on in the streets around him is made comically clear in his
Armistice Day observations.

On "the eleventh day of the eleventh month" he was at Cardiff. "The
town," he said, "went quite mad and, to the everlasting credit of that
rollicking city, not a single case of drunkenness was noted." Cardiff may have
been unlike other parts of the country, but there was for the others a simple
matter-of-fact explanation why drunkards were few. Strong drink, even
the vile official tipple called Government beer which can be brought under
this head only by misuse of language, could not be had.

Public-houses made fair distribution of what they had to eager besiegers
from noon until doors were closed in the afternoon. By then supplies had
given out. Outer doors were padlocked and bolted, shutters were put up, and
in each city of dreadful night where "dowsing" shed its squalor (unlike the
black-out, which held beauty as well as danger) over all attempts at gaiety,
revelry was baulked of its natural design. Resolute fighting-men seized one
of the captured German guns lined up in the Mall, man-handled it up the
Haymarket to Piccadilly Circus and used its muzzle as a battering-ram against
the doors of a hotel.

Otherwise London became very quiet as the eleventh hour of evening
fell. Foreign soldiers were being taught by Cockney Harriets to sing and
dance "Knees up, Mother Brown" round lamp-posts in Trafalgar Square,
but these were isolated groups. The rest of those not content to go home
early formed up in column of route behind one of those self-appointed
commanders who live their brief hour on all such occasions, caring little
whether the ranks behind them are protesting or celebrating; he led them
down the Strand with someone beating a gas-alarm from the trenches in
lieu of brass-band. Thus they marched, sad spectacle of rejoicing under
difficulties, until the encircling gloom caused massed desertion and the
unnamed Garibaldi went on to Temple Bar alone.

To our everlasting credit, you might say, all marched steadily. But if
you were a realist you wondered whether the Government had withheld
supplies to preserve the peace or whether "the trade" had decided to protect
its property. Then again the Armistice had not been long foreseen, and extra
supplies were not available anyway.

Armistice was receding into history before the first London performance
of *The Burgomaster Of Stilemonde* was given at the Scala on January 10, 1919.
That it would not "date" was evident at once. Are there other war plays, that
is, plays written during a war about that very war, about which this could
be said? Ten years later, Mr. Agate was writing, "Sir John Martin-Harvey,
in achieving a masterpiece of quietism, gave one of the most perfect performances I have ever seen. My ears are still filled with the poignant vibrations
of that gently reasoning voice."

CHAPTER II

TWILIGHT FOR ROMANCE

IN a world of shadows some importance belongs to the shadow of a shade. Where are all the actor's real achievements when he is long dead? They are barely one remove from the achievements he merely imagined. As time passes we begin to see *Dante* as Irving intended it, no less clearly than the inchoate performance mortal eyes actually beheld. In the future we may see Binyon's *Arthur* as the Covent Garden triumph Martin Harvey planned in 1919, instead of as it was mounted in actuality by the less lavish resources of the Old Vic four years later.

Although he had no hand in presenting it upon the stage he has some credit for the writing of it; in fact when Laurence Binyon gave the details for a book of references he wrote of this work, "in collaboration with Sir J. Martin-Harvey". At the time the author was deputy-keeper in the Print Room of the British Museum. He had written *Paris And Œnone* for Gertrude Kingston at the Savoy in 1906, and *Attila* for Oscar Asche at His Majesty's in 1907.

There seemed to be some danger that his gifts would be lost to the stage. The proposal was brought to him by two ardent believers in dramatic poetry, eager to discuss it with him both in London and on holiday in the Isle of Wight. "What right have I to dedicate to you what is already so much your own?" he asks in the dedication of the printed work.

The original idea was that Lancelot should be the star part, but at the reading of the MS., Martin Harvey says, "my wife much preferred my expression of the King, and, with Binyon's concurrence, it was decided that I should play Arthur. This necessitated some changes in the latter part of the play, which Binyon willingly made." Yet Lancelot, when the play is read, monopolizes the interest. At Astolat he recovers from his wound in the care of Elaine. In "the Palace at London" the queen flings herself at his head and he manfully resists.

Elaine dies for love of him, and her body is brought down to him by the river steps at Westminster. At a secret farewell meeting with Guinevere he is set upon by traitors and routs them, then carries her off to his stronghold, Joyous Gard. There is a battle in a violent storm until the Pope commands them to make peace. Guinevere enters a convent and from its steps watches the barge in which the three queens bear King Arthur to Avalon.

The mood throughout is solemn, tender, wistful. Even so well-worn a theme is given fresh inspiration (not without an echo here and there of Tennyson) by the new pen. But even while admiring each scene's quiet dignity a reader may understand why Martin Harvey preferred to let it stay

237

on the shelf rather than present it without imposing spectacle. It is possible
to render the poet his due and at the same time question the aptness of his
story for the stage.

The Round Table, as a dim shape glimpsed through the mists of antiquity,
is magnificent. If we are to set eyes upon it, then it must be no ordinary table
of practical dimensions, but splendid alike in size and primitive beauty.
That symbolizes all the life around it. In love, in war, in saintliness these
Britons cannot behave like people of life-size.

Adultery, when committed by such a queen, must have something to
be said for it; and as the splendid sin is not a first-hand experience with most
of us, the great wrong of Camelot—or Westminster, as Mr. Binyon prefers
it—is more credible when the report is barely breathed than when made the
subject of anything so bold as a play. Lancelot and Guinevere lack all the
historic excuses, all the pleas tacit in the erring of lesser, pathetic lovers.
Alike in *Pelléas And Mélisande, Paolo And Francesca*, the lovers are young, the
husbands insensitive, almost brutish. Neither of those brides could be
upbraided with

>   at your age
> The heyday in the blood is tame, it's humble
> And waits upon the judgment.

Neither is given time to grow into a spouse in an atmosphere of home,
where to err as soon as the husband's back is turned creates the squalor of
adulterous propinquity.

Yet the infidelity of Guinevere cannot, at this latter day, be separated
from the body of romance. Why should her story, acceptable to mediaeval
legend and Victorian verse, be questioned on the modern stage? Tennyson
gives the answer. It was not because he doubted his own stagecraft that he
declined to dramatize "The Idylls of The King" for Irving, but because the
excuses to be found for Guinevere in descriptive poetry will not stand the
light of gas or electricity. When set before us in the flesh she has more
kinship with the divorce court than a world where the lures of the flesh
are etherealized.

But this does not explain why the play was shelved. According to his
autobiography, Sir John despaired of the venture when ill-health prevented
Robert Loraine from taking up the part of Lancelot; it was abandoned when
sixteen hundred pounds had been spent on costumes alone. Since then the
mind's eye has dwelt lovingly on visions of that dauntless king exerting his
royal authority over that towering subject, six gigantic feet of honour to be
rooted in dishonour armed cap-à-pie.

Loraine was a genuine warrior. He volunteered for South Africa and
came back frustrated because it had all been so tame where he had marched.
He had been an airman in Flanders, which was near enough to knight-
errantry; he rode his 'plane like an unbroken horse. In a silk dressing-gown

he still looked a man of war, and the hand on his knee was like Otranto's iron gauntlet in Walpole's tale. What a pair for Guinevere to stand between!

Though the vision faded it marked the renewal of the actor-manager's urge to be to London another Irving. In the October of 1919 H. B. Irving died, having in the years of war fulfilled all the prophesies that one day he would employ his solemnity to excel in comedy, as he undoubtedly did as the finicking exquisite in *The Angel In The House*. One of his next productions at the Savoy had been *Hamlet*, deliberate, thoughtful, and with more emphasis than ever on the soliloquies—he restored "How all occasions do inform against me", and made of it one of his most considerable moments. He was not the last of the family to serve the stage, for his son, Laurence, would make his name as a scene designer when he left the R.A.F., and Elizabeth Irving would be the most ethereal of Titanias before choosing to "dwindle into a wife".

Of all the ripples from the old Lyceum's mighty splash the happiest lapped the stage of the Lyric in the April of 1919. There was a revival of *Romeo And Juliet* to satisfy the artistic hunger of Doris Keane. After a thousand performances as the prima donna who loved a parson in *Romance* she said, "I am not only a woman, I am an artist," and insisted upon Shakespeare. The title should have been changed to *Nurse*, for Ellen Terry, remembering some of her lines, romped away with the whole evening. Why doting youngsters in the stalls should have murmured, "Marvellous at her age" is not quite clear. Seventy years are nothing to players not burdened by management.

With Covent Garden on his hands without a Covent Garden production, Martin Harvey had recourse to *Hamlet*. The memory of his last revival was still so fresh that even critics went happily to their work. But something was wrong. Had they or had the production changed? Neither. The proscenium arch was all that was different. Place any masterpiece in a frame too large for it, and the most adoring eyes will make little headway against the handicap of having to ignore the hiatus. The opening of Covent Garden's stage is wider by ten feet than that of His Majesty's. You could not lose yourself in any vista beyond; your eyes stuck at the borders and your thoughts began to surmise how many problems of the kind beset an actor-manager who spent his life moving from theatre to theatre.

Once more *The Only Way* lived up to its title in managerial policy. After coming of age at Covent Garden it resumed its place on tour with *Hamlet*, *The Burgomaster Of Stilemonde* and *The Breed Of The Treshams*. With these the Company embarked for Canada that autumn. Everywhere from coast to coast the players were received as Noah's family received the homing dove— proof of the world's return to normal. In such a holiday atmosphere anyone might have forgotten the strict propriety of dramatic art. Miss de Silva confessed that she did. It was St. Valentine's Day. Shops were decorated with large red hearts. She bought one. Batty, on going to visit his ladies in

The Breed Of The Treshams that night, wore one of them. The audience enjoyed the joke, but Martin Harvey did not. In her own words, she "caught it".

In the New Year's Honours List of 1921 Martin Harvey became Sir John Martin-Harvey, one of the few stage knighthoods to be welcomed without any undercurrent of "What on earth for?" The moment was happily chosen. Touring companies which kept the Canadian Theatre alive upheld the idea of hands-across-the-sea in its most cheerful fashion. Players constantly came back with tales of hospitality in Quebec, Montreal, Winnipeg, Calgary, Vancouver and everywhere else, down to the "smalls". There were not enough companies of sufficient note to maintain interest along this chain of Trans-Canada Theatres, bought up by one company at such generous prices that they could not be left empty.

After celebrating its coming of age at Covent Garden *The Only Way* was still proving itself to be no ordinary play, for on their twenty-first birthdays most modern plays which have managed to live as long make their last gasp and die. The next performance to be notched would be the 2,000th, which would occur during the autumn season of 1921. For this Martin Harvey returned to the Lyceum. Was there ever a theatre which could change in spirit so much while still remaining a theatre? However great the gutting behind the very same old portico when lobbies, cloakrooms, foyers and lounges all vanished to add to the new auditorium with space for three thousand, however drastically the stage had been swept back to the walls, the change between Irving's retrospectively classic repertoire and the up-to-date popularity of record-breaking melodramas was more startling still.

Other theatres, of course, could become vaudevilles or dance-halls, warehouses or police-courts; the distinction of the Lyceum lay in ranging the whole gamut of drama while remaining (apart from that period as a music-hall) legitimate. The Melvilles, who now held control, were forthright men, rich not only in pelf but in knowledge of what the public wanted from the stage. Their grandfather had been a manager, of whom it was said that all manner of young stars, Irving, Kate Terry, Ellen Terry and even John Ryder, had moved in outer darkness while he gave great performances in focus. His son Andrew, who billed himself as Emm, responded to the call of democracy's new audiences and stayed on the road.

Now grandsons, under the lead of Walter, as a playwright the elder and more terrible, had made the name synonymous for drama for the masses, partly because of their faith in powerful parts for powerful—sometimes handsome as well, but always powerful—leading ladies. The heroine of Walter Howard's *Seven Days' Leave* had at the end of the war broken all records for its type with a run of over seven hundred performances, by means of a heroine who sank a German submarine. And seven hundred here would be equivalent to three times that number elsewhere when there is counting of heads.

Martin Harvey as
"The Burgomaster of
Stilemonde"

Rehearsing the Fare-
well Tour of *The Only
Way*

Martin Harvey as "Sydney Carton"
From the Bust by Sir GEORGE FRAMPTON, R.A.

With audiences capable of being stirred, *The Only Way* played to crowds. *The Breed Of The Treshams* and *The Burgomaster Of Stilemonde* maintained this atmosphere of massed enthusiasm night after night. Not that Walter Melville was unduly impressed. Actors, whoever they were, were always ten-a-penny to him. One morning, hearing noises in the auditorium, he left the little office he shared with his equally large and burly brother, to look down from the corner of the dress-circle upon what might be happening in the stalls. There he saw a small kinematograph projector. "Take that damned thing away!" he stormed.

"Don't worry," responded the dulcet voice of Sydney Carton, "I'm making an experiment. You can hold me responsible."

"Hold you responsible!" snorted Leviathan, "you're not worth tuppence."

He would have said the same to Irving himself or any of the tribe of sock and buskin he knew so well. Had he not sent them round the country, twenty trainloads at a time?

Rivalry cannot be ignored. Ainley, fresh from his service as a gunner in France and Italy, went into management at the St. James's as Mark Antony in *Julius Caesar* and Tolstoy's living corpse in *Reparation*, both dramas to win admiration without anyone losing a heartbeat. For popular appeal he relied on *Uncle Ned*—in modern dress without the romance that alone could provide him with a stop-gap. After playing Captain Hook in *Peter Pan* he doffed the purple to play Prospero in *The Tempest* at the Aldwych in 1921. He lacked the rising intonation to make the prosy old fellow bearable; revealed his propensity for first-night mishaps by letting his magic wand fall into two long before the moment came to snap it. Prospero, said Walkley, has the lecturer's pointer and needs only the carafe with tumbler. That was not the author's fault altogether.

For nearly a dozen years Matheson Lang had been able to fall back on *Mr. Wu* to replenish his treasury—the tale of a mandarin who seeks to revenge his daughter upon her betrayer's mother. Yet another stop-gap was added unto him in the summer of 1918 when he tried, as Martin Harvey had done in *Boy O'Carroll*, to act a face in costume. How steadfast the demand for French Revolution romances remained Matheson Lang discovered when he adapted a French play, *Le Chevalier Du Masque*, which guyed them. As *The Purple Mask* it opened at the Lyric in the July of 1918 and added itself to that theatre's impressive list of long-lived productions.

Yet the actor-author found that his own ideas clashed with those of playgoers, who "did not accept it as a skit but were much more inclined to take it seriously as a perfectly straightforward romantic play". The Chevalier Armand, full of tricks, disguises and in-the-nick-of-time exploits, stepped straight into Sir Percy Blakeney's shoes. Author's fees for performing rights abroad accumulated into the purchase price of a house which nearly became Armandville. This brings Martin Harvey into Matheson Lang's book, "Mr. Wu Looks Back":

Q

"This house, by the way, belonged to Sir John Martin-Harvey. One day we were lunching with him and Lady Harvey and told them of the long hunt we had had for a suitable house in St. John's Wood. Up to then we had lived in a flat but we wanted a house with a garden. Harvey said:

" 'Why not buy this one?'

"After lunch he took me into his study and there and then we fixed the whole thing up. It was a delightful old-fashioned house in Avenue Road with a miniature avenue of poplar trees up to the front door, and a quaint tower like an Italian Villa. We lived there for fifteen years until a succession of two bad droughts in two succeeding summers so damaged the walls and foundations that we found one morning, to our dismay, that the house was tumbling about our ears. The nice old-fashioned porch, which we were so fond of, started to lean out towards the road at a perilous angle, and gaps appeared in the outer walls that daylight could easily be seen through."

Some contrast shows itself in the endeavours of these romantics, as each in turn takes the lead. In the September of 1920 Matheson Lang demonstrated how strong a hold over popular imagination was still exercised by the man accursed. At the New he ran Temple Thurston's *The Wandering Jew* for a year and thus added a third piece to his stock repertoire. In between whiles his Shylock and Othello had hinted that he had yet to exert his powers to the full. So far Godfrey Tearle had not ventured into management, but in a round of parts from the conscience-smitten monk in *The Garden of Allah* at Drury Lane, and as a magnificent Othello at the Court, he seemed to be prepared for that leap in the dark.

If Sir John had now brought out another adventure story in costume he would have belonged to this group. By upholding instead his ardent faith, "God in the Theatre", he stood alone. That rigidly moral attitude, which had seemed exalted in wartime, seemed still more so in peace. History records the nineteen-twenties as shameless, because a number of people were undoubtedly so. How singular then for Martin Harvey to have brought out in the midst of this bacchanalia a morality with public rebuke in its title of *Via Crucis*. But was it singular, was he so very exceptional? The period owes its bad name to the antics of thousands. That is true. Great Britain houses millions.

"I have never been reconciled to the exclusion of the spiritual in the Theatre," Sir John declared in the most significant statement he ever made about himself. While arguing that the lesson of a play is more powerfully conveyed than one contained in a sermon, he contends, "Belief that it can be, has, I think, inspired most of my productions."

Æschylus, Euripides, Sophocles, Calderon and Shakespeare, in his view, believed the same. All this should not be accepted merely as an argument, for whether it is true or not is of minor interest. If read as a confession of faith the singularity of the believer is well worth considering.

Other actors have from time to time echoed the sentiment, but then actors will say almost anything when asked for an after-dinner speech, a lecture or an address at some unveiling. To find one who sincerely and consistently and permanently believed that the purpose of the drama was to teach moral lessons, one who would back his opinion with all his energy and all his finances, would require a far wider knowledge of the theatre than the author of this biography possesses, and a claim may be reasonably made that Sir John Martin-Harvey was in this unique. Even without his own words on the subject the evidence of this play is conclusive. Yet *Jedermann*, as it stood, was not spiritual enough. Taking the title from one of Marian Crawford's books he called the English version *Via Crucis*, and designed a transparency to dominate one of the scenes in the shape of Christ's head surmounted by the Crown of Thorns.

Hofmannsthal's work, translated by Dr. Wheeler and the Hon. Sybil Amherst, was staged in a setting by Sir Aston Webb at the Garrick in the February of 1923. There were steps and a clear sky. This was the world where Everyman affirmed his belief in gold:

> The world gains much by this device
> For each one grows, in his own eyes,
> Into a God—with gold he buys
> Men's work and labour, everything.
> He becomes greater than a king,
> Brings tens of thousands 'neath his sway,
> And over all he works his way.
> As Regent he would reign on high,
> There's naught too great his gold can buy.
> He gains the right to keep by law
> Of charter from the Emperor,
> The Land in fief for all his line,
> It doth descend by right divine.
> Yet priceless grants like these are sold,
> Money brings in wealth untold.
> Everyman bows down to gold.

All his worldly friends come to his banquet. It is disturbed by a summons calling him to the journey and to leave his gold behind. Death tells him

> Nothing was given—all was lent
> As soon as thou art gone it will be spent
> By one and then another till his hour strike
> All must depart alike.

At length Everyman brings himself to know that all hopes of reprieve
are vain:

> Now must I to the grave which draws me hence
> Have mercy on me in Thy omnipotence.

"I made insufficient allowance for the exacerbated feelings of our people,"
was the way Martin-Harvey explained the adverse comments of the Press
and the absence of the public. That was the surmise of a mind still in the
clouds. London playgoers in 1923 showed no sign of exacerbated feelings,
whatever might be happening elsewhere. If any notice were taken of
Hofsmannsthal his nationality would have brought him sympathy since
Austria's plight had become known.

The adverse comments were not against him but against an actor-
manager who should dare to proclaim his religious convictions so defiantly;
in fact murmurs against the transparency were so insistent that after the
second night it was withdrawn. There is good reason to believe that Everyman knew nothing of the vitriolic cynicism of the human wilderness around
him. Yet he played the part as though calling the heedless, pleasure-loving
public to repentance. He filled the masterpiece, said Mr. Agate, in his
moving account of it, with something of the quality of Elgar's *Gerontius*:

> "His acting, when Everyman was near to dying, had the hushed
> sweetness of that opening to the second part, so that one was reminded
> of the theme which symbolizes purification by the waters of Purgatory:
> 'Softly and gently, dearly-ransomed Soul.' In Germany Everyman was
> played by a bull-necked Teuton. He would be. Harvey was all spirit,
> and when, at the end, the hooded figure of Death held forth his shadowy
> yet certain arms, it was a very pitiful, childlike figure that they enclosed."

．　　　．　　　．　　　．　　　．

In bare outline the next three or four years of the actor's life appear
uneventful. Most of the time was spent on tour—mainly in Great Britain and
Canada, apart from a season in New York with a tour of the United States
to follow.

What very different ventures the one word "tour" covers! In 1923 the
Martin-Harvey Company travelled an imaginative cosmos. The Fate Tree
of *Hamlet*, the columns of *Œdipus* and the banquet of *Via Crucis* docked
together, and with these plays went not only *The Burgomaster Of Stilemonde*
and *The Taming Of The Shrew* but *David Garrick*, *The Breed Of The Treshams*,
A Cigarette-Maker's Romance and *The Only Way*. Even the lesser lights
seemed to possess for a time the imperishable quality of masterpieces or the
longevity of legend; it was, in fact, a "little play" which brought about one

of the performances Lady Martin-Harvey remembers most vividly. While they were playing the "smalls" they arrived at a town where the electric supply had failed. The play was *David Garrick*. Once again, as at the Shakespeare Hut on the Christmas Eve of 1916, they acted by candlelight. The players felt they belonged to the play. "Then," says Lady Martin-Harvey, "the electricity came on and vulgarized everything."

In 1925 *The Burgomaster Of Stilemonde* had a London season at the Ambassadors. The next year there were engagements at the Coliseum in *The Shewing-Up Of Blanco Posnet*, a one-act play so often billed as a sketch that Mr. Shaw might qualify for membership of the Variety Artistes' Federation. Blanco has presented himself in all shapes and sizes, at one time big and burly, at another time small and rather clerical or professional. He had never been played in so romantic a manner as when Martin-Harvey revealed at the Coliseum in the autumn of 1926 how thin the Shavian varnish is over an essentially emotional tale. Not for the first or last time N. de Silva put so much spirit into the bravado of a bad girl as to suggest that she revelled in these rôles—vindicating the soul of good, she seemed to say, in things evil.

Both stars had found characters so much to their liking that Mr. Shaw's piece had to be taken on tour. It shared the programme with Maëterlinck's *The Death Of Tintagiles*. The prejudice against double or treble bills was now stronger than ever. Yet dates were booked everywhere and the public response was unwaveringly "loyal". The Martin-Harveys could do no wrong. They still attracted youth. They still won the gratitude of the middle-aged and elderly. In the February of 1927 *The Lyons Mail* was added to the repertoire when they were at Golders Green. There was no describing, to intermittent playgoers who feel for the theatre a warmth of feeling less than passion, the thrill of this revival of tradition. Now we linked hands afresh, through the Martin-Harveys, with Irving, with Charles Kean, with the Boulevard.

Four years had passed since *Via Crucis*. In that time Sir John had attempted no new plays. The only one he found in a period of eight years was by the most romantically minded author of the day—Rafael Sabatini. Either with rapier or cutlass his characters could hold their own with those of any man then living, and as long as he wrote the sawn-off sub-machine gun would not be the principal weapon of offence on the shelves of circulating libraries. No novelist was ever less of a buccaneer or swashbuckler. With the quiet, meditative, "listening face" of a compleat angler, he would hear the claims to fame of others whenever he could not escape a crowded dressing-room.

Quiet authors are rare. Being denied the respect shown to actors during rehearsal, drivers at the wheel, or pugilists in training, they have to assert themselves in order to retain enough self-confidence and belief in the importance of what they are doing to carry them on from day to day until anything from a one-year to a five-year plan is fulfilled. Rafael Sabatini had enough inward strength to do without this form of Dutch courage. There was no bluster whatever in his nature. The Martin-Harveys passed the time while doctoring his play restfully, though realizing that *Scaramouche* was "the last romantic" among plays.

For years "Wardour Street" meant costume plays and historical novels just as "sword" was another way of saying "war". Willie Clarkson's vast store of cloaks, ruffs and fleshings still clothed multitudes of the romantically minded at revels or theatricals when the significance of his postal address changed. By that odd chance which made Covent Garden celebrated alike for tenors and cabbages, Smithfield for martyrs and Sunday joints, Piccadilly for staid clubs and strumpets, the farther end of what once had been Willie Clarkson's own particular street now seemed lovely in movie-magnates' eyes. Offices were rented there by one or two film companies, others came by dozens, and then the more prosperous ones built blocks of offices, until "Wardour Street" signified the cinematograph industry to the exclusion of all else.

History did not stand its ground (as the costumier did until he died) but retreated. The new meaning had things all its own way because the old meanings had lost their public. The once intense light of Maurice Hewlett, Seton Merriman, Stanley Weyman, Guy Boothby, Marjorie Bowen and the Baroness Emmuska Orczy flickered and dimmed. There was an undeniable change of taste. For the time being the historical novel seemed as much out of favour as romance on the stage. Yet even with the fashion against him, Rafael Sabatini made headway where many either failed or came to a standstill.

Before the taste of Edward's reign had quite vanished he won a stage success with *Bardelys The Magnificent*. Ten years later he returned to the footlights with enough acclaim to catch the eye of the new Wardour Street. Sheer commercial instinct led the quivering nostrils of its experts to "Scaramouche" because it was a French Revolutionary tale. That it was well told had been known from the start, but before the camera those scenes where the skilled swordsmen of the aristocracy pick off each troublesome reformer until the professional master-at-arms is ready for them gave Ramon Navarro, the idol of the hour, a character to exhibit himself in as attractive as Ben Hur.

That was how the film fans saw things. In the theatre Andre-Louis Moreau had to be bracketed less fortunately. Since *The Only Way*, other tales of the Revolution had been effectively set upon the stage. Nevertheless, it had become ever plainer that "A Tale of Two Cities" had possessed not only a prince among authors but a paragon among plots. That, more than any number of mischances, more even than the rivalry of Ramon Navarro's film, was the handicap the stage *Scaramouche* bore. There has yet to be considered that problem of an audience's mood. So much depends on the set of its faces as the curtain goes up. In London these were listless. In Canada they were not.

The pattern of his beloved master's life now stamped itself on Martin-Harvey's own in its darker colours. An injured leg came into the disciple's story with an ominous hint of ebbing fortune. That there is a difference in the outcome can be ascribed to Lady Martin-Harvey's strong will. While he lay helpless in hospital at Toronto she took the Company on to fulfil their obligations at Winnipeg—keeping in touch with the doctors by telephone. Credit must also be given to the sympathy shown by Canadian audiences. Perhaps British provincial audiences would likewise have stuck to their bargain, though the clause does start with perhaps, but in London the box-office results would have been far different. It simply did not occur to Irving's staunchest "supporters" to turn up at the Lyceum, just to prove their friendship, when he was out of the bill. The West End is not a health resort.

Many months were spent in Canada between 1927 and 1929. At length London's turn came again, and with it an episode of comic relief at a time of depression. The laugh must go against the actor, who bore out Emerson's reference to "that slight taint of burlesque which, in our strange world, attaches to the zealot". Naturally it attached itself to Sir John, and to leave it out would mean an incomplete portrait. His account of a correspondence with Mr. Shaw over *The Devil's Disciple* has its funny side, and whoever misses this can barely claim to have seen him steadily or seen him whole.

Authors were expected to serve the Martin-Harvey Company, often to put its interest before their own—as W. L. Courtney and others of equal eminence did. Merivale objected to no good purpose. Stephen Phillips had the key turned upon him to make him add a special scene—"he wrote a most wonderful interlude for the bibulous trooper of the Spanish wars, but we were, alas! never able to include it". A less patient author, after receiving a list of alterations that were desired, and then an urgent message that his revisions were wanted at once, replied, "Make the alterations yourselves," which by way of interpretation becomes "the play needed a a little further development. This it received with the help of my wife, whose collaboration Mr. Jackson has always generously allowed."

In short, authors were treated in the way Romance had always treated authors—Byron and Tennyson had had to submit as meekly as Shakespeare to Irving's scalpel—until a dramatist of the new school was invited into the operating theatre. "I appealed to Shaw," runs a delicious sentence in the autobiography, "to rewrite portions of the play which I found were confusing the audiences and militating against its chances of success." How perplexing authors were, to be sure. One you had only to lock in a room to be obeyed. Another "promptly replied that I ought to be in the workhouse, that I had flattened out the play as badly as my old master Irving had always flattened out his".

To an onlooker the trouble seemed to be that *The Devil's Disciple* could never be an actor-manager's play. Since the hero has a touch of the prig the play might easily be stolen from him by the easy wit of Burgoyne, who, even on the scaffold, figuratively steals the spotlight with his remark about never hanging a man by an American clock. Granville-Barker, in the original production, reserved this part for himself. In some future production a rising star will change the play's meaning right round by exploiting all the chances the play affords, which points to the fact that no actor has yet written a treatise on the craft of stealing a play.

Audiences never have a suspicion of it. When Ellen Terry's Nurse made Juliet look like the parlour-maid, doting worshippers argued, "She is just being Ellen Terry," which was about as true as saying, "She is just being the Nurse." To see Bottom the Weaver robbed of all his laughs by Quince, the Carpenter (who passes you in the wings murmuring, "Can you blame me?"), is to realize what subtle chess this is. Hamlet was once robbed of his sympathy by Claudius without the audience being astonished. Such a game may be decidedly worth the playing—but not in the Martin-Harvey Company. "You see, my man," said Sir John, "I want you to concentrate your light on my hand." The electrician readily replied: "Yes, sir. On which *finger*, sir?" This tale, meant as an example of devotion to detail, has a sinister ring. But the zealot who never lays himself open to be laughed at is no zealot. Electricians and authors were in the same boat. They all had to serve one man, and for the very good and sufficient reason that he was serving an ideal.

While yet another Canadian tour was in preparation there came disturbing news of Ainley. That he should have proved unequal to the strain of his career was not surprising. For thirty years he had been incessantly engaged in what he liked to call "good work"—part after part all requiring fresh, intense study. Four attempts at management had left him where he was before, with no stop-gap to fall back upon when new plays failed him. No one could represent a man of genius on the stage as well as he; and despite his bluff Yorkshire manner he had the temperament which left him at the mercy of "nerves" on every first night. All the public saw of this were mishaps, almost to be expected after a time. In *Hassan*, most exquisite of all modern poetic plays, his turban started to unroll. In *Prince Fazil* he found, when he tried to rise from his cushions, that one foot was half-way up his red morocco boot and could not be wriggled down again. He seemed to feel nothing but regal disdain, but these were signs and portents.

After the strain of Macbeth the breakdown came. For a time friends spoke as though it were the end. The Martin-Harveys waited until he could travel and then took him to Bonchurch, stayed with him for a while and when they had to sail for Quebec left him in good hands. The front of Jove himself,

> A station like the herald Mercury
> New-lighted on a heaven-kissing hill,

seen by the Islanders when the invalid took his solitary walks, like some beautified Beethoven, in the full blast of the Channel gales, was enough to make even those with the utmost contempt for "foreigners" pause and wonder. Like Martin-Harvey himself, like all the stalwarts of the romantic school, there was no taking him for any ordinary man.

The actor of the natural school prides himself on looking ordinary. When one of the best and most gallant of them landed from the air amid those Hampshire hills where nobody without known grandparents is wanted, he sought to allay the virulent spy-fever by saying, "But hang it all, I'm Ralph Richardson." He looked so little like their idea of an actor that he was lucky to survive. Forgive the digression. What should have been said without this break is that when the Martin-Harveys came back across the ocean Ainley had begun that recovery which led, after two years, to his triumphant return at the Haymarket in the July of 1929 as Fraser in St. John Ervine's *The First Mrs. Fraser*. No mention is made in the Autobiography of all this care and friendship.

The next play came from Frederic Jackson, a playwright of experience which meant far more at this time than a generation ago. Partly because the public preferred films and partly because the provinces lacked enterprise, baffled writers preferred other forms of authorship. It says much for Mr. Jackson's skill and pugnacity that from 1915 onwards his plays had been regularly accepted at the rate of one or two a year. Usually they had been on the light side, as such titles as *La, La, Lucille, Stop Flirting, Just a Kiss* and *Her First Affair* indicate.

In *The King's Messenger* he aimed at a higher mark. Just as a professional humorist had turned without warning to the quasi-supernatural in *The Passing Of The Third Floor Back*, so the brain that contrived *Your Money Or Your Wife* sought relief from being comic. In a Spanish setting he arranged a cross-section of human society under some necessity of justifying its existence. They are travellers who suppose themselves to be held up by a bandit, who is less interested in their purses than their souls.

This King's Messenger was in keeping with the rest of the Martin-Harvey picture-gallery, and the way Miss de Silva rapped out the confession from a supposedly dignified and decorous lady that she led a venally immoral life had a directness that took even the archangel bandit (or whatever his rank in the hierarchy was) aback. One thing definitely was wrong, with perhaps no one on the stage aware of it. The King's Messenger wore a sash of bright scarlet over his black suit. Whenever he stood sideways it revealed the fullness of the actor's figure. Sir John, now approaching three score years and ten, was (temporarily) putting on weight like a man of forty.

To have noticed this may well be to prove that the London critic was hypercritical. The Martin-Harveys had confidence in their judgment. *The King's Messenger* was the play they chose for the eighth Canadian tour—

to be their last. They acted it from Quebec to Vancouver while rehearsing, for the homeward journey, a revival of *The Bells*.

While Irving's disciple returned to Irving's parts, Julia Neilson and Fred Terry revived *The Scarlet Pimpernel* and *Sweet Nell Of Old Drury*. Of all their school it was Matheson Lang who took the boldest course. His needs were supplied by Ashley Dukes, first known as a brilliant young critic in 1909 when he returned from the Continent with a knowledge, very rare at that time in England, of what was happening to the theatre in France, Belgium, Holland, Germany and Russia. His *The Man With A Load Of Mischief* in 1924 challenged the traditional use of costume not, as Shaw had done, by substituting an up-to-date, matter-of-fact manner, but by making his characters speak what an American actress called "a load of English".

After watching the progress of the German plays and novels for some years, he adapted three works in that firm, delicate style he had made peculiarly his own. The subjects were historical. The treatment, though not historical as understood by "historical novel", was entirely free from modernisms. Similarly the characters were seen neither with glamour nor with belittlement. The result seemed to be a hybrid, never cultivated by any other hand so perfectly, between romance and naturalism. It enabled Matheson Lang to mark the zenith of his career in three memorable full-length figures—Count Pahlen in *Such Men Are Dangerous* in 1928, Joseph Süss Oppenheimer in *Jew Süss* in 1929, and Philip of Spain in *Elizabeth Of England*, with Phyllis Neilson-Terry as the queen, in 1931.

Much as actors in general may hate to admit it, theatrical history can rarely be made without the aid of critics. One of Sir John's finest achievements in acting won comparatively little notice because it happened out of range for any but brief chronicles of the time. This was in *The Bells*. With this revival, besides *David Garrick* and *The Only Way*, he toured the provinces on his return to England. In the November of 1932 he played Mathias at the King's, Hammersmith. Again idealism triumphed. Accept the idea that blood-guiltiness and purity of heart could go together and Christ's "sinner that repenteth" is symbolized in our memory of that distraught face, fixed with horror, not of phantoms but of deadly sin.

Was there ever a performance which took so many ordinary pleasure-seekers so completely by surprise? People who wandered in out of idle curiosity came out aglow with enthusiasm, determined to see an actor, whose existence they had taken for granted all their lives, in all the rest of his parts as soon as the opportunity should arise. In a purely romantic rôle there were few thrills in the theatre to equal Martin-Harvey, no matter how near he was to the age of retirement.

Retire? Why, after fifty years of the stage, his hair had but just turned white. The part which had hastened Irving's end at an earlier age was one in which the disciple could throw himself with dynamic energy and make the faces of a new generation flush with praise. Yet it was an achievement in acting without any sop to the craze for new methods of production.

That *The Bells* would lend itself to such treatment Stanislavsky had proved. "My Life in Art" described the production by the Society of Art and Literature in Moscow on November 19, 1896. When deciding to put on *The Polish Jew* in "Who was the murderer?" style, Stanislavsky confessed, "I like to create deviltry in the theatre." He succeeded after this fashion:

> "There rises a storm of nightmare sounds; the hallucinatory sym-phony of sounds is renewed; the stage gradually darkens and a crimson glow appears behind the glass of the door which leads to the stairway. The burgomaster in his nightmare thinks it is a forge and runs to it in order to squeeze the tremendous body of the murdered Jew into the narrow opening of the fiery stove."

It was the twilight of the romantics. New stars of the naturalist school excited hero-worship. In the April Ainley's Hamlet won brief glory for the old style, only to be thrust into the past in less than a week by fervent acclaim for John Gielgud's Hamlet in a performance so directed by Harcourt Williams as to keep the chief character within the framework of the story. But youth had not conquered yet. At the Westminster Theatre, a converted cinema near Buckingham Palace, Ainley outshone all his past brilliance in two sharply contrasted parts.

These were in plays by James Bridie, a Glasgow physician with an unmatched faculty for giving romance a humorous twist. In his *The Anatomist* Ainley played Dr. Robert Knox, veteran of the science of healing, who continues his lectures and research despite the popular outcry against him because of his dealings, in all innocence, with Burke and Hare. In *Tobias And The Angel* the donnish airs Ainley gave himself as the Archangel Raphael, seeing in some minor devil a shady acquaintance of past years in the College of Cherubim, became in an instant one of the great rewards of playgoing in the twentieth century.

After that he prevailed upon the management to accept a new play about Disraeli, then disappeared, and word went round that he was ill beyond all hope of recovery. In the nursing-home he began a real, enduring friend-ship. Afterwards he settled down in a suburban villa where he was content with a quiet life remote from all the fever and the fret of the theatre.

In 1933 Sir John decided to storm London again, more particularly that part of the Strand where he had once walked to and from his interviews with John Ryder. At the Little Theatre over the Adelphi arches he revived *The Burgomaster Of Stilemonde* masterfully enough to demonstrate that he could adapt voice and gesture as easily to an audience of four hundred as to those of two or three thousand.

On moving to the Savoy in the autumn he presented a new play in modern dress. "That taste for the purely dramatic which audiences expected of me" —the way he preferred to put things rather than regard himself as a romantic —was set aside. *If Only Father* was by a young man in whose gifts he believed, and for his sake Œdipus, Hamlet, Gloucester and the great-hearted burgomaster dwindled, to put it bluntly, into a dead grocer.

Here at once is a difficulty not to be calculated in advance—an "imponderable", in present-day jargon. In what circumstances will audiences accept an actor's hint or statement that he is a ghost and when will they not? Hamlet's Father has rarely had any trouble over incredulity and the Corsican brother is jibbed at only when the apparatus is at fault. A whole shipload of actors in *Outward Bound* compelled belief that they were dead, so much so that any number of scared spectators wondered whether they were dead also.

Despite all these and some other instances the odds are against an actor's chance of getting away with it. Even a play by Algernon Blackwood, with a gangrene halo round the spook, disturbed us no more than the lion in *Pyramus And Thisbe* disturbed the ladies. Similarly, *If Only Father*, on the first night, could make no headway. This is not to question the acting. The cast of *Outward Bound* did not *act* ghosts; they just were, without altering their every evening behaviour.

This was an exasperating time. Romance dried up at its source. Nothing inspired by it, either as a play or as a novel to be dramatized, came to Sir John's notice. If he appeared in some other kind of play there was disappointment. If he revived the old romance then, in London, very little interest was excited. People who did come in went away satisfied, but he could not be for ever preaching to the same handful of converted.

Why were the newspapers so unhelpful? That handful blamed the critics, not knowing the difference between the critics of 1933 and those of Clement Scott's day concerning one essential of their work. Scott patted himself on the back for the rate at which he could turn out a column of copy; the space was there and his task was to fill it. His successors had to fight for a few inches of space and put forward good and sufficient reasons why they should be given it.

The first night of a new play was justification enough, but the revival of a well-known play was not. Few editors or news-editors would willingly yield the space needed for any but a bare mention of "facts" for *The Lyons Mail* or *The Bells*. Those vivid impressions that are left when a critic writes immediately after a performance, before they can be sicklied o'er with the pale cast of thought, rarely found their way into print when Mathias, Lesurques and Dubosc came back to the stage—wraiths of St. Lyceum and yet figments powerful enough to make the stranger to these old ways of the theatre exclaim, "Why have I never heard about this before?"

One character from Dickens had been, and still was, the most enduring in a repertoire of enduring parts. Why were no others from the same teeming brain included? When imagination pictures the actor of Sydney Carton in a series of roles from David Copperfield to Pip, some regret must be felt that he never tried at least to duplicate his success. Towards the end of his active career, before the period of farewell tours began, he did take up another character from Dickens, but this time it was not a straight part, not a hero to be endowed with that bright, wistful eagerness which suited Victorian youth so well.

Another effort had been made to adapt "Great Expectations" for the stage. Though W. S. Gilbert attempted the task, no version had been a noteworthy success; scene after scene has dramatic possibilities, but the novel as a whole is too much for anything less than a trilogy. Early in 1935 the new one went into rehearsal at the Westminster under the title of *The Convict*. It opened in February with Martin-Harvey as Abel Magwitch. All the magic of Dickens radiated from him; directly he spoke you sensed the world of sinister doorways, of benevolence indoors and starving outcasts on the other side of the railings, of a vast jungle of wintry murk with dim vistas of flickering street lamps, of black-and-white contrasts between comfortable family circles and begrimed evil.

Nothing could mar our delight in the rich romance of that portrait, and when a fault could be noticed that added to the enjoyment. It was so typical of Martin-Harvey that despite the careful training of his observant eye he had never been near enough to life in the poorer London streets to know how to eat with a clasp-knife. In obedience to the author's clear direction Magwitch certainly took out his when sitting at table, but with his left hand he picked up the fork.

The younger generation may see nothing in this, but any Victorian child who watched goggle-eyed the navvies at breakfast by some evil-smelling gas main in a hole in the road could go through the motions of their fascinating table (without a table) manners. First the spade becomes a frying-pan; it is, of course, steel-bright clean; it has been carefully scraped by the clasp-knife, which in proper use enables you to cut food and convey it to your mouth with the right hand only, thus leaving the left hand free to juggle frizzling bacon upon the spade over the watchman's perforated bucket of red-hot coke. The clasp-knife is preferred to the table-knife because it makes of the table-fork an article of supererogative effeminacy.

Some inward laughter at the actor's refinement at keeping his thumb out of the plate where it ought to have had serious work to do could not be resisted. The mistake would have ruined any ordinary performance. This one was far from ordinary. It gave added colour to Dickens. We shall always think of Magwitch in such shape, even though not with a table-fork.

When the run of *The Convict* at the Westminster ended, Martin-Harvey arranged to take it on tour under the title of *The Scapegoat*. In this Lady Martin-Harvey won a truly notable success as Miss Havisham. She had not wanted the part; she declined it at first; she accepted only at her husband's entreaty and she took no pleasure in it. But because she had so little liking for it she gave it, in her own phrase, "all she had".

Provincial playgoers praised her ardently. The more they admired her the more she flinched. The hard, vindictive character was repellent to her. The production was never brought to London, but the widespread opinions of approval enable a chronicler to record it as one of their outstanding works.

Travel was a family heritage. Muriel Martin-Harvey, whose career began as a servant in *Pelléas And Mélisande* at the Lyceum in 1911, played many characters on the New York stage, and toured Canada and Australia. Jack Martin-Harvey, whose interests included miming and dancing, took part in Reinhardt's open-air production of *A Midsummer Night's Dream* at Oxford in 1933. The producer had asked for a hill and a lake. Some rising ground was discovered at not too great a distance, and some excavation was hastily made to hold water. Into this, each chilly June night, Jack Martin-Harvey, scared by the ass's head on Bottom's neck, had to fall. In the cause of art he contracted pneumonia—and survived to appear in still more "open-air Shakespeare".

THE PROPHET SAMUEL

IN what was now so remote a period that you linked it rather with the Norman Conquest than the present, Martin-Harvey had acted his first Barrie part. That occurred when he replaced H. B. Irving in *The Wedding Guest*. Now, thirty-six years later, came his second. The Scot who so queerly blended a belief in fairies with sour realism had brought his whimsy about never growing up into his actual existence. He drew his fountain-pen in the service of Elisabeth Bergner, whose girlish form fulfilled his quaint but modish ideal, and vowed to write a play especially for her on a subject she should name.

The MS. of *The Boy David* came into being at her behest, and Charles B. Cochran undertook to give it the cast and setting of a great occasion. The very names by themselves were enough to stir the blood. Expectation came to fever heat. Then Mme Bergner was ill. Another date was chosen. Then Mme Bergner had a film engagement. By now the fever had abated. Even so a new Barrie play, with the names of Martin-Harvey, Godfrey Tearle and Ion Swinley beside Bergner's in the bill could not but be an event.

But the ebb and flow of popularity are queer. Praise was given very grudgingly to Barrie during the last years of his life. His reputation reached the phase which all reputations have to pass through, of being generally assailed; and it seemed to stay there. That was a sign of its vitality. But he had no influence on, and was little influenced by, the time. While *The Admirable Crichton* was being written his contemporaries were ardently affirming or denying the equality of man. You would never guess from the way he handles the idea that it was ever anything but a toy. The refusal to admit that ideas are more than playthings is evident in all his work.

Otherwise, there are several Barries. There is the Scot who made the housekeeper in *The Professor's Love Story* describe certain visitors as "just English". There is the Englishman by adoption who wrote *The Admirable Crichton* and *Quality Street*—far more English than the average Englishman. There is the practical joker of *Rosy Rapture* (composed for Gaby Deslys in the midst of war), of the film called *The Real Thing At Last*, of *The Truth About The Russian Dancers*, and that unsolved murder mystery, *Shall We Join The Ladies?* There is also the teller of fairy tales who began light-heartedly with *Peter Pan* and *A Kiss For Cinderella*, and grew more and more pessimistic in *Dear Brutus* and *Mary Rose*.

It can be seen also in *Quality Street*, where Phoebe grows so old and tired

over school books that the dashing Valentine Brown cannot recognize her
on his return from the wars, and tragedy is averted only by restoring her to
youth. In this way it is the comedy of the girl who refused to grow up. In
Mary Rose the refusal lasts too long for a happy ending, but the trick is the
same. Put back the clock—put back the clock for one but not for all. It
would not happen to Phoebe in real life, not to a Phoebe who had to give
all her vitality to a school. Her story is as incredible as the adventures of
Mary Rose on the island that liked to be visited.

When Barrie's magic was new these plays made so delightful a surprise
that only the hypercritical thought of inspecting the illusionist's machinery.
When the public grew acquainted with his manifestations of the supernatural
familiarity bred contempt. Playgoers were like small boys who had been taken
to see a conjurer once too often. But it was they who had aged, not the
Barrie heroine, who was what the public wanted even when some other
author created her.

This became apparent when Mme Bergner played Shakespeare's
Rosalind, bending downwards until she gazed after Orlando with her head
between her knees, in a film which Mr. P. L. Mannock called *Elisabeth And
Her German Arden*. Whether she was really and truly Shakespeare's little girl
may be doubted, but there is good reason to believe that when Barrie saw
her he recognized the Barrie heroine. Whatever it was that enslaved him to
this ideal, whether or not it was the kind of yearning that made him sigh over
the unborn dream-daughter in *Dear Brutus*, the whimsy now had him in
thrall. *The Boy David* was a heart-breaking experience. The postponements,
trying for any nerves, bore heavily on a man of his years.

When the play was first mentioned to him, Martin-Harvey saw himself
as Saul. With a vigour as great as many men possess in middle age he would
have presented an impressive figure whatever his stature, but Barrie's unerring judgment had set him down for Samuel. In typescript the part read
well, mainly because of a vision scene—but this was cut. He was disappointed, but barely as much as hinted at this. Instead, finding that the
postponements left him with time on his hands, he despised the idea of
resting for a while, and rather than make the most of August for a holiday
went straight into rehearsals of the most ambitious revival he could possibly
have thought of.

In one of those courteous letters he sent to editors, Sir John had mentioned on some other occasion that he had in mind "a good many innovations", and added, "the public, I think, are generally interested in such."
Time, which "makes of our sweethearts corpses or wives", much more
easily transforms innovations into conventions. When Œdipus returned
to Covent Garden in the September of 1936 the surge of supers through
the auditorium was just one of the methods of handling stage crowds.
The interest now was far less in the general effect than in Œdipus, in the
Jocasta of Miriam Lewes, the Messenger of Franklin Dyall and the Creon

of Baliol Holloway. You could still admire all these, though you had time to reflect why you were not carried away.

Classic tragedy had become taken for granted since Sophocles in the Reinhardt vein had been the nine days' wonder of January, 1912. Some matinées of other Greek tragedies in 1920 at a music-hall (with the rumble of tube trains *obbligato*) had startled us so much that Ancient Greece could not startle us more. Professor Gilbert Murray had been preparing us in print for the discovery that Euripides had a strong affinity with twentieth-century realism. Sybil Thorndike, whose leadership of the Manchester School had been won ten years before in plays of drab modern domesticity, now blended the realistic and the classic; and as the subject was the price that had to be paid for war, we were stirred as we had never expected to be stirred in the theatre again. Siddons herself could not have surpassed that Hecuba and Medea—Dame Sybil herself was never so divinely inspired again.

After *The Trojan Women*, with its pressure on current affairs, *Œdipus Rex* receded a long way off. And yet that performance was still vibrant, still impressive, still (so it would prove when the new image would remain clear ten years after) memorable. The best compliments are unintentional. The recollection of those last appearances at Covent Garden was of Martin-Harvey in his prime. Much later you suddenly stumble on the plain fact that he was then seventy-four years of age. Merely to stalk on buskins up and down steps would test most of us at such a time of life. He did so serenely while he undoubtedly *acted*. You have to go back to the father of the modern stage, to Thomas Betterton, to find anything approaching—not equalling—it.

At last, in the November of 1936, *The Boy David* was ready. There was a first night in Edinburgh which restored theatrical prestige to the Athens of the North. The kilt and lace ruffles gave to the audience that touch of grandeur which an audience in no other capital could try to emulate with any better hope than looking like a masquerade. After that performance changes were made. A sequence of scenes that represented David's dream was deemed a mistake and omitted. "Although the cut scene was particularly beautiful (John magnificent) the play was bettered by dropping it," ran Cochran's verdict. Unfortunately, the news that one or two young actresses had lost their parts went the rounds in the West End when public goodwill, as Cochran had already noted, was lost.

Directly you entered His Majesty's on the night of December 14 you felt that something had gone wrong. What was it? Perhaps your mind was haunted by the phrase about choosing five smooth stones out of the brook, and beset by bias against any attempt to imagine David's boyhood without them. Or perhaps the prejudice was a preconceived one against any possible association, even the slightest, of the ruddy young shepherd with acting which would not grow up. That was not it. A woman's voice

R

probed into the murk with the remark, "I keep fumbling for my prayer-book." Hope deferred had made the heart sick. To impress such an audience, not necessarily the public, was uphill work. There should have been electricity in the air to welcome such a performance.

There were many fine moments in it. Best of all was a single line spoken by Martin-Harvey. He had what only the veteran of the stage can ever hope to have, and then only the veteran who has laboured. That was why Barrie, with unerring eye for exact casting, had chosen him for this scene. It was designed by a master-painter (Augustus John) as a simple farmhouse—how simple had not been evident until the stranger entered. He had that un-purchasable power, authority. When he said quietly, "My name is Samuel," the ears of audiences brought up in the Protestant faith rang with a clangour of echoes from childhood's unnumbered Sundays:

"And it came to pass at that time, when Eli was laid down in his place, and his eyes began to wax dim, that he could not see;

"And ere the lamp of God went out in the temple of the Lord, where the ark of God was, and Samuel was laid down to sleep;

"That the Lord called Samuel . . .

"Therefore Eli said unto Samuel, Go, lie down: and it shall be, if he call thee, that thou shalt say, Speak, Lord; for thy servant heareth. So Samuel went and lay down in his place.

"And the Lord came, and stood, and called as at other times, Samuel, Samuel. . . ."

All the old awe of the name, that neither time nor pawnbrokers could dispel, John Martin-Harvey evoked the moment he uttered it. His voice travelled down dim corridors of the mind, reawakening old wonder at a child who heard the living word of God, the child whom God had called by his name, Samuel.

The star could not play higher than that, no matter how high she stood in the theatrical heavens. Nothing like that complete capture of a play had been witnessed since Ellen Terry, likewise with the authority of three score years and ten, swept Romeo and Juliet aside to turn the tragedy of lovers into the comedy of a nurse, lines or no lines. But Ellen Terry's triumph took some part of the evening. Playgoers may rack their memories in vain to find another night when three syllables crowned a life's work with glory in one overwhelming instant.

It was, if you will, an example of the art of knowing what your audience knows and letting that do your work for you—not as simple as it sounds, of course, because though the principle is like the penny-in-the-slot machine there is no penny and no slot. This particular example would not have existed but for the fairly plain fact that if fifty years are spent generating power, that power will then operate at the mere touching of a switch. Fifty years spent in acquiring the habit of slinging heavy trunks upon the spine enable a railway porter, when ageing, to carry a prodigious load, and art, after all, is not so very different from other activities of the human frame.

In an unsigned article an actor who had "walked on" in the Martin-Harvey Company wrote, "Sitting in the stalls one night at His Majesty's watching *The Boy David*, a very well-known young star of to-day turned to me and said, 'You know him, don't you? I have never seen him before to-night; I did not know what acting was until now.'" Youth in 1936 might fairly make the confession.

There is no forgetting his last new part. This was in *Tuberin 5*, adapted by Peter Gray (Lady Martin-Harvey) from the Viennese success, *Hans Mueller*, which he brought to the King's, Hammersmith, in 1937 at the opening of an autumn tour with Blackpool, Birmingham, Newcastle, Edinburgh, Glasgow and Manchester in the itinerary. While the play itself fades into a confused mass of all the stories ever told about selfless healers at war with selfish authority, Professor Paul Gurdner himself, standing by a table as young Jack Harvey had loved to stand before an earlier generation of playgoers, is as clear as though his portrait hung before us now. In a world of great discoveries, with 1937 heading for the future, he stood for a calmer society that had not believed in change and could not quite believe in it now.

In a delicate way, a little sad in its dignity, he seemed an aristocratic Rip Van Winkle, trying manfully to acclimatize himself to a laboratory atmosphere with new-fangled apparatus and words. As there was nothing to bear out this view of the character in the play, we listened inattentively to the dialogue and let our sight dwell lovingly on the valiant little figure. He could never have been called the Grand Old Man of the theatre, no matter what his age. He could never have looked old enough for that. But he could, and did, look proudly and maturely Victorian.

One detail in the way he dressed had significance. It appeared to be an oversight, though this would be strange in an actor so meticulously respectful for history that Reresby, just for one example, made his rivals look like New Year revellers in costumes hired for the night.

The theatre is frequently taken off its guard by plays of contemporary life where the cast may dress as it chooses to dress in real life. Sir Seymour Hicks used to tell how Hawtrey, rehearsing a scene where he was supposed to have arrived after a long railway journey, asked the young producer whether he should wear a blue suit. "Brown, don't you think?" was the answer, and with this Sir Seymour always raised a shout of laughter.

But a wit with such command of effect could raise a laugh with each letter of the alphabet. Since brown is the colour of comfort in hats, great-coats, jackets, socks and shoes, while a blue suit has to be straight from the press if its wearer wishes to look unlike a sanitary inspector, the producer was as right in answering the question as Hawtrey was in putting it. Any close observer knows how rarely such questions are ever put by scores of actors who dress to please themselves.

One of the grandest profiles ever publicly exhibited in London regularly went with a modified Gladstone collar which suited it. Times changed, clothes changed, *dramatis personae* changed, physical deportment changed. Still that collar persisted even with soft shirts and deportments not unwaveringly poker-back, until you could not see the play for the collar.

Then again an actor of exceptional good looks, in a part inclined to elegance, came on in the double-breasted blue reefer, "Polo" collar and black tie which are, by time-honoured custom, the signs aboard ship that the skipper is going ashore. The actor, imagining that what pleased him as a private person must naturally express the taste of the fictitious person in the play, might argue that only the captious would object. On the other hand, the onlookers who would assure him that they "saw nothing wrong" might well be unconsciously led along a false line of expectation by this misdirecting clue. Anything untoward that an actor wears is, as we discover at our first charade, quintessential scenery.

No apology need be made for a running commentary about acting in general in an actor's biography. The point of the foregoing is the colour of Professor Paul Gurdner's shoes. They were bright tan, worn with a blue suit in the fashion of King Edward's day, usual then and surprisingly unusual in 1937. Irreverent youth quoted a line or two from the popular ballad, "Brahn Bewts", with its hero who wore them on wrong occasions, because youth had no notion that blue serge and tan leather ever went together.

Is this a trifling point? But if a Rip-Van-Winkle effect had been intended, then the colour of those shoes would have been a very fine example of what has been called the power of "making clothes act". Memory, which has let all the rest of *Tuberin 5* run through the mesh, retains a portrait, not so much of the part as the actor. Perversely or not, we treasure it all the more for that reason.

We did not wish to see Martin-Harvey in modern dress. The life of to-day gave no scope for his free, flowing movement. It hampered him in the use of imaginative detail, restricted the range of a voice that needed to flow in the Shakespearean half-chant, and sobered a countenance that otherwise delighted in ease of grimace. *Tuberin 5* served his need for an idealism of the kind extolled by Joseph Conrad as not beating its wings in blind flight but standing, open-eyed, with feet firmly planted on the earth. Still the new twentieth-century mode meant shackles for him.

Modern acting expresses a new attitude to life. What that is might be indicated by an exchange of views between an Englishman and a group of Hungarians. When they were entertaining him in Budapest he was surprised to find the duel still customary there and they were surprised to learn that in England it was obsolete. "But what," he was asked, "happens when you quarrel?" He answered, "We just don't quarrel." That seems to be what the stage mirrors. It avoids all the violence that is inherent in both the romantic and the classical. It values the smooth as a driver values smooth-running.

This is not a style midway between the other two, it is a new style altogether. It needs some understanding, and to this end the best testimony yet provided comes from confessions in "George Arliss By Himself". We may regard him as a contemporary of Martin Harvey, for he played in *Pelléas And Mélisande* with him and Mrs. Patrick Campbell at their first matinée. By 1940, when his book was published, he had become one of the foremost champions of the style universally accepted—he was acting for Hollywood films. He has no theories to expound. He merely expresses his personal feelings when he contemplates parts as varied as Shylock, Richelieu and The Third Floor Back.

In preparation for *The Merchant Of Venice* at the Broadhurst, New York, in 1928, he consulted the records of great tragedians. He tested each emphasis and gesture in moments that had either held the audience spellbound or roused them to a furore of applause. "When I spoke them," he says, "they sounded just like me trying to be clever, and not a bit like Shylock." Lytton's *Richelieu* was resurrected not for the stage but the screen. Old players and playgoers prophesied how great he would be in its finest moments, but they were quite wrong—"I have never been able to rise to those great moments." The work of Jerome K. Jerome he declined:

"I defy anyone not to have believed in Forbes-Robertson in the play, with his glorious voice and his magnificent profile, but I have always found it very difficult to be convincingly celestial in the theatre."

It is not just Mr. Arliss speaking. These particular reactions to definite parts at certain moments could be matched by so many players in conference over plays during the same period that they indicate the general state of mind in the theatre. The dislike of raising the voice that tested a human being's claim to be civilized had also, naturally, become a major rule of acting. Grimace stopped; almost all gesture, unless tying a bootlace or lighting a cigarette can be called gesture, caused a scare.

To be even slightly dogmatic is not in keeping with all this; nevertheless, the general aim does seem to be to get as far away as possible from *The Bells*. Things have to be flattened out—a process that Gerald du Maurier made definite when he revived the most celebrated of all drawing-room dramas, *Diplomacy*, in the spring of 1913, with each "telling line" left out. Effect again wavered in the scales against illusion, but the Russian way of rehearsing Russian plays—which demonstrated, for example, how much grief gained by being inaudible—made the illusion of actuality seem the one virtue.

There was a great deal more in it than that. The word "tempo", borrowed from the music-hall, was used as though it signified some new thing. It did not. Timing has always been recognized as of importance by competent stage directors. The new thing deserves to be called rhythm. Of old there had been pace, varying from gradual to rapid according to the requirements of everything from tragedy to farce. By varying this a performance could keep interest alive when "flattening out" would have proved monotonous. Much fuss was made over "team-work", no new thing, and liable to disappear directly any member of the team became an actor-manager—no new thing either.

The public at large, even more than regular playgoers, became excited over all actors in the latest style. One celebrity's self-restraint was such that no one could tell whether he were expressing emotion at white-heat or expressing nothing at all. But as the auditorium's ardour cooled there was a winnowing. The players who were left compelled admiration even from the oldest Tories of stalls and gallery, for the modern style. It was at the zenith of this conquest that paragraphs appeared about the making for John Gielgud of a new stage version of "A Tale of Two Cities". Martin-Harvey, having the farewell tour of *The Only Way* in mind, felt some concern. There was reason for this; in the contests of Hamlets the traditional had suffered by comparison with the new. With this in mind he wrote to John Gielgud, who handsomely agreed, at once, to postpone his project.

While *The Only Way* was taking its farewell of the provinces Sir John received an honour which he prized next to his knighthood. It came from Scotland and deserves to be noted in refutation of the deep-rooted belief that the Scots are incurably clannish.

Glasgow strengthens that opinion by preferring Highland legends to the world's stock of fairy stories—at least that impression has been spread abroad by the Princess's Theatre, which offers Christmas pantomimes under Scottish titles and once substituted Bonnie Prince Charlie for Prince Charming. Yet Glasgow in our times accepted an English actor (Scottish on his mother's side) as heir to the playgoing fervour once bestowed upon the real McKay, whose popularity among his ain folk made their refusal to accept a substitute proverbial. Martin-Harvey had ever been the city's idol. Now the University conferred the degree of Hon. LL.D. upon him in the June of 1938 to celebrate his seventy-fifth birthday.

On the journey back he fell ill and had to take to his bed when he reached East Sheen through bronchial trouble. Yet no sooner was he on his feet than he prepared to resume his farewell tour which had been planned to last until Christmas. The Last Romantic fought hard for his faith, disregarding all the weaknesses of the flesh to keep some of the fragrance of the past alive in a world set on realism. It was like maintaining a flower-garden in a Black Country landscape; and then it was like cultivating a vineyard on the slopes of an active volcano.

There was no mistaking those rumblings. Once you had heard them you had, to adopt the pet word of the hour, to turn realist. Romance did perish As though submitting to the verdict that it had to be uprooted, the remains of its old haunts in the Strand yielded themselves up to auctioneers' gavels. The Lyceum, at the same time as the Gaiety, became an empty shell, ready to be demolished in order to make room for a traffic roundabout.

Before the walls could be destroyed a wider destruction threatened. Undeterred by war talk the Martin-Harveys had everything in readiness for their autumn tour, and how much that meant is proved by *Picture Post* for March 18, 1939, which made the rehearsals front-page news, with photographs inside of Sir John, the pince-nez and the powder-puff of Irving in his hands. But the whole scheme of life could no longer be relied on. There was no certainty about booking a special train in which the company had always travelled. Members of the staff left to start war work. Suddenly the whole fabric of their tangible dreams tumbled down, as Lady Martin-Harvey says, "like a pack of cards".

Their chauffeur, a fine mechanic, told them, "I've got to go on duty to-night," and a much-valued stand-by vanished out of their lives. The old Rolls-Royce, for which they felt something like affection, was commandeered. For Lady Martin-Harvey, with her failing sight, this was a heavy blow, for she was now cut off from all her interests in life, a prisoner in a home distant from everything except other homes.

"The bottom," she says, "fell out of my life." She tells, in her vivid phrases, of Sir John's unremitting endeavours not to yield to fate. He made journeys to Town, though he had to walk considerable distances and then strap-hang in buses. He was greeted with smiles by the girls who now caused the familiar jingle to be altered to:

> Punch, sisters, punch, sisters,
> Punch with care,
> Punch in the presence of
> The passengaire,

and carried on "flirtations with a conductress", according to the lively story he brought home. He never grumbled. He was always at work. Like John Philip Kemble, he delved like a labourer in his garden.

War invaded even his quiet backwater of London. Richmond Park was an armed camp, and when its headquarters were first wired some telephone calls meant for its staff became wrong numbers in Primrose Cottage. Even modern war, in all its hideousness, exhibits a touch of glamour in unexpected places. Man-power was short. Girls took over manly duties.

The sentinel at the gates a stone's-throw away was tall and most divinely fair. A playgoer thought of Offenbach, but this was no idle *vivandière*, and far too intent on duty to throw her life away like Ouida's Cigarette. She really did mean war. In the midst of it *The Times* printed news of the sale of stage furniture, "The mahogany bureau, two carved wood armchairs, and two oak high-back chairs," used by Sir Henry Irving and Sir John Martin-Harvey in *The Bells* and *The Lyons Mail.*

Our understanding of life through the eyes of four score years is limited. So few of us experience it, so very few of us can look back upon it, that we are content to have no knowledge of it. But surely the old heart is deserving of sympathy like the young heart; its disappointments must move us and its valiant courage stir us. The gallant old trouper, still trusting to his "splendid spur", had struggled to the end, only to be frustrated by forces strong enough to frustrate the world.

Together Jack and Nell went back to their favourite garden seat to talk it over. What should they do next? The time would come for farewell tours with play after play from their repertoire. Meanwhile there was the radio for the public. The loyal provinces, as a vast whole, more especially, would still be glad to hear their voices. They talked of Sydney Carton and Mimi on their way to the scaffold, of Rat Reresby and Batty in disgust with the world, of the Burgomaster and his fate-entangled daughter, of Hamlet's wait in the graveyard while Ophelia's funeral approaches, of the soldierly wooing of Kate by King Hal, of Everyman and his guiding Good Deeds, of all the long procession of brave things attempted, bravely done, down the long years—back to the daily walk though London's Arden when they were boy and girl together.

They had looked from the bridge into the still waters and dreamed this almost unending dream, and now they were looking down the same vista backwards. It was all strange, hauntingly incredible. They were still Jack and Nell, still eloquent in the very same deep understanding. On, always on, had been their aim. They must keep on, always on, with their work. In the garden the shadows were deepening.

Labour and sorrow were not apparent in Sir John's bearing after four score years. Disregarding the dangers of London in time of war, he gave us the fruits of his long, rich experience in lectures about plays and players. But he was not satisfied with this. At home he still planned. Hour after hour he spent discussing with Lady Nell, as her friends called her, how the difficulties of the next tour could be overcome.

While still looking ahead, still eager, still undaunted, he had through weakness to take to his bed. He would, he thought, be at work again soon. And in this spirit, unconquerable romantic, master of his fate to the very last, he died.

The end bears the date May 15, 1944. His wish had been for a grave in the little cemetery at Bonchurch, and there he had long ago become the owner of a plot of earth against this day. But the Isle of Wight was now a prohibited area. He was buried instead at East Sheen, near his home. A memorial service was held in "the actors' church" of Covent Garden, and there, by the lectern where he had paid his last tribute to Ellen Terry, stood Henry Ainley whom we, as a body, would never see again.

Lady Martin-Harvey had now, for the first time, to live without hope. That was the plight of many in the years ruled by savagery, but philosophic reflections over the condition of humanity are not the answer to individual problems. For half a century a spirit had shaped itself to be interminably at odds with all the manifold resistances of that complicated machine we call "theatre".

Every working moment, from early morning until midnight, all Lady Nell's energy had been concentrated on what was to happen between curtain-rise and curtain-fall on a long succession of nights in the imminent future. Life to her was, apart from response to the needs of people in distress, almost entirely directed to that.

"You must have such wonderful memories," she was told. But to live on memories is a way of life that, like any other way, cannot be enjoyed by those who have not fitted themselves for it. She had never looked back. The present and the call it made on will, nerves and energy had been her training.

Now the present was cluttered up with all those domestic cares which were more than enough for those fully capable of looking after themselves. With failing sight, cut off from the world she knew, in a house far from the hub of the district where each day's difficulties could be tackled, she saw no difference between one day and another, beyond lesser or greater perplexity over food, lesser or greater daylight at her chair by the window. There was the companionship of her son and daughter at frequent visits, but life still had its gaps.

Sometimes a friend would call, sometimes a voice would linger on the telephone, and then at the mention of *Hamlet* or *Via Crucis* or *The Burgomaster Of Stilemonde* footlights would seem to dazzle between her eyes and the great darkness, a bolder ring than ever heard before would sound in her voice, and the glorious warfare of spirit against inertia would fight its battles over again. These days are sad—but how brave the old days were. The glory cannot be taken away.

At no very distant date the centenary of Martin Harvey's birth will arrive. Then those who wish to mark the event will lament that an actor who lived in an age when the art of Thespis at length found means to perpetuate itself left so few records. Considering his unquestioned right to a place in theatrical history he was not closely observed by critics. For the simple reason that he spent so much of his life on tour he did not win a nameable fraction of the descriptive pages devoted to Irving.

The film studios will have little to offer posterity. When Martin-Harvey acted before the camera, moving-pictures barely as much as claimed any relation to art. Little remains, either as celluloid or in living memory, of what the cinema turned *A Cigarette-Maker's Romance, The Breed Of The Treshams,*

The Lyons Mail and *The Only Way* into. But Lady Martin-Harvey describes the film of *The Burgomaster Of Stilemonde* eloquently. On his way to execution Cyrille Van Belle has to walk to the rose-garden that was his pride, through the conservatory. He stops for an instant beside a pot in order to tend a bent branch and then moves on, in his usual gait, to face the firing-squad.

The radio recorded his voice. Sir John and Lady Martin-Harvey's last performance together was in *The Burgomaster Of Stilemonde* at Broadcasting House. Then plans were mooted for making a fresh dramatization of "A Tale of Two Cities", and he responded with zest to the proposal that he should play Dr. Manette. This came to nothing. Yet it is easy to imagine how the stir that is in the pages of Dickens would have again been brought by him to life upon the stage. Among the immortals his shade may make the great wraiths of Dickens and Shakespeare the better acquainted with each other—a fantastic conceit, if you like, but in him there was something of each of them.

THE END

INDEX OF PERSONS

134–149 (*The Only Way*), 150–1 (*Don Juan's Last Wager*), 151–2 (*Ib and Little Christina*), 153 (*The Wedding Guest*), 155–7 (*A Cigarette-Maker's Romance*), 159–60 (*After All*), 162–3, 167–9 (*The Breed of the Treshams*), 170, 173–4 (*Hamlet*), 178–80, 181 (*Boy O'Carrol*), 183 and 187 (*The World and His Wife*), 188–9 (*Richard III*), 189–90 (*The Lowland Wolf*), 193–4 (*Great Possessions*), 195 (*The Corsican Brothers*), 196–7 (*The Last Heir*), 199–209 (*Œdipus Rex*), 213–14 (*The Taming of the Shrew*), 215–16 (*The Faun*), 217 (*The Conspiracy*), 220, 223–4 (*Armageddon*), 225–30 (His Majesty's season), 230 (*David Garrick*), 231–3 (*Rosemary*), 234 (lectures under shell-fire), 235–6 (*The Burgomaster of Stilemonde*), 237–9 (*Arthur*) 239 (Canadian tour), 240 (Knighthood), 242–4 (*Via Crucis*), 245 (*The Shewing-Up of Blanco Posnet, The Death of Tintagiles, The Lyons' Mail*), 246 (*Scaramouche*), 247–8 (*The Devil's Disciple*), 249 (*The King's Messenger*), 250–1 (*The Bells*), 252 (*If Only Father*), 253–4 (*The Convict, The Scapegoat*), 255–8 (*The Boy David, Œdipus Rex*), 259–60 (*Tuberin 5*), 261–6

Martin-Harvey, Lady, 7, 9, 13–14, 90–5 (at the Lyceum under Irving), 101–2 (Vacation Tours), 109 (*Widowers' Houses*), 110 (*The Foresters*), 113–14 (*Don Quixote*), 126–9 (*Pelléas Et Mélisande*), 134–149 (*The Only Way*), 150–1 (*Don Juan's Last Wager*), 156 (*A Cigarette-Maker's Romance*, 159–60 (*After All*), 162–3, 167–9 (*The Breed of the Treshams*), 176, 179, 183 and 187 (*The World and His Wife*), 189–90 (*The Lowland Wolf*), 191, 197 (*The Last Heir*), 205, 208, 209–210 (*An Idyll of Seven Dials*), 213–14 (*The Taming of the Shrew*), 215, 223–4 (*Armageddon*), 226–30 (His Majesty's season), 230 (*David Garrick*), 231–3 (*Rosemary*), 235–6 (*The Burgomaster of Stilemonde*), 237–9 (*Arthur*), 239–40 (Canadian Tour), 242–4 (*Via Crucis*), 245 (*The Shewing-Up of Blanco Posnet, The Death of Tintagiles, The Lyons' Mail*), 246 (*Scaramouche*), 247–8 (*The Devil's Disciple*), 249 (*The King's Messenger*), 250–1 (*The Bells*), 252 (*If Only Father*), 253–4 (*The Convict, The Scapegoat*), 259–60 (*Tuberin 5*), 261–6

Martin-Harvey, Jack Seaforth Elton, 254, 265
Martin-Harvey, Muriel, 254, 265
Mason, A. E. W., 160
Maude, Cyril, 122, 218
Melingue, 61, 159
Melville, Walter, 240–1
Meredith, George, 5
Merivale, Herman, 46, 48, 50, 73–4, 81, 108, 150, 166
Montague, C. E., 113, 169–70
Moore, Nelly, 174
Murray, D. L., 7
Murray, Professor Gilbert, 200, 204, 207

NAPOLEON I, 37, 39, 109, 135, 167
Navarro, Ramon, 246
Neilson, Julia, 153, 165, 169, 198–9
Neilson-Terry, Phyllis, 250

ODELL, E. J., 80
O'Neill, Frank Bernard, 159
O'Neill, Norman, 188
Orczy, Baroness, 169
"Ouida", 23

PARKER, Louis Napoleon, 217–18
Pertwee, Roland, 125, 128
Phillips, Stephen, 9, 24, 102, 154, 160–1, 163, 173, 192, 196–7, 217, 223–4
Phillips, Watts, 55
Pinero, Sir Arthur Wing, 122, 223
Playfair, Sir Nigel, 214
Price, Nancy, 229

READE, Charles, 46, 61, 63, 73
Reinhardt, Professor Max, 202, 206, 217, 254
Réjane, Mme., 135
Richelieu, 47 (sketch), 95
Roberts, Lord, 145, 149
Robertson, Forbes (*see* Forbes-Robertson)
Robertson, T. W., 62–3
Rodway, Philip, 21
Rorke, Mary, 183, 197
Ross, Herbert, 102, 122
"Rutherford, John", 167–9, 181
Ryder, John, 48, 50, 70, 82–4, 141
Ryder, John (the Younger), 84